The Pursuit of Pleasure

THE PURSUIT OF PLEASURE

Gender, Space & Architecture in Regency London

JANE RENDELL

RUTGERS UNIVERSITY PRESS
NEW BRUNSWICK, NEW JERSEY

First published in the United States 2002 by
Rutgers University Press, New Brunswick, New Jersey

First published in Great Britain 2002 by
Continuum International Publishing Group Ltd,
The Tower Building, 11 York Road, London SE1 7NX

Library of Congress Cataloging-in-Publication Data

Rendell, Jane, 1967–
   The pursuit of pleasure: gender, space and architecture in Regency London /
Jane Rendell.
      p.   cm.
   Includes bibliographical references and index.
   ISBN 0-8135-2980-8 (cloth: alk. paper)—ISBN 0-8135-2981-6 (pbk.: alk. paper)
   1. Architecture and women.   2. Feminism and architecture.   3. Space
(Architecture)—England—London.   4. Architecture—England—London—
19th century.   5. Women—England—London—Social conditions.   I. Title.

NA2543.W65 R46 2001
720′.82′09421—dc21   2001019291

British Cataloguing-in-Publication information
is available from the British Library.

Copyright © 2002 by Jane Rendell

Manufactured in Great Britain

Contents

List of Figures

Acknowledgements

This book began life when I was an architecture student in 1988. Nicky Smailes, a close friend studying politics, came home one day with a present for me. It was a book called *Making Space: Women and the Man-Made Environment*, written by the feminist architectural cooperative Matrix, a practice I eventually worked for. A decade on, whether it is thinking about the relationship of feminist theory and architectural history or exploring the questions feminism asks of architectural practice, I continue to be fascinated by the various intersections of feminism and architecture. It seems Nicky's gift sparked something important for me – the question of how two different areas of knowledge can be related and how this might provide the potential for reciprocal transformation. Taking a feminist approach to architectural methodology was not something that my architectural educators (with the notable exceptions of Russell Light and Sally Schaffer) took seriously, particularly in the studio. Because I was interested in non-formal political ideas that come from outside architecture, Isi Metzstein, the professor I fought (and laughed) most with, once told me that he believed I had never had an architectural idea in my life. But I thank them, for by continuously discouraging the incorporation of feminism into the objective practice of architecture, they fuelled my rebellious nature and so this work.

Over the past five years writing this book, my research has been funded by the British Academy. Their financial support allowed me first to complete my MSc in the History of Modern Architecture at UCL and then my doctoral research at Birkbeck College, University of London. Over that time, numerous institutions, colleagues, students and friends have given support in many other ways – the space to teach, talk about and publish my work. I'd like to acknowledge all those at Winchester School of Art, the University of North London, the Bartlett School of Architecture, Chelsea College of Art and Design and the University of Nottingham, who provided such exciting discussions in the classroom and in the pub. Many of their voices, often with very different interests, are within this work: Judy Attfield, Sue Ayton, Faye Carey, Katherine Clarke, David Clews, David Connearn, Matthew Cornford, David Cross, Emma Davis, Julia Dwyre, Miche Fabre-Lewin, Lucy Harris, Sophie Horton, Neil Leach, the 'Desiring Practices' team (Duncan McCorquodale, Katerina Rüedi and Sarah Wigglesworth), Malcolm Miles, Diane Ghirardo, Rex Henry, Jonathan Hill, Sue Hubbard, Barbara Penner, Mario Pettruci, Annie Richardson, Sue Ridge, Clive Sall, Paul Sweetman, Lynne Walker, Pamela Wells and many others. Thank you also to Michael Lock and John Simpson, Beadles of the Burlington Arcade, for their time and thoughts; to Mr Parkinson of the Oxford and Cambridge Club, for showing me around the club; to Mr Edmunds, the Secretary of Boodle's Club, for allowing me complete access to Boodle's Club and its archives over the summer of 1995. Thanks to the Guildhall Library, especially Jeremy Smith, and the British Library, for permission to reproduce some of the images in this book. I am also delighted at Sharon Kivland's generosity in allowing me to use 'Allure' from her series 'la bonheur des femmes' (2000) for the front cover of this book. Thank you also to Mike Goldmark of Goldmark and the poet Aidan Andrew Dunn for permission to reprint a section from his amazing epic poem *Vale Royal*, and to the University of Nebraska Press and Hélène Cixous for permission to reprint a section from *The Book of Promethea*.

But I must especially thank Lynda Nead for her focus, warmth and critical insight; Tristan Palmer of the Athlone Press for his ongoing enthusiasm for my work; Ben Pitcher of Continuum for his patience and care; Deborah Millar, Steve Pile and John Whiteford for shared rambles; Joe Kerr and Alicia Pivaro for being strangely familiar and Adrian Forty for his precision in thought as well as in camera work. A big thank-you goes to Iain Borden for his belief in my ideas, his meticulous mind, his curious ability to stimulate and soothe, and for providing me with my one-time intellectual and emotional home. Finally, to my family – Alan, Beth, Sarah and David – this book is for you.

CHAPTER 1

The Pursuit of Pleasure

In wide arcs of wandering through the city
I saw to either side of what is seen,
and noticed treasures where it was thought there were none.
I passed through a more fluid city.
I broke up the imprint of all familiar places,
shutting my eyes to the boredom of modern contours.[1]

And all my theories skilfully and gracefully took up position
in my own starry night. There was an order. They obeyed my
wishes so well that even though they came from me, they
surprised and taught me, and even though they were no
more than hypothesis and illusion, they always took me to a
safe harbour as easily as any real boat. In the end, going from
illusion to illusion, one also comes to understand the world.[2]

In contemporary urban and architectural discourse, we are increasingly
obsessed by figures which traverse space: the flâneur, the spy, the detective, the prostitute. The literary flâneur, or city stroller, in his role as man
of the crowd and detached observer of city life has become a central
motif in discussions of urban experience – through movement the
flâneur maps space. A trope among postmodern critics, the flâneur first
appears in Charles Baudelaire's poems of 1850s Paris, but features most
famously as a dialectical image in the work of cultural critic Walter
Benjamin. For artists and writers, from romanticism, to Dada, to sur-
realism, to the situationist international, to fluxus, to conceptual art and
to contemporary work, urban roaming, drifting or flânerie has defined a
particular approach to creative practice.[3]

The flâneur represents for me urban explorations, passages of revelation, journeys of discovery – what Michel de Certeau might call 'spatial
stories'.[4] Through the personal and the political, the theoretical and the

historical, we all tell spatial stories, we exchange narratives of archi-tecture in, and of, the city.[5] Inspired by a desire to 'know' the past as a woman, to understand the gendering of architectural space in early nineteenth-century London, this book tells one such story. It is the story of my pursuit of pleasure, theoretical and historical, following the rambler, a figure who roamed the streets of early nineteenth-century London, prefiguring the more famous Parisian flâneur.

A historical understanding of architecture in the city is not adequately framed through one specific and self-contained discipline – architectural history. Rather it is located in the places where ideas are exchanged about the city between geographers, sociologists, film-makers, artists, cultural theorists, literary critics, architects and urban dwellers of all kinds. This 'interdisciplinary' state of knowledge allows new kinds of spaces and alternative modes of interpretation to emerge. In this more fluid state, knowing the city is always contingent, forever in flux. As a historian, I may tell my spatial stories about architecture somewhat differently from any other kind of storyteller. Certainly, my stories are inspired by a desire to 'know' the past, to 'tell it as it was', and, if possible, to 'explain' it. But I am not sure 'knowing' history is as easy as it might seem. At times historians do present their findings as obvious – who else can dispute our reconstruction of places dwelt in before we were born, today transformed beyond recognition, left as traces in obscure documents which only we will ever read? But what if our 'attempts at disclosure' are not as revealing as they seem, what if, as Steve Pile has suggested, 'the unknown is not so easily known'?[6]

Historical epistemology is a complex area. The (hi)stories we tell of cities are also (hi)stories of ourselves. My interest in architecture and in history is embedded in my fascination with the politics of sexual differ-ence. My position as a feminist makes a difference to the way in which I know. Negotiating a meaningful relation between the personal and the theoretical is central to much feminist work. With myriad feminisms, there can be no single way of knowing the city. But who I am raises important questions about the ways I proceed, about my methodology. Who I am makes a difference to how I read and what I write. It makes a difference to the way I do things, to what and how I can know.

'Knowing' the city invites, and invokes, a need to know the self, the one who seeks knowledge. This female subject places herself in complex relation to her subject matter. She is desirous of knowledge, but also fears her need to know. For her, clear and certain knowledge, 'knowing' without doubt, is a masculinist pursuit, one which assumes knowing oneself. To make purposeful decisions about historical lines of enquiry and interpretative strategies, one must first know one's own mind. But what we call objective historical knowledge cannot be separated from a fluid network of cross-linking, constantly shifting and reciprocal relations between outer and inner worlds. The urban past, the cities we seek to know, can only be made in our own blurred self image.

In my pursuit of historical knowledge, in my search to understand architecture and gender in nineteenth-century London, I entered poignant forms of exchange – searching, thinking, reading, writing. Two texts seduced me, one a feminist polemic, the other an urban narrative from the 1820s. These two created places of methodological struggle – dialectical sites where questions of spatial and historical knowledge were raised, where I was offered alternating and tantalizing glimpses of the relation between theory and history, between my desirous self and the city, the object of my desire.

The first time I read the French feminist psychoanalyst and philosopher Luce Irigaray's essay 'Women on the Market', I was overawed.[7] Irigaray's text was a critical and poetic expression of the anger I felt about women's oppression. Her writing fired me as it has many others. For me, 'Women on the Market' served as a political manifesto, a source of creative inspiration and a theoretical tool-kit. I read it in the park, on the bus, in bed. The more I read Irigaray, the more I felt I knew about the way in which space was gendered in nineteenth-century London. Yet I had not looked at a single piece of primary evidence. I had not entered the British Library nor even contemplated visiting archives. I was thinking profanities in the sacred space of historical knowledge.

Starting with Karl Marx's critique of commodity capitalism, Irigaray argues that women can also be understood as commodities in patriarchal exchange. As a commodity, woman's value resides not in her own being but in some standard of equivalence. For Irigaray, commerce is an exchange played out through the bodies of women, as matter or as sign. Men make commerce of women but not with them. In Irigaray's version of patriarchy, men and women are distinguished from each other through their relationship to property and space: men own property/

women are property; men own and occupy spaces and women/women are space.

Irigaray's work suggests to me a way of thinking about the gendering of space which is dynamic. Rather than the static binary of the separate spheres, space can be considered gendered through a series of shifting relations of exchange. As men and women traverse space, their positions and pathways vary according to personal, social and cultural desires, and to relations of power, class, race and nationality as well as sex, gender and sexuality. The spatial patterns composed between them, both materially and metaphorically, are choreographies of connection and separation, screening and displaying, moving and containing. In these relations of exchange, Irigaray's work suggests that men move and look whereas women move or are moved between men, as commodities – as both objects and signs of exchange. Reading 'Women on the Market' made a significant difference to the way in which I imagined architectural space in early nineteenth-century London might be gendered.

I had discovered Irigaray through passion, but now, from the labyrinth of my personal desire, a more abstract theoretical stance emerged. Theory told back to me what I already knew, but in a different language, one which seemed to speak objectively rather than subjectively. It was a voice which could reasonably influence the way I knew and understood events in the past, the way I did history. Before I had looked at any primary documents, I could speculate, within reason, about how space might be gendered in early nineteenth-century London. In theory. I pursued the ramble from a theoretical perspective.[8] But theorizing the personal is one thing, historical textual analysis is another, the two are in constant negotiation. Each document I chose to examine offered me a different form of knowledge, held influence over what I could know.

The second text that held my attention was Pierce Egan's *Life in London* (1820–1),[9] an example of an early nineteenth-century ramble.[10] Rambling, as I later describe more fully, can be defined as the pursuit of pleasure, or the exploration of urban sites of leisure and entertainment by men. Here, in *The Pursuit of Pleasure* I look briefly at the cartography of the ramble in London overall and then focus on a particular part of the ramble, London's St James's, an area bounded by Pall Mall, Piccadilly, St James's Street and the Haymarket, shown in figure 1.[11]

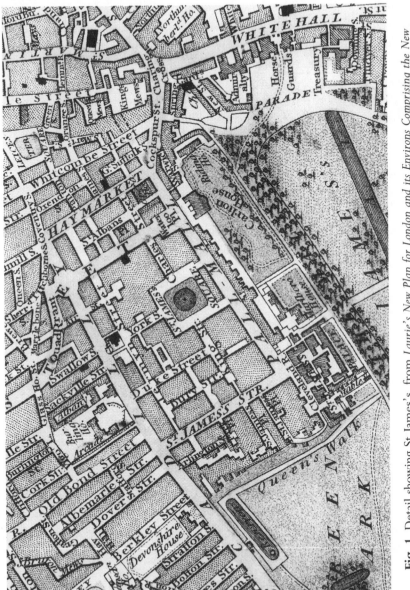

Fig. 1 Detail showing St James's, from *Laurie's New Plan for London and its Environs Comprising the New Buildings and Recent Improvements, Being an Original Survey to John Outhett* (London: Richard Holmes, 1 January 1821)

Represented as the most élite upper-class, or more precisely, aristocratic neighbourhood in London,[12] and from the late eighteenth century
onwards, a predominantly masculine district, St James's offers a highly
specific urban site through which to explore ideas of gender and space.
My investigation takes me to a number of architectural spaces – streets,
clubs, assembly rooms, opera houses and theatres – all places of
upper-class leisure.

Although, a large number of west London family residences were
located in Mayfair, north of Piccadilly, St James's, south of Piccadilly,
was a district where there were plenty of places of temporary residence
for single men. Bond Street and St James's Street had been fashionable
shopping streets for men in the seventeenth century. Activities connected with Parliament were also located in the male spaces of this
district, in drinking and sporting venues and in the clubs of St James's
Street and later Pall Mall. Coinciding with the parliamentary session,
was the London season which ran from February to July, peaking in May
and June. At this time of year St James's was the focus of upper-class
public entertainment.[13] The most prestigious and fashionable places of
leisure, such as Almack's Assembly Rooms and the Italian Opera House,
had been located in the area from the eighteenth century, but in the
early nineteenth century the area was also developed, as part of
John Nash's urban improvements for the west of London, as a luxury
shopping district for men and women.

Methodologically, the sites of ramble, the activity of rambling and
figures such as the rambler provide significant new objects of study for
architectural history and allow the development of new theoretical
models for organizing historical enquiry and architectural analysis. Typ-
ically, architectural history has dealt with form, style, physical modifica-
tion and spatial typology. Considering the production, reproduction and
representation of urban space through rambling creates a new conceptual and physical map of what the city is. The perpetual movement of
the ramble places urban locations in temporal and sequential relations,
framing social events, activities and rituals in time and space. In search of
pleasure, in constant motion, rambling represents the city as multiple
sites of desire. Architecture is redefined as a space of related social
interactions rather than as a series of isolated and static objects.

This chapter then is a pursuit of pleasure which works in two directions, from the theoretical to the historical and from the historical to the theoretical; from Irigaray's 'Women on the Market' to 1820s London, and from *Life in London* to the gendering of architectural space through rambling. I start by placing Irigaray within a broader context in two ways. By examining how her work fits into existing models of feminist architectural history, I suggest that Irigaray's theoretical work can extend the discipline by its implicit suggestion that new methodologies which deal with issues of movement and vision are adopted. By positioning her in relation to feminist accounts of the gendering of space in other disciplines, I suggest that Irigaray's writings point to a more fluid understanding of the interrelation between public and private space. I then move on to describe how rambling texts in general, and *Life in London* in particular, are important because they allow us to discuss some of the broader theoretical issues in more specific terms.

THE PURSUIT OF THEORETICAL PLEASURE: 'WOMEN ON THE MARKET'

> The economy – in both the narrow and the broad sense –
> that is in place in our societies thus requires women to lend
> themselves to alienation in consumption, and to exchanges
> in which they do not participate, that men be exempt from
> being used and circulated like commodities.[14]

Architectural history can be broadly described as a practice which studies the history of buildings. Although approaches vary, traditionally, architectural historians have tended to concentrate on defining 'architecture' as those buildings financed by wealthy and influential patrons and designed by prestigious architects, analysing this architecture in terms of form, style and type. Critical approaches to architectural history have been made by those concerned with the politics of architecture, specifically with issues of class. So-called 'marxist' architectural history entails seeing buildings as the products of the processes of capitalism and, as such, to be implicated in the political, social and cultural values of dominant classes and élite social groupings.[15] Initially interested in looking at the production of architecture, marxist architectural historians are now exploring the representation, reproduction and consumption of architecture.[16] This involves a consideration of the ways in which architecture is a setting for everyday life, both a scene for the reproduction of social relations, but also for the consumption of architecture through occupation. But although marxist architectural historians have considered the social production of architecture, and also its reproduction through image and text, seldom has this work been from a feminist perspective.[17]

Some feminists have been concerned with women's exclusion from architecture and, following reformist tactics, sought to establish a history of women architects by uncovering evidence of women's contributions to architecture.[18] They have studied the history of women's fights for inclusion in the predominantly male profession, their place in architectural education and their role as practising architects.[19] Such work, although useful in providing new material, rarely questions conventional definitions of architecture or the architect. Other feminists have focused their critique on the gendered nature of the profession and the practice of architecture itself, and sought to redefine architecture in ways that differ radically from existing models.[20] One such approach has been to look at the ways in which gender difference impacts on both the making and the using of built space. The suggestion here is that the predominance of men as producers of built space creates problems for women as users of these so-called 'man-made' environments.[21] Another approach has been to question traditional associations of women with certain kinds of environment – vernacular structures and domestic interior. Implicit within this work is a critique of architectural value systems in general, and a suggestion that women have different priorities in the design of built spaces and the organization of their production.[22] Such work raises important issues for the practitioner and the critic concerning the role of the architect and the definition of architecture. But although useful in providing the architectural historian with new material, this work does not raise questions of historical methodology, concerning status of the architectural object and the kind of analysis relevant to the objects of study.

To date, much feminist work in architectural history has remained internal to the discipline. Only recently, following the publication of Beatriz Colomina's edited collection of essays, *Sexuality and Space* in 1992,[23] has the work of feminists in other fields – such as psychoanalysis, philosophy, cultural studies, film theory and art history – been reflected in collections of work in feminism and architectural studies.[24] What such work provides is an interdisciplinary context for a feminist critique of architectural history, one which expands the terms of the discourse by making links, through gender, with methodological approaches in other academic disciplines. Feminist theory can provide useful tools and models, drawn from other fields, for critiquing architectural history, redefining both the academic context in which architectural history is located and the methodology of the discipline itself. It does so in two main ways, by questioning the actual material which architectural histor-ians choose to look at, and by rethinking, from a gender perspective, the intellectual criteria through which this material is interpreted. It is worth just briefly sketching out some of these critical positions.

The perspectives of marxist geographers, namely David Harvey and Edward Soja, and marxist philosopher, Henri Lefebvre, have been highly influential in describing the dialectical relationship between society and space – that space is socially produced and that space is also a condition of social production.[25] Feminist geographers, such as Liz Bondi, Doreen Massey, Linda McDowell and Gillian Rose, have developed and extended much of this work, arguing for attention to gender as well as class difference in the production of space.[26] They suggest instead that gender difference patterns space in a way very different from class or race for example.[27] Like geographers, anthropologists also suggest that, as material culture, space is intimately bound up in daily life, social activities and personal rituals. The earlier work of feminist anthropolo-gists, Shirley Ardener, for example, on 'public' and 'private' realms, kinship networks and social relations of exchange has been particularly important in examining the differing spaces men and women are allocated culturally, and the particular role space has in symbolizing, maintaining and reinforcing gender relations.[28]

In these disciplines, whether understood as social space and/or material culture, architecture is taken to be integral to the built environment as a whole. Users and builders, therefore, as well as designers, are seen as producers of space. In putting forward a critique of the privileged status of architecture and the role of the architect, and in suggesting that architecture is continually reproduced through use and everyday life, geographical and anthropological approaches have been and remain influential to architectural historians.[29] The twin notions of 'social space' and 'material culture' pose two key questions for feminists interested in architectural space: 'how are gender relations manifest in space and material culture?' and, equally, 'how are spatial relations manifest in constructions of gender?' These two questions are explored thoughout this book, implicitly if not explicitly.

Although important for thinking about the dialectical relation of gender and space, the disciplines of geography and anthropology are largely silent on the importance of representational systems, such as architecture, in mediating between gendered identities and urban spaces.[30] It is within visual culture – fine art, photography and film – that feminist analysis has been more attentive to the issue of representation.[31] Gender, representation and space intersect in a number of ways. For example, in two-dimensional art forms, women may be used as a sign, an empty signifier, to represent abstract concepts such as beauty or evil; while in three-dimensional space, qualities such as liberty or patriotism may be embodied in public statues with female forms.[32] Although the female-sexed body might represent notions of the 'feminine', gender itself is a form of representation. Historical documents too are gendered representations.[33] As such they often marginalize women's relation to public space.[34] And as we shall see later, gendered signifiers in historical representations often highlight concerns with other political issues such as class and race.[35]

Representations of space or architecture may also be gendered, not only through the inhabitation of space by men or women as geography or anthropology would suggest, but also through representations of such patterns of occupation. Representations of cities and individual buildings too may be gendered, both in terms of their formal similarities to biological bodies in shape, colour, texture, but also in relation to other gendered notions, such as domesticity. For example, in associating the city with the feminine or the labyrinthine, connections have often been made between the chaos of the city, the uterine form of the female body and the patriarchal notion of the unknown, or the other, as an unknowable entity. In order to look at the ways in which gender is constructed and represented in signifying systems, feminist theory has used psychoanalytic as well as semiotic models. Feminist art historians in particular have drawn on psychoanalytic concepts in order to discuss how subjectivity is sexually differentiated, and how gender difference is structured by the relations of looking and being looked at, desiring and being desired.[36]

The turn to psychoanalysis in order to deal with the differences between women has been criticized either for being ahistorical and universal or for relying too heavily on specific case studies. Certainly these are not problems easily dismissed, but by operating in an area of overlap between biological and social accounts of sex and gender difference, psychoanalytic theory suggests that differences between men and women cannot be simply explained one way or the other, either as the predetermined and natural result of biological difference or the socially determined result of various forms of class, gender, racial and sexual relations. Instead psychoanalytic theory offers an understanding of the unconscious ways in which we acquire sex and gender characteristics, insights into the construction of the gendered subject and subjectivity, and various accounts of the connections between the suppressed elements of the unconscious and the feminine.

In America, the psychoanalyst Nancy Chodorow based her theories of sexual difference on psychological development. Drawing on, but critiquing, the work of Sigmund Freud, Chodorow argued that women's social role as mothers had a differing effect on the psychological development of boys and girls.[37] Female children learnt to connect to objects, since their mother was the same sex as themselves, whereas male children learnt to separate themselves from objects, since their primary parent was a different sex from themselves. This resulted in a difference in psychology, what Carol Gilligan termed an 'ethic of care' in females, and a need to empathize, relate and connect.[38] In France, the situation was somewhat different. Feminist psychoanalysts, namely Hélène Cixious, Luce Irigaray and Julia Kristeva took other approaches. Again proceeding from, but ultimately rejecting, the work of Freud and Jacques Lacan, these feminists considered the constructions of self and subjectivity in the work of Freud and Lacan to be gendered – based on the male subject and male subjectivity. Although all three feminists replaced the phallocentricism of Freud and Lacan with new ways of thinking about the construction of the female subject, here the focus is only on the work of Irigaray.[39]

The underlying project in all of Irigaray's work to date, although this

intent has changed in the form of its articulation, has been an exploration of female subjectivity from a position of difference. Her earlier
writings, arguably more poetic in tone than the later work, are highly
theorized and focused feminist critiques of male psychoanalytic and
philosophical traditions.[40] In these texts, Irigaray argues for a relation
between the sexes which is not determined by the equation male/female
where female is defined as not-male. This is not to argue for the reversal
of the hierarchy of male and female, placing the female in the position of
dominance, but to challenge the opposition itself by showing that the
feminine and female sexuality exceed the complementary role that they
have been assigned in the opposition male/female. Irigaray has argued
that 'any theory of the subject' has always been appropriated by the
masculine; when women submit to such theories they either subject
themselves to objectification by being female or try to re-objectify
themselves as masculine subjects.[41]

Irigaray proposes an alternative subjectivity based metaphorically on
the female body with a different syntax of meaning. The symbolism of
two lips – both oral and vaginal – challenges the unity of the phallus
because of their self-contained eroticism. From the phallic point of view
the vagina is a hole, or a flaw, but when viewed as a founding symbol, a
new configuration of meaning occurs. The 'one' of the male subject
becomes 'two' constantly in touch with each other, in which they are
not separated by negation, but interact and merge, not unitary, but
diffuse, diversified, multiple and decentred.[42] For Irigaray, the spaces of
an alternative female symbolism, based metaphorically on 'two lips', are
concerned with notions of openness and exchange.[43] This provides the
starting point for imagining new forms of relationship between men and
women as equal but different subjects. It is this more cultural perspective to sexual difference that Irigaray has addressed in later work.[44] So
that as well as providing a feminist critique of women's existing position
in patriarchy, Irigaray's writing also offers men and women a more
'utopian' position.

Irigaray's work is located at the centre of a debate over essentialism
and constructionism – is being a woman an essential attribute or a
constructed one? For example, feminists who believe that the cause of
women's oppression and difference can be found in material circumstances – social and historical – critique the use of psychoanalytic

theories for understanding the construction of the female subject as anti-material and ahistorical – as essentialist or pre-given and innate. But to insist on female difference does not necessarily mean this difference is constructed outside social and historical contexts. As Elizabeth Grosz has so eloquently argued, the differently sexed female body may be considered a product of social and physic forces, constructed or produced though culture.[45]

One of the key issues in Irigaray's work has been her analysis of sexual exchange. Along with feminist anthropologist Gayle Rubin, she has been influential in arguing that within the masculine economy of patriarchy women are feminine products of exchange.[46] In structuralist anthropology, for Claude Lévi-Strauss, the exchange of women is fundamental to all kinship structures. As objects and signs, women are essential commodities in systems of exchange.[47] Irigaray's 'Women on the Market' and Rubin's 'The Traffic in Women'[48] critique the concept of exchange, as conceptualized in marxist economics and structuralist anthropology, from a feminist and psychoanalytic perspective. Rubin has argued that it is the exchange of women which reproduces male power and gender structures within the family and kinship systems.[49] For Irigaray, it is because commerce is made of women but not with them, that the power relationships between men and women appear to be dependent on the relationships between men, thus reinforcing patriarchal social order.

Irigaray's conception of woman-as-commodity – the object of physical and metaphorical exchange among men – reworks Karl Marx's analysis of commodities as the elementary form of capitalist wealth to show the ways in which women are the commodities of patriarchal exchange.[50] Marx argues that when goods are produced for exchange in the market they come to be seen as having two forms – their natural form and their value form.[51] In his materialist analysis of the commodity, Marx makes a distinction between exchange and use value. The use value of a commodity is determined by physical properties, whereas when goods are produced for exchange in the market they are seen not only as articles of utility but as inherently valuable objects with special mystical properties.[52] For Irigaray, like the commodity in marxist analysis, the female body as a commodity is divided into two irreconcilable categories.[53] Women are utilitarian objects and bearers of value, they have use value and exchange value, they represent natural value and social value. In Irigaray's symbolic order, women have three positions: the mother who represents pure use value, the virgin who represents pure exchange value and the prostitute who represents both use and exchange value.[54]

Implicit in Irigaray's work on the three variations of the female commodity – mother, virgin, prostitute – is the importance of space and property. For Irigaray, mother, or natural use value, is both the sign and the place of use value. As mother, woman is off the market, excluded from exchange. Defined as use value, mother is confined as and in private property. Similarly, virgin, or natural exchange value, is both the sign and place of exchange between men. As virgin, woman is on the market, but once violated, she is taken off the market, removed from exchange among men, confined as and in private property. The prostitute does not fall into the binary opposition of use or exchange value, private property or market. Once used, the prostitute is not defined solely as use value, confined as and in private property. Instead the prostitute remains on the market, both useful and exchangeable.[55]

Prostitution amounts to *usage that is exchanged* [. . .][56]

Irigaray provides useful ways for thinking about private, public and the gendering of space through the figure of the moving or exchanging prostitute. 'On the market', for Marx, relations of exchange can only function between property owners.[57] For Irigaray, in patriarchy, only men, as the only property owners, can perform acts of exchange. In Shannon Bell's reading of Irigaray, the prostitute is not the object of exchange between men, but the subject of exchange, she exchanges her own use value. As seller and commodity in one, the prostitute is a moving subject who actively intervenes in the male exchange economy. It is this 'ambiguous unity in the prostitute of use and exchange value which positions her as a speaking subject'.[58] We could extend this in order to argue that women 'on the market' occupying the public spaces of patriarchy, potentially determine their own movement and perform acts of exchange. They therefore are perceived as threats to patriarchy and represented as objects and signs of exchange – Irigaray's woman-as-commodity.

Irigaray's strategy, the way in which she relates her conception of the woman-as-commodity to the marxist commodity, has been the subject of much feminist debate. Given the importance of style or rhetoric in her work – the way an argument is made – this issue seems critical. Abigail Solomon-Godeau has described the relationship as a structural homology.[59] But Irigaray herself suggests that the relationship she is making is an analogous one.[60] Toril Moi has argued that Irigaray uses mimicry, that it is through her imitation of marxism that Irigaray exposes the flaws of phallocentric discourse.[61] Whether homologous, analogous or an imitation, what remains important for a discussion of gender and space is that Irigaray has suggested a relationship between two different economies using the notion of 'exchange' to allow a point of cross-over. In Margaret Whitford's view, by juxtaposing one conceptual system with another, Irigaray's use of exchange allows associations to be made between the analysis of one system and another.[62] It is this fluid concept of 'exchange' that I draw on to explore a dynamic analysis of gendered space, where men are represented as exchanging and moving and women are represented as moved or exchanged between men. These spatial patterns composed between them describe a choreography of desire: of mobility – freedom and constraint/ connection and separation and of visuality – looking and being looked at/display and secrecy.

Female movement, both conceptual and physical, is important to Irigaray. She has argued that it is women's connection with nomadism that has caused their confinement within the 'prison-house' of the male symbolic order.[63] She suggests an alternative and celebratory way of conceptualizing women's relation to movement through the figure of the angel. The angel circulates as a mediator, an alternative to the phallus, who rather than cutting through, goes between and bridges. The angel cannot be represented in patriarchal terms since she rethinks the organization of patriarchal space and time. It is difficult I think to generalize the connection between movement and sex, to suggest that all women would like to, or are equally capable of moving. But in my opinion, this is not what Irigaray is about, rather her mode of operation is suggestive, she is providing us with the opportunity to imagine new possible relations that women might have with space.

The angel is that which unceasingly *passes through the envelope(s)* or *container(s)*, goes from one side to the other, reworking every deadline, changing every decision, thwarting all repetition.[64]

This corresponds closely to much other work in postmodern feminism, where new ways of knowing and being are discussed in spatial terms – 'mapping', 'locating', 'situating', 'positioning' and 'boundaries'. Employed as critical tools, spatial metaphors constitute powerful political devices for examining the relationship between identity and place. *Where* I am makes a difference to who I can be and what I can know. For example, Donna Haraway's 'situated knowledges', Jane Flax's 'standpoint theory' and Elsbeth Probyn's notion of 'locality', all use 'position' to negotiate such ongoing theoretical disputes as the essentialism/constructionism debate.[65] In bell hook's passionate claim for the margin to be understood and occupied as a place of radical difference, the exploration of difference in female identities through race and class is explicitly spatialized.[66] And most clearly paralleling the angel in Irigaray, Rosi Braidotti's notion of the 'nomadic subject' provides an important 'theoretical figuration for contemporary subjectivity'. The nomad describes an epistemological condition, a kind of knowingness (or unknowingness) that refuses fixity, that allows us to think between, or to think 'as if'.[67] Here the work of feminist philosophers, originating with an investigation of the subject, creates an interesting intersection with the work of feminist geographers, starting with an interest in space.[68]

Relations of exchange, defined through capitalist and patriarchal culture, interlock with relations of display and consumption. Exchange takes place through the transactions of consumption – desiring, choosing, buying, owning, using and displaying commodities. Consumption as a socio-economic activity is becoming increasingly important especially in the fields of anthropology and cultural geography. And for marxist work in many disciplines, an interrogation of the sites and modes of production has shifted to those of consumption.[69] In traditional marxist critique, consumption, a compensation for alienated wage labour, is viewed as a passive activity. But recent work discusses the important and pro-active role that consumption plays in the formation of identity. By consuming, possessing and displaying certain goods the consumer identifies him/herself with a status, life style or social identity.[70] Consumption may be understood as the result or the producer of desire and/or need. The relationship between the three is complex. Psychoanalytic accounts, for example those of Freud, consider attitudes towards consumption to be reflections of the desires of early childhood development – passive, regressive and oral.[71]

Consumption can be seen as important in the lives of women and the constitution of femininity.[72] The role of consumer may be seen as an empowering one, a source of self-identity and pleasure in the public realm.[73] In the early nineteenth century, it was through the development of commodity capitalism that women were encouraged into the city as consumers, both for the home and for themselves.[74] But such a view is complicated by patriarchal ideologies and practices which suggest that female consumers do not necessarily consume for themselves, but 'consume vicariously for the head of the household' in order to represent male status.[75] Places of consumption reinforce this ideology by representing women as objects of visual consumption in order to sell goods.[76] In this way, women 'on the market' may be considered both consumers and commodities.[77] Historically, it was in places of consumption, legitimated zones of pleasure, where women's presence (as consumers) was most obviously felt in the city.[78] Consumption, by virtue of the fact that it is neither production nor reproduction, runs against the grain of the separate spheres ideology, and so such spaces were represented as sites where social codes were transgressed.[79]

The theory that consumer goods communicate cultural meaning through social rituals – possession, exchange, grooming and divestment – helps to account for the importance of the visual in spatial activities such as dressing, shopping, and promenading. In certain forms of psychoanalysis, it has been argued, unequal gendered relations of looking are created as men and women acquire their sexual identities. For example, in the work of Freud, the fears of castration which arise in the boy child as a result of looking at the mother's body, cause him to invent fetish objects to stand in for the mother's lack of phallus. Here looking is active and gendered masculine, being looked at is passive and feminized.[80] This model of the male gaze and the female spectacle, although binary in nature and over-simplified, provides a useful starting point for thinking about the gendering of space through looking.[81] In the first instance, it allows us to consider men as looking subjects and women as looked-at objects on display in public spaces in the city. Connections can be made between the spatial qualities of urban places and femininity as 'to-be-looked-at-ness', where certain parts of the city may themselves be treated as spectacle.

Laura Mulvey has argued that various kinds of visual pleasure are constructed through relations of sexual difference.[82] For example, sco-pophilia, what Freud called the desire to look, is stimulated by struc-tures of voyeurism and narcissism which both derive pleasure in looking. Voyeurism is a controlling and distanced way of looking in which 'grat-ification is obtained without intimacy' and where pleasure is derived from looking at a figure as an object.[83] Narcissistic pleasure is produced by identification with the image and can be considered analogous to Lacan's mirror stage – just as a child forms his/her ego by identifying with the perfect mirror image, so the spectator derives pleasure from identification with the perfect image of themselves in others. In both voyeurism and narcissism the look is active and the object is passive. But while the looked at object of voyeurism is prohibited and has therefore been considered female in heterosexual discourse, the looked-at object of narcissism involves self-identification and so may include other men. Here the rambler and other male figures encountered on the ramble can enjoy looking, but also being looked at. Indeed displaying through con-suming requires an exhibition of the body to be looked at both by women and by other men.

However, this model is far from ideal. First, the distinction made between 'looking' and 'being-looked-at' can be a false one – more often these are reciprocal positions. Second, there are different kinds of look. For example, looking as 'seeing' allows multiple and different view-points, whereas looking as 'gazing' is a more sustained operation of vision that implies authority and surveillance.[84] Third, any attempt to reverse this construction is problematic. It is only possible for a female spectator 'to look' if she is identified with an active male, or to consider the construction of female identity in relation to being looked at. Iriga-ray's work once again is useful here, since she utilizes the operation of mimicry as a conscious and subversive strategy for destabilizing the masquerade, or woman's role as spectacle. Irigaray suggests that by deliberately assuming the feminine style of masquerade assigned to them, by deliberately flaunting spectacle and speech, women can uncover the mechanisms which exploit them.[85] For example, by taking herself to market and naming her price, it could be argued that the prostitute occupies a mimetic position. She mimics male discourse and in so doing disrupts the male economy exposing at its foundation the exchange of women.

We can summarize now the feminist and theoretical line taken by Irigaray: that women are exchanged, both socially and symbolically, as commodities with use values (sex and/or child-bearing and -rearing) and exchange values (signifiers of male wealth in terms of property and commodities); and that men organize and display their activities of exchange and consumption, including the desiring, choosing, purchasing and consuming of female commodities, for others to look at in public space. It is this theorized and abstract discussion of interlocking relations of exchange, consumption and display in Irigaray's work which provides a critical framework for examining how relations of moving and looking were represented as gendered in *Life in London*, my second starting point, the second text that seduced me.

THE PURSUIT OF HISTORICAL PLEASURE:
LIFE IN LONDON

This day has been wholly devoted to a ramble about London,
to look at curiosities.[86]

My decision to focus on the 'ramble' and its particular role in representing early nineteenth-century London as a series of gendered spaces demonstrates a number of criteria. The chosen historical period is significant for a number of reasons. The years of the Regency between 1811 and 1821 and the reign of George IV between 1821 and 1829 are important for feminists interested in gender and space for historiographic reasons. We could argue that, since these decades precede the full-blown mid nineteenth-century urban manifestation of the 'separate spheres', they offer us an opportunity to look at the crucial moments of early formation.[87] But I suggest that the large amount of feminist research which has been conducted within the mid- and late nineteenth century has resulted in a perception that the separate spheres ideology is

somehow 'fixed' in the Victorian period. So rather I argue that representations of gendered space in any patriarchal culture will play an important role in 'placing' men in dominant roles in relation to public and
private spaces, but just how such representations are configured depends
on specific historical conditions. In the early nineteenth-century ramble,
particularly if we look at the texts published in the 1820s, there is an
emphasis on placing men as visible explorers of the city.

Conceptually there are a number of problems with the very loose
ways in which the terms public and private are defined.[88] The terms have
been used in various ways in different discourses to refer to social and
spatial metaphors, spatial forms and architectural layouts, kinds of property ownership, attitudes towards political liberty and citizenship, types
of activity.[89] Further, their changing meanings are made even less clear,
by the fact that since public and private are cultural constructions, their
definitions change historically.[90] There is a great deal of ambiguity here
then concerning the terminology of the separate spheres. For example,
in terms of property ownership, places owned by private individuals for
public usage may be classified as private property as opposed to state or
crown property, or public space as opposed to family homes. Further,
when graduations from public to private are considered in terms of
social activities, from formal activities where certain distances between
people are maintained, to intimate activities which involve bodily contact and exposure, such as sex, bathing and sleeping, it is important to
note that these are not necessarily mapped onto public and private space
in ways which reinforce each other. For example, formal activities may
occur in private places, whereas intimate activities may take place in
public space. Finally, and with reference to spatial morphology and
typology, outside spaces are usually defined as public, and inside spaces
as private, regardless of ownership or the kinds of activity taking place
there. So we can see that the description of the city as public within the
separate spheres ideology is rather crude considering that the urban
fabric incorporates individual private homes which may vary in their
composition possibly to include a large open space accessible to the
public.

It is perhaps more useful to consider the changing meanings of public
and private in relation to patriarchy.[91] Patriarchy varies historically,
geographically and culturally and in relation to other social structures,

such as capitalism. As such, it is an adaptable and flexible social structure, but one which always works to control the exchange of women
among men.[92] Partly defined by the terms themselves, patriarchy also
forms an important way of shaping public and private space. Sylvia
Walby has argued that public patriarchy is segregationist and private
patriarchy exclusionary.[93] In private patriarchy, the patriarch controls
women individually and directly in the private sphere of the house,
whereas in public patriarchy the institutions of the public domain maintain control of women. But exactly how these two types of patriarchy
are related depends, I argue, on specific historical circumstances.

Shifts in kinds of patriarchy produce different genderings of space.
The emergence of commodity consumption as an important economic,
cultural and social activity in the early nineteenth century emphasized
conflicts between capitalism and patriarchy, both social systems desirous
of controlling public urban space. As capitalism required an increase in
the number of women entering the city, as low-paid workers and as
consumers for home and family, forms of private patriarchal control
centred on the family and home, shifted towards the intensification of
public patriarchal struggles to control women's use of the city as a
whole. As we will see in a later chapter, male-only spaces such as the
clubs of St James's marginalized women's access to public space through
exclusion, whereas legislation, such the Vagrancy Acts, controlled
female urban movement in a complex yet codified manner.[94] In less
clearly enforced but equally powerful ways, subsequent chapters argue
that the ramble also articulates an attempt to reduce the presence of
women in public space.

The rising importance of various middle-class groups, not least
religious ones, was particularly significant at this time in emphasizing the
problems signified by the presence of women in public places. Whereas
working-class women in the city were largely ignored by middle- and
upper-class commentators, their gender rendered invisible through their
class position; the presence of middle-class women in the city as consumers and workers was a concern. Fears that their own female property was on display to other men instilled the need to extend and
intensify controls over women in the city. Women's public presence
threatened the values of emergent bourgeois masculinities and
represented fears of public disorder where class hierarchy could be

overturned. The mid-nineteenth century saw a return towards a more private mode of patriarchy involving the intensification of domestic ideology, defining 'woman' as a signifier of social stability, respectability and domesticity for the lower classes to look up to.

There has been much theoretical discussion over how forms of representation inform women's relation to the city historically. It is clear the problem operates at both a material and ideological level, but the exact role of representation in constructing or being constructed by this relationship is a matter of feminist debate. Cultural historians, for example Elizabeth Wilson, have been concerned with re-establishing a positive connection between women and the public realm by reclaiming the city as a space of female enjoyment through literary evidence.[95] Such a move disputes the work of sociologist, Janet Wolff, who has argued that literary and visual forms represent the separate spheres ideology in such a powerful way that the liberating potential of lived experience as a counter-practice is denied or at least obscured.[96]

Both Wolff and Wilson engage critically with various forms of representation to discuss women's relationship to the city. While Wolff argues that cultural representations – the almost exclusively male literature of modernity – work to deny the connection of women to the city; Wilson uses positive representations by women of their life in cities to assert that women occupied and enjoyed urban public space. Clearly, urban experience can only be understood historically through cultural representations, but, as Lynda Nead points out, it is important to consider how gender ideology does not precede, but is produced through these representations.[97] Given that feminist historians differ in their political stance, one might prefer to account for the ways in which women have been oppressed, while another chooses to write a history of struggles for liberation, it is also important to recognize the influential role played here by the historian in choosing and interpreting cultural representations as forms of evidence and in discussing the ways in which they reconstruct particular versions of history.

Griselda Pollock's work has also considered women's relation to public space, specifically through a study of visual representations – the paintings of male impressionists. From her study of such paintings, Pollock constructs a model of gendered space which shows how the paintings correlate certain kinds of women with particular spaces in the city – 'ladies' are found in parks and theatres, 'fallen women' in the backstage of theatres, cafés, follies and brothels.[98] Pollock's analysis starts to suggest that the gendering of space is configured in a far more complicated manner than the separate spheres ideology suggests and that a more fluid and complex analysis of the gendering of space is required.

The Pursuit of Pleasure sets out with such a mode of analysis in mind, one which pays attention to variations in definitions of public and private and their interrelationship, to the specificity of context and to the different kinds of spatial distribution of activities taking place within buildings themselves. By developing a discussion of movement and vision, enacted through activities associated with consumption, display and exchange, the ramble provides us with a good historical example for exploring the gendering of space in this way. The spatial configuration of the places of the ramble goes beyond the notion of the separate spheres and the city as unproblematically male, public and external. The public sphere of the city, London, represented through rambling, is reconceived as both public and private, outside and inside, institutional and domestic, formal and intimate, urban street and domestic home, and so starts to dissolve the boundaries of binary definitions. Public and private spheres are shown to co-exist and overlap, the boundaries defining them changing over time and in relation to morphology, ownership, activities and occupations.

The rambler moves through a series of haunts or places of pleasure in a city composed of internal and external spaces. These spaces can be interpreted as both private in terms of ownership or intimacy, and as public in opposition to the domestic realm. For example, male clubs are private in terms of membership and their function as alternative domestic spaces for unmarried men, but they are also public as places of entertainment outside the family home; while opera houses put on stage, on public display, emotional states usually considered personal and intimate.

The male rambler demonstrates the possibility of re-examining the relation of 'male' and 'masculine' not as a pre-given pairing, but instead as social constructions, constructed in relation to one another and in relation to femininity. The rambler's masculinity is articulated through different modes of representation – dress and language; through various social activities – fornicating, gambling, drinking and sporting; and in relation to differing and gendered positions governed by relations of vision and movement – display and concealment, mobility and constraint. The rambler was a man who liked to be on display, a feature associated with femininity in patriarchal ideology.

This is where Irigaray's work also provides such a useful theoretical starting point, a place to reconceptualize the gendering of space as a form of 'choreography'. This might also be understood as a sequence of moves performed by and between men and women in space, at a material and an ideological level. These moves, or perhaps we could call them spatial practices, develop as responses to the demands made on men and women by patriarchal and capitalist culture. They are therefore not necessarily liberatory for women. Although, as I have earlier described, much of Irigaray's work does provide us with ways of theorizing women's resistance to patriarchy and imagining alternative kinds of feminine space, that is not my main purpose here. Rather I am interested in investigating how Irigaray's work can allow us to explore the ways in which particular texts, in this case the ramble, represent male spatial practices and operate ideologically to define male and female mobility and visuality in public space.

The kinds of places visited by the rambler in early nineteenth-century London were sites of leisure and pleasure. Some, such as theatres, opera houses, pleasure gardens, parks, clubs, taverns and streets, were familiar places of entertainment where pleasure was sought through engaging with those outside the immediate family, sometimes strangers. Such interactions within the public spaces of the city involved various forms of social exchange and display – walking, talking, watching, dancing, eating, drinking and sporting. But for the first time during this period, particularly in London, new places of leisure emerged as important to urban enjoyment. These sites were related to the rise of commodity capitalism and represented the commodification of urban leisure, adding shopping or commodity consumption to the list of upper-class leisure pursuits. The pursuit of pleasure through commodity consumption focused on the desire for commodities, their purchase through money exchange and the public display of consumption.

As well as acknowledging the role of the body's pre-given capacities for desire, cultural historians emphasize the role of material conditions in instigating the need for consumption. For example, the 'birth of consumer society' in the eighteenth century has been explained as the coincidence of certain social and technological conditions.[99] While mass production offered the possibility of buying more consumer goods, it was class stratification which increased the need to represent status through the purchase of objects.[100] For Thorstein Veblen, social competition was the motive force of this consumer revolution. Rank and social status could be made visible through the display of consumption – visible waste and ostentatious expense. His notion of 'conspicuous consumption' follows the principles of conspicuous waste and leisure. Wealth, luxury goods, manners, decorum, surroundings and the ability not to perform degrading productive work are displayed in order to attract envy and admiration.[101] Veblen's ideas provide a useful starting point for exploring the ramble as a form of consumption which indicated the status of wealthy young bachelors, as a display of conspicuous waste and leisure through activities such as shopping and gambling.

According to Veblen, modern consumption is based on a two-way model of 'emulation' and/or 'distinction', where lower groups emulate the modes and manners of the higher, while higher groups adopt strategies of distinction to keep a distance from the lower. Georg Simmel's 'trickle down' theory also explains change in fashion as a result of two conflicting principles. In Simmel's case, adjacent social groups adopt strategies of 'imitation' and 'differentiation', where the subordinate groups imitate and the superordinate groups differentiate in response.[102] Such two-way models are of limited use, however, since they deal with a restricted number of groups and are reductive in describing the direction and flexibility of the actions such groups might take. In considering the important role of consumption in determining the relative status of the nobility and bourgeoisie in the early nineteenth century, while we could argue that the newly wealthy members of the bourgeoisie 'emulated' or 'imitated' the aristocracy by acquiring titles, buying offices and marrying into the nobility,[103] the response of the nobility, the traditional landed élites, was not to adopt a policy of 'distinction' nor to 'differentiate' in response, but rather, between the 1780s and 1820s, to marry into the bourgeoisie in order to acquire new wealth.[104]

A number of other theorists of consumption provide a complexity to this class distinction model. Gilles Lipovestsky, for example, argues that the potency of consumption to operate as an instrument of class affiliation and distinction varies historically; when certain classes are wealthier, more mobile and less homogeneous, changes in consumption are particularly rapid.[105] Colin Campbell also highlights the importance of historical variation – at different times different groups adopt different actions.[106] While Lipovestsky emphasizes the relation between the struggle at the top and the threat of the working classes, Campbell stresses the key role played by intermediate groups. Pierre Bourdieu also emphasizes the importance of strategies of distinction in representing ever more subtle differences of good taste.[107] Bourdieu argues that instead of requiring an unlimited stock of new commodities, the acting out of distinction through use as well as purchase, allows objects to represent multiple meanings.

In the early nineteenth century, commercial cities like London provided an increasing availability and variety of fashion items and a growing number of places in which to display the self. In urban dwellers, such as the rambler, this led to an increase in the awareness of style and a greater desire to articulate a sense of identity through distinctive consumption.[108] Richard Sennett has argued that a shift in social relations in the rapidly increasing centres of urban population in general led to a transformation of public spaces, from places where social contact was intimate and sensual, to places where the emphasis was on surface appearance, display, fashion and eroticism.[109] Different distances in the space between people, from distant to intimate, allow a variety of communication systems to evolve. Both clothing and language, for example, can be understood as systems of meaning, but by operating over varying distances they provide clues to social identity, but not in the same ways.[110] Spoken language, with its large vocabulary and ability to convey complex variations, such as accent, dialect, rhetoric, irony, metaphor or scepticism, can communicate subtle differences in an intimate setting; whereas clothing, read more easily from a distance, can display meaning about status and social dynamics rapidly and flexibly in urban spaces.[111]

Ideas concerning the role of consumption as a means of communicating social status are important in understanding the early nineteenth-century rambler and his position as conspicuous consumer in public space. The approaches of Lipovestsky, Campbell and Bourdieu allow us to explore the complexity of the relations between various male figures in the ramble in ways which appear to oppose the earlier two-way explanations put forward by Simmel and Veblen. For example, as we shall see, the aristocratic corinthian's emulation of the working-class bruiser's dress, language and posture describes an attempt to differentiate himself from the bourgeois dandy by emulating and appropriating the identity of a male below him both in terms of class. When considering this appropriation of the streetwise demeanour, clothing and cockney slang of the working-class coachman, Bourdieu's work is particularly relevant. Following models which emphasize the importance of intermediate groups in establishing competing identites, dandies express an attempt to distinguish themselves both from those below and those above them by adopting austere dress codes and exclusive spatial practices.

As a gendered urban movement, rambling provides a new conceptual and theoretical model for feminist architectural history. Examining the figures and spaces of the ramble enables us to explore how gendered identities and spaces are produced, reproduced and represented through activities – consumption, display and exchange. Rambling represents gendered space as fluid and complex, varying according to time, to specific urban location and to the spatial patterning within buildings. Gender relations are articulated spatially and visually, through movement and containment, viewer and viewed. The relation between gendered identities and architectural spaces is shown to be one of flux. In short, studying the ramble allows an elaboration of the dialectical relation between architectural history and critical theory from a feminist perspective.

The concept of rambling is introduced in chapter 2, while chapters 3 to 5 deal in turn with specific architectural spaces in St James's visited in the ramble: the male club, the assembly room and the opera house. In chapter 2, I describe how the rambler articulates his masculine identity through his visuality and mobility. The various other male figures of the ramble – corinthian, bruiser, dandy – are outlined as examples of conflicting and reinforcing representations of public masculinity. The female figure of the cyprian or prostitute and the other females conflated with her, such as actresses and dancers, are described in terms of their status as commodities and spectacles in the ramble.

Chapter 3 explores the notion of gendered space through varying configurations of public and private with specific reference to a number of clubs in early nineteenth-century London's St James's. The male-only venue of the club is considered to represent public masculinity through two forms of male control over space: first, patriarchal mechanisms which exclude women and second, fraternal mechanisms which exclude certain men. The chapter outlines how the male club also operated as a private space within the public realm, both as a space of intimacy and domesticity rivalling the familial home, and as a site of private property and exclusivity. The male clubs of St James's, specifically the four at the top of St James's Street: Boodle's, Brooks's, Crockford's and White's, were frequented by men of the same class who controlled space to assert their social and political allegiances and rivalries. The exclusivity of the first-floor gambling room, a place of secrecy and privacy, is contrasted with the ground-floor bow window, a site of public display and exclusivity. Male leisure pastimes, such as drinking, sporting, gambling, are explored as social and spatial practices which, by establishing shared codes of consumption, display and exchange, represent public masculinities.

Chapters 4 and 5 discuss different aspects of the gendering of public spaces through the control, rather than the exclusion, of women. Almack's Assembly Rooms, described as a 'marriage mart', provides an example in chapter 4 of a space where women were exchanged between men as marriageable commodities, in the form of titles, land and money. Such exchange was carefully controlled by the establishment of tight entrance policies and the internal division of assembly rooms into places which encouraged the manipulation of courtship though supervised activities, like dancing and cards.

Chapter 5 examines a different form of exchange, the exchange of looks rather than property. In the Italian Opera House varying positions of looking, gazing, displaying and masquerading constructed a series of differently gendered spaces. Rambling texts represent women in the auditorium, performing on stage and sitting in the audience in boxes, as feminine spectacles – positioned as the foci of the male gaze. But conversely, these texts also describe how the male patrons offered themselves as objects of display in boxes on stage and in fop's alley in the pit. The ancillary spaces of the opera house provided a secondary array of visual spectacle. Here ramblers watched cyprians in the foyers and saloons and, in the green room, male patrons of the opera and ballet had a privileged audience with their favourite female performers.

Chapters 2 to 5 each explore how space is gendered through different pursuits of pleasure in the city. Each chapter goes beyond a discussion of public and private to show how in public places of leisure, interactions take place in different ways through relations of exchange, consumption and display. The relation of the male rambler, represented as a moving, looking, consuming subject, to the female cyprian, represented as a passive, displayed, commodified object, is critiqued as a reductive and binary model. Considered from a more reflexive and dialectical position, men and women are shown to be situated in sets of complex relations, as both objects and subjects, often simultaneously. Each chapter demonstrates how different social relations of moving and looking are emphasized according to specific configurations of site.

It is the conceptual device of the urban ramble which allows each individual site of urban leisure and enjoyment to be considered as part of an integral network of spaces of pleasure across London. In chapter 6, these different locations are brought together with a particular emphasis on the figure of the cyprian, a patriarchal representation of the public woman, but also of the city itself. Egan's sequel to *Life in London*, *Finish . . . to Life in and out of London*, written eight years later, places a different emphasis on the pursuit of pleasure in the city.[112] Instead of offering fun and satisfaction, the public places of the ramble are shown to bring with them physical and moral downfalls. The life of enjoyment lived out by the rambler is represented here through a narrative of decline and retribution, discussed metaphorically through the decay and collapse of the body of the female cyprian. No longer a visual spectacle and desired object, the figure of the cyprian, featured as a site of disgust, articulates fears concerning the unfettered activities of rambling.

CHAPTER 2

Life in London

The gaze of the flâneur articulates and produces a masculine sexuality which in the modern sexual economy enjoys the freedom to look, appraise and possess.[1]

We have already taken a promiscuous ramble from the West towards the East, and it has afforded some amusement; but our stock is abundant, and many objects of curiosity are still in view.[2]

Fig. 2 George and Robert Cruikshank, 'The Corinthian Capital', Pierce Egan, *Life in London; or, the day and night scenes of Jerry Hawthorn, Esq., and his elegant friend Corinthian Tom, accompanied by Bob Logic, the Oxonian, in their Rambles and Sprees through the Metropolis* (frontispiece)

The verb 'to ramble' describes incoherent movement, 'to wander in discourse (spoken or written): to write or talk incoherently or without natural sequence of ideas'. As a mode of movement, rambling is unrestrained, random and distracted: 'a walk (formerly any excursion or journey) without any definite route or pleasure'.[3] In the early nineteenth century, the verb specifically described the exploration of urban space, only later, by 1879, was the term rambling associated with planned rural excursions.[4]

An urban activity generated through the pursuit of pleasure, rambling involved visits to places of leisure – assembly rooms, opera houses, theatres, parks, clubs, sporting, drinking venues and shopping streets. Ramblers were young, single, heterosexual and upper-class men, one of a number of new urban masculinities which emerged in London rambling texts in the late eighteenth and early nineteenth centuries. Other urban males included the corinthian, or upper-class sporting gentleman; the bruiser, or working-class boxer; and the dandy, or aspiring man of fashion. Their different identities were articulated through verbal language, dress codes and through activities such as gambling, drinking, sporting, fornicating and the consumption, display and exchange of commodities which took place in a series of specific sites throughout London. *The Pursuit of Pleasure* explores the ways in which rambles, specifically Pierce Egan's *Life in London*, represent early nineteenth-century London through a series of gendered figures and spaces.[5]

LIFE IN LONDON: THE RAMBLER AS READER

> Our motto is be gay and free
> Make Love and Joy your choicest treasures
> Look on our book of glee
> And Ramble over scenes of Pleasure.[6]
>
> *Pleasure* was the word – *Gaiety* the pursuit.[7]

The rambling genre has its origins in books published from the sixteenth century onwards which, while delving into the London underworld and pretending to be authentic and sensational, actually revealed little more than graphic detail. These texts professed that their aims were to warn 'country men and women' against the corrupting influence of the city.

Despite such alleged intentions, the tone of such texts was partly moralizing but also partly titillating. By alluding to aspects of danger in a seductive manner, 'Johnny Raws' from the country were tempted by the excitement of urban life, rather than informed as to the location and activities of the sophisticated criminals of the town. The key distinguishing feature of the so-called 'spy' tale is its structure.[8] This takes the form of a journey through the city, told as an urban narrative, half fiction/half fact, in which various country gentlemen are initiated to the adventures of city life under the guidance of streetwise urban relatives. These streetwise characters are represented as 'knowing' individuals already wise to the delights and entertainments, as well as the tricks and frauds, of the urban realm.

Throughout the eighteenth century, spy texts focused on stories of criminals, robberies, prostitution and pictures of the seamy side of metropolitan life.[9] At the same time, the term ramble appeared alongside spy and was used in an interchangeable way, although the emphasis differed slightly. While earlier spy texts were fascinated with the darker aspects of urban life, such as crime, the ramble was more involved with excitement in the form of fun and pleasure. However, this is not to say that rambles were not interested in the excitement of discovering the unknown. For example, although daytime or Sunday rambles usually passed through sites already familiar to the rambler; night-time rambles involved visiting places usually out of bounds to the rambler. In combining elements of suspense and danger, this attitude represented a form of urban masculinity inherently concerned with aspects of knowing.[10] By the first decades of the nineteenth century, some publications continued to follow earlier models and focus on the detection and exposure of criminal codes.[11] However, in others including Pierce Egan's *Life in London*, Jonathan Badcock's *Real Life in London*, William Heath's *Fashion and Folly* and Bernard Blackmantle's *The English Spy*, the emphasis had shifted from the earlier texts in significant ways.[12]

Unlike the earlier books which were primarily scripted and included only a few black and white woodcuts, these new rambles were highly visual documents, composed of a combination of text and image, with coloured lithographs, engravings and etchings, providing a place where urban dwellers could look and read. *Life in London*, for example, describes itself in terms of visually based urban knowledge: as a 'complete cyclopedia', allowing its readers to 'see life'.[13]

ON THE DIFFERENCE BETWEEN WHAT IS GENERALLY TERMED 'KNOWING THE WORLD' AND 'SEEING LIFE'.[14][sic]

Written by Pierce Egan (1772–1849) and illustrated by the caricaturists, George Cruikshank (1792–1878) and Robert Cruikshank (1789–1856), *Life in London* was one of the most popular rambling texts of the early nineteenth century.[15] Moving from site to site in the pursuit of pleasure, *Life In London* describes the rambles of three young males as they explore London in 1821. The three men, as shown in figure 2, are Corinthian Tom, a young London bachelor and member of the aristocracy, with an inheritance and a London residence – Corinthian House; Robert Logic, Tom's drinking companion, an Oxford student also with an inheritance living at the Albany chambers for bachelors off Piccadilly; and Tom's cousin, Jerry Hawthorn, from the same class background, a fine sportsman and drinker, but represented as somewhat lacking in credibility as a male due to his rural origin. If *Life in London* has any narrative plot it is of Jerry's initiation into urban lifestyle and manhood.

In their intention to inform the reader about the city, rambling texts could be described as guidebooks to the city.[16] But unlike traditional guidebooks, spy tales and rambles are only semi-documentary, their intention is more sensational, to excite and produce a pleasurable response in the reader. Although the places described are real, the manner of their selection is not comprehensive, but highly subjective. Only those places deemed to attract pleasure seekers are featured. Unlike traditional guidebooks, ramblers describe sites in terms of the activities going on within them rather than as objects. They also organize their material differently. Rather than describe districts or relate sites by location or type, places are linked through time as part of a journey, more like the accounts of London in the diaries of contemporary visitors.[17]

In their structure rambles could be described as 'spatial stories'.[18] As traditional stories or fictions, rambles are lacking, there is no narrative plot and the characters are not developed; instead the motivations are spatial and thematic – the desire is to move through the city in the pursuit of pleasure. Excitement is developed in the reader by visually juxtaposing image, written text and different typographic techniques. Contrast is an important aspect of rambling. Both in the narrative and the engravings, *Life in London* prioritizes the diversity of social experience, portraying the paradoxes of city life as the main source of urban pleasure.[19] The experiences of Tom, Jerry and Logic are structured around contrasts, social and spatial, from high culture to popular culture, from grand interiors to dark streets. The most important contrast represented is between the two extremes of London – east and west.

> The extremes, which in every point of view are to be met with every day in the metropolis [. . .] ornament London, and render it the delight and happiness of society.[20]

In the early decades of the nineteenth century, the City of London and the eastern districts surrounding it were commercial and industrial zones, inhabited by the working classes, including a large number of immigrants, most numerously the Irish, often in slums.[21] Such areas, particularly St Giles and East Smithfield, feature in *Life in London* as the places where 'real' life is to be found. The west was populated by members of the upper classes, nobility and wealthy bourgeoisie, who had moved out of the City, first to Covent Garden and Soho, later to St James's and Piccadilly.[22] The consequence of these movements created a considerable degree of social segregation in London between the racially mixed, working-class east and the 'white' upper-class west. The differences between the west and east were further marked by temporal patterns: the late-rising leisured upper classes were found in the west and the early-rising industrious working classes in the east. In *Life in London*, Jerry's metamorphosis into upper-class urban dweller is represented by a change in his daily routine, from getting up at dawn, to going to bed at dawn.[23]

This social contrast was reflected in the urban topography of east and west. As well as the status and wealth of the residents, patterns of land ownership and government legislation affected the kind of urban spaces produced in both areas.[24] The London jurisdictions of the City of London, the City of Westminster and the counties of Surrey and Middlesex, had different legal and institutional structures and attitudes to building.[25] Due to the nature of the collaboration between the landowners and speculators, the only areas of planned development during the eighteenth century occurred in the west. The 1774 Building Act and the various building guidelines set out by the landlords produced a structured set of urban spaces with wide, straight, regular streets with new squares, footways, street paving, sewers and houses built to a uniform design.[26] The early nineteenth century also saw the design of a number of urban improvement schemes in the west of London, such as Regent Street; prestigious pieces of architecture, such as Carlton House; and new spaces of public entertainment, commercial leisure and commodity consumption – theatres, parks and arcades; all of which reinforced the development of a sophisticated urban culture.[27] In contrast, and partly caused by differences in property rights, the east, outside the boundaries of the city, sprawled haphazardly, fragmented and chaotic, with narrow and irregular streets, crowded rookeries and slum areas.

In *Life in London* the ramble uses contrast as a structuring form to represent the diversity and flux of London life.[28] The juxtaposition of visual images and written text forces the reader to move constantly between word and picture.[29] Typographically, the graphics are animated by the use of conflicting cases, exclamation marks and italics. Egan moves relentlessly between different urban scenes in the manner of an on-the-spot reporter, using rapid language, lively slang terms and sensationalist tactics. The result is a textual creation of a picturesque city where contrast and juxtaposition operate to create effect and to suspend reality. Egan compares this literary technique to that of painting.[30]

The writers and illustrators of *Life in London* adopt literary and visual motifs which combine fact and fiction, in order to simultaneously attract and distance the reader, locating the city both as reality and fantasy.[31] Much of the amusement and excitement in reading the ramble comes from blurring real and imaginary figures. For example, the three main characters, Tom, Jerry and Logic, are supposedly modelled on the three creators of the book.[32] Corinthian Tom represents George Cruikshank; Robert Logic, Pierce Egan; and Jerry Hawthorn, Robert Cruikshank. The two main female characters, Corinthian Kate and Sue, represent well-known London courtesans.[33] The low-life characters refer to prostitutes and beggars familiar to Londoners.[34] The illustrations are also partly based on 'real life'. George Cruikshank drew the characters in his local tap room and the sets Robert Cruikshank designed for the theatre production of the book were reproductions of the interiors of real London places.[35] Egan's own experience as a sport journalist enters the text when his notebook, his 'reader', is lost or stolen as a result of a drinking spree.[36] The copy is treated journalistically, with detailed asides, contemporary gossip, character sketches and the use of colloquial sporting slang and flash cant in order to emphasize that this was a representation of 'real' London life:

> Tom is sluicing the ivory of some of the unfortunate heroines with blue ruin whom the breaking up of the SPELL has turned-up without any luck, in order to send them to their pannies full of spirits. Jerry is in Tip Street upon this occasion and the Mollishers are all nutty upon him, putting it about, that he is a well-breached Swell.[37]

The simultaneous representation of London as both reality and fantasy allows the reader to be excited by certain acceptable aspects of 'real life', such as scandal and gossip, but to be comfortably distanced from other more disturbing issues like poverty, crime, prostitution and drunkenness. Egan uses a number of devices to achieve this. The trope of the camera obscura, discussed in more detail later, creates an isolated distance for the reader to watch real life from. Representing socially distressing events as spectacular and comical also produces a psychological space between reader and the scene portrayed. For example, the beggars and prostitutes in a tavern in the east of London are described textually and visually as jolly figures enjoying life. A similar picture of 'drunkenness, beggary, lewdness, and carelessness' in a late-night coffee shop in Covent Garden is made spectacular by pointing out its novelty value: 'quite new to thousands'.[38] In this way, Life in London provided an opportunity for readers to experience the urban realm in a form that everyday life, with its class barriers created by élitism and fear, did not allow. It provided its readership with controlled and pleasurable views of the potentially dangerous 'other'.

Life in London was issued initially as a monthly publication from September 1820. These monthly publications were then reissued as a book in two editions in 1821, then again in 1823, 1870 and 1904.[39] For the upper and middle classes who could afford the more expensive original, there were tantalizing views of the dangerous territory of east London. James Catnach's twopenny broadside version of *Life in London* with black and white woodcut imitations of the original etchings appeared in 1822. This appealed to a larger audience both in terms of cost and circulation, providing the working classes with glimpses of the exclusive life styles in the west.[40] *Life in London* was incredibly popular in the decade after its publication in 1821. The book was imitated, translated and exported to foreign locations.[41] But it was probably as a theatre production, accessible to those who could not read and those with low incomes, that it reached its greatest audience.[42]

The popularity of *Life in London* has been attributed to a combination of factors, including technological innovations, the adoption of new marketing techniques by booksellers, such as serial publications, an increased consumption of printed material in general and rising literacy rates among certain groups of society, predominantly the working and middle classes.[43] It has also been argued that the popularity of this specific kind of text stemmed from its ability to satisfy in its readers an increasing desire for urban identity, one being articulated simultaneously in other art forms including city entertainments, architecture and urban planning.[44] Contemporary publishers recognized a new urban market of second-generation city dwellers fascinated by town life – specifically literate, young, middle- and upper-class men.[45]

Many of these new urban readers were bachelors. In the early nineteenth century, among the upper classes, the nobility and the gentry, fear of social derogation in marriage produced a high proportion of lifelong bachelors. This was particularly true for younger sons who, not benefiting from primogeniture, had to accumulate wealth before they could marry.[46] Living as a single man allowed a different expression of masculinity from that required by marriage and fatherhood, emphasizing instead a lifestyle described as 'libertinism', which focused more on sporting, gambling, drinking and whoring.[47] But while the figure of the male rambler in his pursuit of pleasure may have appealed to certain single young men, *Life in London* was also attacked by members of the bourgeoisie for its vulgarity and by religious movements for its immorality.[48] Egan's responses to such criticisms, namely the book's encouragement of vice, anti-work ethics, drinking, prostitution, brutal sports and betting, are stated at the outset of the sequel, *The Finish to the Adventures of Tom, Jerry and Logic in their Pursuits through Life in and out of London*, discussed later in this book.[49]

Activities represented in *Life in London*, such as pugilism, cockfighting, dog fighting and drinking, and the language used deriving from flash, cant and slang dictionaries and boxing treatises suggest that the text was out of bounds for respectable women. However, the availability of domestic household items decorated with images from *Life in London* – fire screens, printed tea-trays, cushions and fans – indicates that the book may have appealed to the presumably female consumers responsible for the purchase of such commodities. This speculation on the female readership of *Life in London* is reinforced by the fact that Francis Burney's *Evelina* was given a new title, *Female Life in London*, when it was reprinted in 1822.[50] It may be that there was a female audience who identified with urban life, perhaps with the male rambler.[51] Although, as we shall now see, the rambler's interest in the pursuit of women would have made this relationship more complex than simple identification.

THE PURSUIT OF PLEASURE: RAMBLERS AND CYPRIANS

> we have taken a promiscuous ramble from the West towards
> the East, and it has afforded some amusement; but our stock
> is abundant, and many objects of curiosity are still in view.[52]

The ramble is related to the pursuit of specifically sexual pleasure – 'to go about in search of sex'.[53] 'Ranging' and 'rangling' are terms which describe closely linked activities also connected with random movement and sexual pursuit – 'intriguing with a variety of women'.[54] The ranger is defined as 'a penis' or a 'rover, wanderer, rake'.[55] Such words, especially rambling or ranging, featured in the titles of a large number of contemporary magazines concerned with sex.[56] Many of the publishers of these texts had links to pornography, some produced and even authored fake memoirs of prostitutes.[57] Others continued a tradition of publishing lists which described locations and descriptions of various London prostitutes.[58]

In the ramble, many of the women encountered in the streets and public spaces of the city are represented as highly desirable and described as 'cyprians'. The word cyprian is defined as: 'belonging to Cyprus, an island in the eastern Mediterranean, famous in ancient times for the worship of Aphrodite or Venus [goddess of love]' and as 'licentious, lewd, in the eighteenth and nineteenth centuries applied to prostitutes'.[59] As in nineteenth-century Paris described by Benjamin where the prostitute is the only female figure of all the social characters — collector, ragpicker, detective, flâneur and gambler — to occupy public space; the cyprian is the only female who figures in the ramble.[60] In rambling texts, the mothers, daughters and virgins in assembly rooms, such as Almack's, as well as actresses, singers and dancers in theatres and the Italian Opera House, are represented as cyprians. However, although the term is used to describe courtesans and ladies of fashion, it is often connected with place as well as class. 'Flash Nancy, Gateway Peg and Black Sal', working-class women discovered by ramblers in *Life in London* in taverns in the east and on the streets around Covent Garden, are not referred to as cyprians but as mollishers.[61] This distinction is an important one, since the only factor distinguishing the attractive and enticing cyprian from the so-called common prostitute is her dress or surface appearance. This ambiguous identity, is underscored by her shifting location, the cyprian is represented in a series of different venues, from middle- to upper-class indoor and outdoor places of leisure as well as the street.

In the eighteenth and early nineteenth centuries, a number of words derived from or sounding like Greek, such as nymph, cyprian, paphian and corinthian, were adopted to refer indirectly to prostitution. The ambiguous meaning of such 'foreign' terms allowed them to be used suggestively to subvert codes of decency through innuendo. The common term corinthian, for example, could mean noble or licentious. For the Roman architectural historian Vitruvius, the corinthian was the superlative architectural order, distinguished by its decorative capital. Here corinthian implied superiority indicated through decoration. As a nobleman, Corinthian Tom was an ornament of society, decorated, refined and well-balanced; but in slang terms, the term 'corinth' also meant brothel, making reference to the Greek view of the ancient city of Corinth as a wealthy place full of debauchery.[62] In certain forms of slang, corinthians were defined as 'frequenters of brothels' and connected to rakes or 'lewd, debauched fellow[s]'.[63] In *Life in London*,

Corinthian Tom is described as fond of 'modest fair ones'. He pursues, flirts, drinks with cyprians and is even said to spend the 'weight of his purse' on them. However, Corinthian Tom never directly visits a brothel and his rambles are never represented as lewd, but as frivolous, harmless fun.[64]

The term corinthian also had a double meaning in relation to women. For Vitruvius, the corinthian order was a feminine one distinguished from the more matronly Ionic by being slender and girl-like. Corinthian represented virginal qualities but also the licentiousness of a city such as Corinth, whose patron was Aphrodite. Aphrodite, goddess of love in Greek mythology, originated in the east, in Cyprus or Cytherea. This added an erotic and an exotic element to the term.[65] Used to describe women, cyprian or corinthian could imply a high order of decoration.[66] For example, in fashion magazines, the term 'corinthian trimming' was used to refer to the decorative borders of women's dresses in the early nineteenth century.[67] But associations with Aphrodite also suggest an alluring and enticing aspect to external display. The cyprian was a spectacle – an object of display – her body was the site of the rambler's desire and gaze. In *Life in London*, Corinthian Tom's partner, Corinthian Kate, was represented as a cyprian, and as exemplified in figure 3, a visually appealing female figure.[68]

In his pursuit of attractive women, the figure of the rambler certainly represents a number of characteristics that young, heterosexual men would wish to identify with – moving, looking and desiring in the city. But Tom, Jerry and Logic each also represent slightly different aspects to the rambler. Tom differs from Logic, but shares with Jerry, skilled sportsmanship. Tom differs from Jerry, but shares with Logic, the streetwise knowledge of urban dwellers. Although all three men share a delight in drinking and pursuing women, Tom is the most likely to 'get the girl'. Coming from the country, Jerry is seen as slightly foolish and the unsporty Bob Logic always ends up with prostitutes defined as 'low' by their dress. In the ramble, three other male figures feature, the corinthian, the dandy and the bruiser. Each of these figures represent different aspects of male urban identity articulated through various forms of display and consumption. Ramblers, corinthians, bruisers and dandies are represented as competing and bonding with each other in ways which correspond to the more theoretical discussions of consump-

Fig. 3 George and Robert Cruikshank, 'An INTRODUCTION –
Gay Moments of *Logic, Jerry, Tom* and *Corinthian Kate*', Pierce Egan, *Life
in London; or, the day and night scenes of Jerry Hawthorn, Esq., and his
elegant friend Corinthian Tom, accompanied by Bob Logic, the Oxonian, in
their Rambles and Sprees through the Metropolis*

tion outlined in chapter 1. Combinations of emulation and distinction
and the adoption, rejection, appropriation and transformation of differing styles of dress, kinds of speech and ways of using space all contribute
to the construction of competing urban masculine identities.

MOBILITY: THE RAMBLER AS CORINTHIAN

CORINTHIAN TOM'S unceasing Anxiety to mix with the
World uncontrolled.[69]

For the rambler, mobility was a critical aspect of his masculinity and
public urban identity. His mobility was both social and spatial. His
dominant class position allowed him to mix with a variety of social
classes and to move freely between the exclusive clubs, opera houses,
assembly rooms in the west of London and the working-class taverns and
other leisure spaces in Covent Garden's Holy Land and further east in
East Smithfield.[70] This mobility is most clearly represented in *Life in
London* by juxtaposing a scene in Allmax, a tavern in the east, see figure

4, and Almack's exclusive assembly rooms in the west, see figure 5. This contrast indicates the rambler's ability to experience both sides of the city – the prerogative of the dominant upper- or middle-class male:

> This will be a rich treat to you Jerry, and the contrast will be more delightful; more especially, as the time is so short that we shall pass from All-Max in the East to Almack's in the West almost like the rapid succession of scenes in a play.[71]

In *Life in London*, it is the idealized figure of the corinthian who best represents the mobility of the rambler. Unlike the dandy, whose desire to display exclusivity would not take him east, the corinthian mixed with both classes and moved freely from east to west in search of pleasure.[72] In social rank, the corinthian was 'the highest order of swells, where swell referred to a 'well-dressed' or 'highly dressed' man.[73] Definitions suggest that this hierarchy, like 'the supereminence of that order of architecture', was determined by decoration or 'superlative articles of dress'.[74] But unlike a swell whose rank was one only

Fig. 4 George and Robert Cruikshank, '*Lowest "Life in London"* – *Tom, Jerry,* and *Logic* among the unsophisticated Sons and Daughters of Nature at "ALLMAX" in the East', Pierce Egan, *Life in London; or, the day and night scenes of Jerry Hawthorn, Esq., and his elegant friend Corinthian Tom, accompanied by Bob Logic, the Oxonian, in their Rambles and Sprees through the Metropolis*

Fig. 5 George and Robert Cruikshank, *'Highest "Life in London" — Tom and Jerry "sporting a Toe" among the Corinthians at ALMACK'S, in the West'*, Pierce Egan, *Life in London; or, the day and night scenes of Jerry Hawthorn, Esq., and his elegant friend Corinthian Tom, accompanied by Bob Logic, the Oxonian, in their Rambles and Sprees through the Metropolis*

determined by dress, 'a man highly dressed is a swell, however circum-stanced in pocket', a corinthian, although expected to look good, also had to be of a certain class:[75]

> no man who ever performed any duty or service for hire (except Doctors, lawyers, parsons and statesmen) can possibly be a real swell, certainly not a Gentleman, most indubitably not a Corinthian.[76]

A crucial aspect of the corinthian's mobility was expressed through his class. This defined his leisure time and gentlemanly attitude, as well as his character, politeness, generosity, good humour and, most import-antly, his sportsmanship. Corinthians were described as 'sporting men of rank and fashion', first-class boxers, fencers, hunters and drivers.[77] Unless a man joined 'heartily in the sports of the turf or the ring', giving or taking lessons, he could not be considered a corinthian.[78] Tom repre-sented the archetypal corinthian, a gentleman with property in the form of land and money, known for his elegant manner, fashionable clothes and his sportsmanship.[79] For Egan, corinthianism suggested the possibility for male bonding in a hierarchical class-based society, through shared sporting and drinking activities.

In *Life in London*, if we refer back to figure 2, the corinthian column depicted in the frontispiece can be argued to be a metaphor for social order.[80] This image shows the relationship of a number of different social classes. At the top of the column are the 'ups' or 'the flowers of society', the King and the nobles; next are the merchants or 'respectables'; at the bottom are the 'downs' or 'the mechanicals – the humble labourers and the human vegetables'. For Egan, the 'ups' and 'downs' provided the 'varieties of Life in London', but although he enjoyed class variety, as a monarchist and nationalist, he accepted class hierarchy.[81] In *Life in London*, those in the corinthian capital – king, court and corinthians – sustain all the other orders. Here, the corinthian represents an ideal version of class society, where all classes exist but each in their own place. He also represents an idealized masculinity, an upper-class man who knows his place and is proud of it, but who is also happy to mix with those beneath him, as long as order is maintained. According to the creators of the text, the corinthian's most admirable qualities, his desire and ability to mix with all classes of society, were also reflected in George IV, to whom *Life in London* is dedicated:

> It is only by means of a free and unrestrained intercourse with society, most gracious sire, that an intimate acquaintance is to be obtained with englishmen.[82]

Tom's, Jerry's and Logic's position at the centre of the column engaged in talking and drinking represents their desire to mix with different classes through socializing. The view that class difference can be overcome through shared social enjoyment is a romanticized one. Social mobility only works one way, from a position of privilege. The ramblers could visit the east of London, but characters from the east could not socialize in the west.

As London developed into an busy centre of consumption, the role of streets as spaces allowing the flow of people and goods, became increasingly important as zones of trade and commerce, administration and entertainment. The eighteenth century saw a number of improvements in lighting, paving and drainage, which both increased and facilitated the movement of people on the streets and also provided a social space for visual display and consumption.[83] But standards of street improvement varied across London. Although some streets in the west and the City had stone kerbs and raised pavements, the east remained less accessible.[84] These areas were the hardest places in which to install and maintain improvements such as lighting and paving, since residency was more transitory, property ownership less systematic and the streets themselves less defined.[85]

John Nash's work in the first decades of the nineteenth century in the fashionable, commercial and residential areas of west London around Piccadilly focused on celebrating urban movement.[86] Nash combined classical elements of town planning, from continental cities such as Paris and Versailles, with romantic aspects drawn from the English picturesque tradition, where urban elements, streets, buildings and the flow of traffic were treated like landscapes.[87] Regent Street, designed with promenading and walking in mind, was nicknamed 'Corinthian Path' in rambling texts, see for example figure 6, indicating its high-class and fashionable status.

It is, in my opinion, a peculiar beauty of the new streets, that, though broad, they do not run in straight lines, but make occasional curves which break their uniformity.[88]

Another figure who represented mobility in the ramble was the bruiser. Understood to be a 'gentlemanly pursuit', boxing appeared to cut across class and political boundaries in the search of patriotic unity. Pugilism was admired in both the radical and tory press and at major contests the audience consisted of members of all classes.[89] The working-class bruiser or 'one skilled in the art of boxing' represented another version of idealized masculinity through his sporting physique.[90] His physical form was compared to the celebrated beauty of the classical Greek hero.[91] Boxing publications, best sellers in the early nineteenth century, were accompanied by images of stylized heads and torsos.[92] But as well as representing idealized physical attributes, pugilism also promoted admirable social aspects of masculinity – sportsmanship, courage, gallantry, calmness, tolerance, fair play and honour. These qualities were considered 'good' and enhancing of masculinity in relation to the kinds

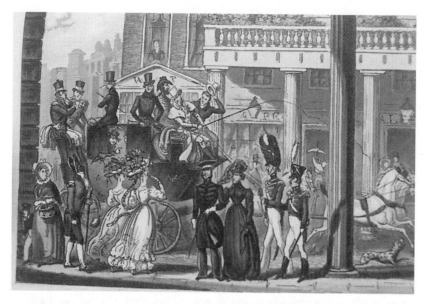

Fig. 6 Robert Cruikshank, 'THE GRAND LOUNGE: Regent Street to Wit', Pierce Egan, *Finish to the Adventures of Tom, Jerry and Logic in their Pursuits through Life in and out of London*

of 'bad' excessive emotions and passions associated with effeminacy.[93] The boxer through his 'principles of generosity and true courage' was a man who prioritized a particularly English ideal of manhood.[94]

> The taste for exhibitions of this kind, are I believe, entirely peculiar to this nation; other countries have their gymnastic and athletic exercises but the English are singular in their exercise of the fist, and are curious in this manner of settling disputes.[95]

Sport was specifically linked to other leisure pastimes, especially drinking.[96] On the title page of *Life in London*, a drinking flagon is shown among various rambling accoutrements.[97] For men of different classes the sharing of private drinking and sporting activities offered opportunities for male bonding, as did the adoption of fashionable styles of dress and language.[98] One of the ways sporting societies, such as the Pugilistic Society and the Four-in-Hand coaching club for example, established their identity was through the adoption of specific dress codes.[99] But the relationship between working- and upper-class men was not simply the creation of egalitarian bonds through sport. A contemporary etching suggests that high fashion for the upper-class male was intrinsically linked to the adoption of the habits of pugilists, coachmen and criminals: if a man desired to be 'a modern man of fashion' he should 'dress like a coachman', 'study boxing and bull baiting' and 'speak the slang language fluently'.[100]

> The Merit of Captain Grose's Dictionary of the Vulgar Tongue has been long and universally acknowledged. But its circulation was confined almost universally to the lower orders of society; he was not aware, at the time of its compilation, that our young men of fashion would at no very distant period be as distinguished for the vulgarity of their jargon as the inhabitants of Newgate.[101]

Appropriating aspects of working-class culture – sporting, drinking and language (flash, cant or slang) – was, it seems, an essential aspect of an upper-class fashionable masculinity. This kind of behaviour has been termed 'urban slumming' or 'urban native', and has been compared to that of the riotous urban mohawks of the eighteenth century.[102] The language adopted was that of working-class criminals, 'a kind of gibberish used by thieves and gypsies, likewise called Pedlar's Greek, French, the slang', and known as flash lingo or 'the canting or slang language'.[103] Dictionaries of flash, cant and slang first appeared during the eighteenth century as part of the research of Frances Grose (1731–91) into the origins of vernacular urban speech. Grose differentiated between the canting language favoured by young men which stressed aspects of urban criminality and burlesque phrases which emphasized rural, superstitious and folkloric traditions.[104]

Grose's research drew on the work of Samuel Pegge (1743–1800) who had made connections between cant and cockney.[105] Pegge opposed the views of contemporaries, such as Samuel Johnson, who held that classical languages represented universal truth and that primitive and vulgar English belonged to a morally and intellectually inferior culture.[106] Instead Pegge argued that cockney, or contemporary London vernacular speech, was not a corrupt form of language.[107] Reclaiming cockney meant being proud of being a Londoner and was an important part of urban masculinity.[108] In the early nineteenth century, strictly speaking, cockney was a nickname given to those who lived in the working-class eastern parts of London 'within the sound of Bow bells'.[109] However, attempts were made to extend the term geographically in order to allow aristocratic men living in west London to link themselves with aspects of working-class identity.[110]

The importance of cockney slang in the construction of middle- and upper-class urban masculinities is expressed by the number of revised editions of Grose's dictionary specifically directed at students and sporting men.[111] The publication of flash dictionaries, rambling tales and boxing treatises by the same publishers, often as two-volume sets (sometimes written by the same authors), indicates a language of masculine culture common to rambling and sporting.[112] The private sporting language used among the members of the 'Fancy' – pugilists, spectators and patrons – reinforced the secretive aspects of flash and its importance in male bonding.[113] A shared knowledge of flash or cant allowed young men to 'talk bawdy before their papas' and provided a code from which others were excluded.[114]

> A kind of cant phraseology is current from one end of the Metropolis to the other, and you will scarcely be able to move a single step, my dear Jerry, without consulting a Slang Dictionary.[115]

Sporting lingo or slang was represented as a language used and understood only by men, and as such indicates an attempt to exclude women from certain aspects of male culture.[116] When a woman was described as 'sporting' the reference was usually a sexual one.[117] Women who got involved in sport as fighters were considered as 'raffish' and promiscuous and judged in terms of their sexuality rather than their sporting skills.[118] By establishing their mutual difference from women, sporting culture played an important role in creating links between different kinds of men.

But as well as making connections between men of different classes, sporting activities also maintained class hierarchies. In general, competitive aspects of sport establish, and are determined by, the dominance of certain male groups over others. Histories of the commercialization of sport show that events and players become increasingly controlled by promoters and patrons and that these more privileged groups devise rules to protect their own interests.[119] This was certainly the case with pugilism, where promoters sought fighters to defend stake money and attract crowds. The illegal status of pugilism necessitated the economic and legal support of the nobility, who as wealthy patrons often employed fighters permanently.[120] Such a relation was not one of equivalence though. The fighter's superior sportsmanship might have provided his patron with social status, but despite the admiration the upper classes held for local and national boxing heroes, these men were ultimately defined by their working-class status.[121] They could never be corinthians.

> no fighting man by profession can be a swell, he is tulip, if he dresses thereafter, and looks swellish :– 'tis esteemed the first grade towards Corinthianism, which he can never reach by any possibility whatever.[122]

VISUALITY: THE RAMBLER AS DANDY

The Dandy – swell of the Bon Ton.[123]

Visual pleasure, Freud's scopophilia, is another critical aspect to understanding the rambler's identity, in terms of looking (voyeurism) and being looked at (exhibitionism) or both (narcissism). The rambler's precedent, the London spy, was represented as a voyeur; his successor, the Parisian flâneur, has been associated with a 'mobile, free, eroticized and avaricious gaze'.[124] Like the flâneur and the spy, the rambler also liked to look and in rambling texts this looking is connected to aspects of exploring and knowing. By adopting a 'camera obscura' view of the city, Egan's ramblers in *Life in London* become voyeurs, possessing 'the invaluable advantages of SEEING and not being seen'.[125] For example, when visiting a low life tavern, a site of potential danger, the ramblers don disguises which serve to distance them from the scene.[126] On a visit to Newgate, the reality of the scene where prisoners are preparing to die, is also suppressed by the adoption of a panoramic and distancing view.[127]

Similar elements of spectacular and detached observation were also created at this time in other cultural forms. These included schemes for urban improvement, such as Nash's original plan for the west of London, new popular forms of entertainment, like panoramas and dioramas, and the social caricatures of graphic artists.[128] Connections can be made between the pleasures of viewing the city through the controlling and framing techniques of the camera obscura and the pleasures of viewing the female body, as we shall see in a later discussion of the cyprian.

Aspects of looking highlighted by the secretive spy, looking but not wanting to be looked at, shifted in the decade following the Napoleonic Wars, with the return of military men from Europe, especially Paris, bringing with them new French fashions and a flamboyant style of military dress. As we have already discussed, the visual excitement of revealing secret activities became supplemented in 1820s rambles and spy texts by the thrill of fashion, display and spectacle, represented through the figure of the fashionable rambler, a self-conscious man demanding to be looked at. The rambler could be argued, on the one hand, to be an exhibitionist who enjoys being looked at, on the other, to be a narcissistic spectator who derives pleasure from looking at the perfect image of himself in others. Ramblers' bodies could be described as sites of narcissism and/or exhibitionism where identities are 'displayed' through surface, size, volume, demeanour, gesture and relations of imitation and distinction in dress.[129] In early nineteenth-century London, sites for this kind of public display became increasingly important with many architectural spaces, as well as bodies, designed specifically to enhance visual pleasure. Such places provided the rambler with locations for 'conspicuous consumption', to display his body, money, leisure time and his masculinity to other men and women. Indeed Egan describes London as the 'looking-glass for TALENT'.[130]

Nash's urban and architectural designs for early nineteenth-century London parallel concerns with the presentation of self through ramble and highlight the importance of visual consumption and display – spectacle – in urban experience. These new spaces of leisure and promenade were spaces of anonymous encounter and visual contact, where pleasure and satisfaction were to be found through looking. Regent Street, from Piccadilly Circus to Oxford Circus, was planned and designed as a street for shopping and visual consumption from the outset. The northern part of the street contained several houses, but lower down towards Piccadilly, the buildings were based on arcades and the principle of mixing commerce and residential use. Shops were to be on the ground floor of the buildings, with accommodation for shopkeepers and their families on the mezzanine floor, and the floors above let as expensive lodgings for visitors or as apartments for bachelors.[131] In the designs for Regent Street, the Haymarket Theatre and the Italian Opera House, including its colonnade, were intended to work as attractive foci:[132]

> [T]he Balustrades over the Colonnades will form Balconies to the Lodging-rooms over the Shops, from which the Occupiers of the Lodgings can see and converse with those passing in the carriages underneath, and which will add to the gaiety of the scene.[133]

Rambling tales represented fashion as essential to the construction of male urban identity, with the differences between town and country styles of dress strongly stressed.[134] On arrival in the metropolis, country relatives are first redressed in urban fashions. For example, in *Life in London* (see figure 7), Jerry undergoes an 'elegant metamorphose'. His 'rustic habit' is discarded for fashionable top-boots, white cord breeches, a green coat with brass buttons and a neat waistcoat.[135]

Fig. 7 George and Robert Cruikshank, '*Jerry* in training for a Swell', Pierce Egan, *Life in London; or, the day and night scenes of Jerry Hawthorn, Esq., and his elegant friend Corinthian Tom, accompanied by Bob Logic, the Oxonian, in their Rambles and Sprees through the Metropolis*

In the eighteenth century, new modes of dress had rejected court hierarchies, adopting instead simple and practical styles, derived from the dress of the sporting country gentleman. The classic example was the John Bull (the typical Englishman) outfit consisting of everyday riding clothes – a top hat, a simple neckcloth, a small coat (cut away in the front), a waistcoat, breeches fitting into riding boots and a stick.[136] By the 1820s this 'look' had become modified to suit urban lifestyles and developed into a city aesthetic. The adoption of simple styles made it even easier to obscure social rank through dress, so increasingly subtle codes were used to establish exclusivity.[137] Stories and anecdotes concerning Beau Brummel, the archetypal dandy, express this focus on dress codes well. Brummel is known for his rejection of finery in favour of a sparse and precise style of dress and his obsessive attention to detail in terms of cleanliness, cut and fit, rather than frills and decorative trimmings.[138]

Although accounts of, and dates given for, the origin of the word 'dandy' seem to vary greatly, common to all definitions is a love of fashion.[139] This interest in appearance, represented as problematic to the dandy's masculine identity, is used in a number of ways to articulate concerns with aspects of social transgression, race- and class-based, as well as sexual.[140] Like the cyprian, the surface appearance of the dandy was a key feature of his identity. It was represented as a form of disguise, making his class 'origin' hard to determine. The dandy was believed to be a man from the middle classes who sought to emulate the leisured life of the aristocracy and reject bourgeois notions of thrift and hard work.[141] Elements of ridicule in representations of dandies, served to circumvent the class threat their social aspiring attitudes raised. The dandy's interest in fashion was marginalized by many who considered him a 'fashionable non-descript[s]'.[142] By describing his appearance in terms of exaggerated and feminized forms, such as waists pinched-in with stays and ineffectual behaviour, gendered signifiers were employed as a means of disempowering the dandy.[143]

Then again, the race of men! they are neither men, women, lapdogs, nor monkeys! but a mixture of all![144]

However, such representations are somewhat ambiguous with respect to sexuality and gender. It is certainly the case that attention to physical appearance in terms of surface skin is characteristically associated with 'feminine' extravagance rather than say the bare strength of the bruiser's physique. But these representations tend to signify effeminacy more often than femininity and so suggest homosexual tendencies in the male. To complicate things further, the dandy's sleek and unadorned appearance, complete with tight-fitting pantaloons and padded shoulders, has been interpreted as a highly erotic version of 'unpainted masculinity' in contrast to the highly decorated masculinities preceding him.[145]

Attitudes towards the dandy's style of dress were also closely tied up with the Napoleonic Wars and the political rivalry between France and England.[146]

> Men of fashion all became dandy soon after that, having imported a good deal of French manner in their gait, lispings, wrinkled foreheads, killing King's English.[147]

Although dandies rejected finery, they were compared to the elaborate Macaronis, aristocratic youths who adopted French fashions in the 1770s on return from their grand tours.[148] The appearances of both kinds of men were both ridiculed as foppish and effeminate, even though the two groups defined their masculinities very differently, the Macaronis through decoration, the dandies through simplicity. Here a feminizing representation worked to disable threats of a racial kind; a country such as France posed a serious political and military problem to England. The figure of the dandy as both effeminate and frenchified was used by the English government and its advocates as an attack on the French, accusing them of effeminacy, decadence, sexual anarchy and sodomy.

Representations of the dandy as 'feminine' attempted then to reduce the threats provoked by various deviant identities – homosexuality, French nationality and middle-class aspirations. It could therefore be argued that it was in order to differentiate themselves from these transgressive and feminized identities that aristocratic urban youths chose instead to adopt the manners and dress of the working-class coachman and the pugilist who represented manly, heterosexual and patriotic values.

One of the most common representations of the dandy concerns 'cutting' or ignoring acquaintances in the street.[149] Another story associated with Brummel, his apology at having been seen as far east as Charing Cross in London, reinforces the dandy's obsession with exclusivity, but expresses it from a spatial perspective.[150] In representing exclusivity rather than mobility, the dandy opposes the value systems signified by the corinthian. The relationship between exclusivity and mobility in representations of the dandy and the corinthian is by no means a binary one, nor is the relation of social identity to spatiality one of reductive expression. On the one hand, social desire, for either exclusivity or mobility, can be reinforced by the adoption of certain spatial practices; on the other, urban design can work to encourage certain social attitudes.

If we return for a moment to Nash's Regent Street, we can argue that the same spatial solution worked both to reinforce desires for social exclusivity and class hierarchy as well as express a desire for movement and promenade as previously discussed. Nash's decision to place Regent Street between the dense network of Soho streets to the east and the more spacious layout of streets to the west, could be described as economic, land bought cheaply in the east was sold for a profit in the west, but it was also ideological, the spatial division kept the 'rookery' or 'holy land' of St Giles in the Fields away from the upper-class west.[151] The design of Regent Street supported the view of the middle classes who wished to make a display of their class status in urban terms by promoting improvement schemes which emphasized the difference between themselves and those 'beneath' them.[152]

> The new street will provide a boundary and complete separation between the Streets and Squares occupied by the Nobility and Gentry, and the narrow Streets and meaner Houses occupied by mechanics and the trading part of the community.[153]

MOBILITY: THE CYPRIAN AS FEMALE RAMBLER

Nymph of the pavé.[154]

In the early nineteenth century, women who worked in the public realm, such as shopgirls, domestic servants and actresses, were likely to be represented as prostitutes. Male commentators assumed that these working women supplemented their incomes with 'real' prostitution.[155] And although statistical evidence from surveys of prostitutes' previous occupations shows that many prostitutes were involved in such professions, it is not the intrinsic nature of 'public women' or 'working women' to work as prostitutes, but rather a result of the poor terms of their employment.[156] Keeping late hours and frequenting places visited by men, both theatres and opera houses, but also cafés and dancing establishments in the same urban districts, actresses, singers and dancers were more likely than any other public woman to signify transgressions through their occupation of public places. Indeed, according to contemporary commentators, actresses and other women who visited theatres, if not already prostitutes, were more than likely to become prostitutes.

Of all the places for intrigue, down right lascivious and intemperate intrigue, there is nothing in London equal to the King's Theatre. Almost all the ladies in their turn fall victims to the Venus-like inspiration which hovers round, and lives in the atmosphere of this cyprian palace.[157]

If the simple presence of women in the city is here considered a defiance of the ideology of the separate spheres and represented in terms of a problematic set of morals, then figures who articulated women's movement in the urban realm were likely to be perceived as even more threatening. Even in female magazines where women readers were encouraged to walk as a suitable form of female exercise, their movement was thought to require careful regulation. Women were asked to walk only in certain ways, at certain times and with a companion. Moral implications are raised here, I argue, with the intention of curbing the self-determined movement of women.[158]

There is another argument which should be of importance to a modest lady – that a morning walk would not cause those reflections on her reputation, which evening promenades too often occasion.[159]

Representations of cyprians in rambling tales also conflate issues of mobility and morality. For example, cyprians spotted in the park by ramblers are given the names of birds, such as Sparrow Hawk and the White Crow, and described in terms of flight, lightness and speed: as 'lady birds' and 'birds', moving with 'lightness and mobility of spirit', 'energy of body and spirit', 'flightiness' and 'moral frailty'.[160] Such descriptions indicate the cyprians' ability to move freely, but also suggest that lightness and mobility be understood in terms of morality. Like the rambler, the cyprian is an urban peripatetic, her identity is defined by her movement. But she is not simply the female equivalent of the male rambler. While the movement of the rambler is celebrated in relation to his activities of urban exploration and the pursuit of pleasure, the movement of the cyprian is cause for concern. For example, as figure 8 shows, cyprians in rambling tales were often shown being reprimanded in places and by figures responsible for keeping law and order, such as courtrooms, magistrates and nightwatchmen. As we shall later see with reference to *Finish*, the sequel to *Life in London*, the mobility of the urban female, specifically her link to the street, was considered to be the cause of her eventual destruction.

Fig. 8 George and Robert Cruikshank, 'Bow Street, *Tom* and *Jerry's* Sensibility awakened at the pathetic Tale of the elegant Cyprian, the feeling Coachman, and the generous Magistrate', Pierce Egan, *Life in London; or, the day and night scenes of Jerry Hawthorn, Esq., and his elegant friend Corinthian Tom, accompanied by Bob Logic, the Oxonian, in their Rambles and Sprees through the Metropolis*

If we take Irigaray's interpretation of patriarchy as the exchange of women as commodities between men, it follows that women moving in the public realm would represent a threat to patriarchal culture and require repositioning as objects or commodities to be circulated between male consumers for their visual and sexual consumption. It is interesting to note that in early nineteenth-century slang the word 'commodity' was commonly used to refer to 'a woman's commodity' or sex, but that a clear differentiation was made between the 'private parts of a modest woman and the public parts of a prostitute'.[161] A modest woman was a private commodity, whereas a prostitute was a public commodity.

In line with the representation of the cyprian described above, it is certainly possible to argue that male authors of rambling tales attempted to circumvent the threat of female agency posed by self-determined moving women in the city in various ways, either by representing female motion merely as a response to male desire or by suggesting that it was in some way a transgressive act. The construction of representations which conflated women in public space with the cyprian and linked female mobility with sexual immorality, might have expressed indirectly a latent wish to control female sexuality but certain forms of legislation did this in a far more direct way. While reading rambling texts could result in female readers internalizing patriarchal control mechanisms, the law worked in a much more obtrusive way to restrict female movement.

Although streetwalking or nightwalking was not itself a crime, women's movement on the street was controlled through legislation, such as the Vagrancy Acts. The amendments to the Vagrancy Acts of 1822 controlled female urban movement by associating 'Night Walkers' with the term 'Prostitutes' for the first time and defining this group of women 'wandering in Public Streets' as 'idle and disorderly Persons'. The Act required that unless 'common Prostitutes and Night Walkers' gave 'a satisfactory account of themselves' they would be liable for up to one month's hard labour.[162] Further amendments to the Vagrancy Act in 1824 which removed the term 'Night Walker', shifted the definition of disorderly behaviour to 'riotous or indecent' and expanded the description of the public realm to include 'any Place of Public Resort'.[163]

We have so far discussed the movement of the cyprian as problematic, with a focus on the ways in which representations of the city such as rambles sought to restrict this mobility. This is one feminist perspective Irigaray's work offers, that we understand how gendered representations work to control women, but it is also possible to take a slightly different angle. If we consider Irigaray's notion of the angel, then we can shift our interpretation of the rambler's pursuit of cyprians. Instead we can explore the cyprian's relation to her own mobility in terms of women's nomadic status. The rambler's movement may have defined his urban masculinity, but the cyprian was also defined by her position in public space. This positionality can only be understood as mobile, since as well as being related to the street – a space signifying movement – the cyprian is located in a dispersed network of spaces around the city, as we shall see further in chapters 4 and 5. The cyprian is a moving locus in the ramble, her body is also the focus of the rambler's gaze but, further still, she is the stimulus, the reason for the rambler's movement. Without the cyprian there is no male movement, ramblers would not ramble.

VISUALITY: THE CYPRIAN AS FEMALE SPECTACLE

The Rambler in the public streets,
Admires at everything he meets [. . .]
Ladies you'll find of every class,
In shape, just like the hour glass [. . .][164]

In public space, the displayed surface of the body is usually a covered one, composed of a close relationship between the cover or the clothes and what is covered or the fleshy body. At different historical periods, the exposure of different parts of the female body signify very specific meanings associated with 'appropriate' behaviour. A correct amount and kind of covering might represent decency in terms of honesty or modesty; whereas an incorrect covering might represent indecency or aspects of transgressive behaviour. Fashionable clothing for women of the upper classes in England in the first two decades of the nineteenth century was a highly minimal costume adopted from post-revolutionary Paris, inspired by the democratic politics of ancient Greek culture.

Gowns were of a semi-transparent full-length white fabric, worn with minimal undergarments and stockings. Sparse, revealing and décolleté, the waist was raised to draw attention to the breasts.[165] Referring to classical antiquity, the material was dampened so that it clung to the body like drapery, presenting the body as a sculptural form.[166] Fear of French politics meant that by the end of the 1820s, the exposure of the breast and the transparency of this simple white gown were considered immoral in England.[167] Writers in fashion magazines read by the middle and upper classes connected such 'nakedness' with political radicalism.[168] Visual emphasis in female fashion shifted from the bosom, once thought of as 'the most beautiful ornament of the sex', to the waist, where increased slenderness was considered beautiful in the female form.[169]

In the early nineteenth century, the month of the year, the time of day, the location and the type of activity engaged in, all had an effect on the amount and kind of covering considered appropriate for women. Women's magazines recorded such specific rules governing women's dress as 'fashion'. For example, uncovering or displaying the top of the breasts was only considered decent at night in special venues, such the theatre, and for certain occasions, such as masquerade balls. The issue of 'covering' was connected here with a number of themes around decency and morality. Clothing was expected to be neither too revealing nor too obscuring of the body that lay beneath. Covering too little meant display of the body or immodesty; covering too much meant display of clothing or dishonesty. Both 'excesses' were connected with prostitution. An excess of flesh represented exposure and wantonness; an excess of clothing in the form of dress and decoration represented artifice and vanity.

A woman proud of her beauty may possibly be nothing but a coquette; one who makes a public display of her bosom is something more[170]

a lady with a well turned ankle should never wear her petticoats too short: cheap exhibitions soon sink into contempt. A thousand little natural opportunities occur to disclose this attraction without any ostentatious display of their own. No ornament for the leg or foot can be too plainly elegant.[171]

transparent habits [. . .] dresses of glass [. . .] at first adopted by courtesans and soon followed by females who imitated them in more than one particular [. . .][172]

Such comments in women's fashion magazines worked to regulate female dress. Concerns with exposure and decency in the public place of the street were also expressed in the controversy around the amendments to the Vagrancy Acts of 1822 and 1824.[173] The morality of dress was a constant theme in representations of women inhabiting public leisure haunts of the aristocracy, such as Hyde Park and the opera.[174] Rambling texts also made connections between public female identity and surface display. In *Life in London*, in one image of two women in the street at night, see figure 9, the time of day and their location combined with the amount of their breasts shown revealed, defines them as cyprians.[175] As well as wearing too little, cyprians were also believed to wear too much. They were distinguished by their fancy clothes and considered to be motivated by 'allure', 'principles of lust, idleness, or avarice' and 'love of dress and of superior society'.[176] Whether clothed in too much or too little their appearance was problematic – duplicitous and/or extravagant. Like dandies, the cyprian was a site of contested debates about inappropriate surfaces.

The issue of the surface takes on a special relevance in relation to the role of actresses and dancers. Although the displays of intimate emotions or parts of the body not normally seen in public were located on the stage, within the context of the imaginary space of a theatrical, dance or operatic performance, the making visible of the private in public created a problematic juxtaposition that became the defining feature of such women. For example, the life of the most famous actress of the early nineteenth century, Madame Vestris, who appeared in a number of plays and operas between 1821 and 1828, at Drury Lane and the King's Theatre, was represented in terms of the blurring of public and private distinctions. A large amount of literature about her 'public' life was published in the form of 'private' memoirs, supposedly authored by the actress herself.[177] These texts are structured by a twisting of the meanings of public and private, where 'public' represents the exposed and immoral behaviour of a brazen cyprian and 'private' represents the intrigues and deceit of secret sexual liaisons.

Fig. 9 George and Robert Cruikshank, '*Tom* getting the best of a Charley', Pierce Egan, *Life in London; or, the day and night scenes of Jerry Hawthorn, Esq., and his elegant friend Corinthian Tom, accompanied by Bob Logic, the Oxonian, in their Rambles and Sprees through the Metropolis*

There are others who are proud of exhibiting their charms before the public, and who are as eminent in their various professions, as lewd in their course of life. [. . .] If we look to the boards of Covent Garden, and Drury Lane, we have melancholy proof how genius is vilely prostituted at the shrine of Plutus and Venus.[178]

It is possible to interpret such instances in relation to men's anxieties concerning their inability to detect the 'true' identity of a women, either in terms of class or morality (virtuous woman or prostitute), resulting in a desire to represent the surface as a site of intentional female deceit. But Irigaray's theory of mimicry is useful here in suggesting that on such occasions we might re-interpret this deception in relation to the female subject herself, and instead explore ways in which she is actively engaged in constructing her own surface.

woman must be nude because she is not situated, does not situate herself in her place. Her clothes, her makeup, and her jewels are the things with which she tries to create her container(s), her envelope(s). She cannot make use of the envelope that she is, and must create artificial ones.[179]

Irigaray's theoretical work certainly provides us with an interesting interpretative dilemma in relation to the rambler and cyprian. On the one hand, it is possible to use her view of the woman-as-commodity to interpret the ramble as a representation of gendered space where men's need to present themselves as the only moving and looking subjects in the city results in a positioning of women as the loci and foci of male desire – as cyprians or exchangeable commodities. On the other, the critical strategy of mimicry and the imaginative potential offered by the figure of the angel, suggest that we re-focus on women's agency, their ability to move and to choose how to be looked at, as cyprians or stimuli to male desire. The following three chapters explore these themes and tensions between history and theory, between men and women, between rambler and cyprian, in a number of different architectural spaces represented in the ramble: the male club, the assembly rooms and the theatre and opera house.

CHAPTER 3

The Clubs of St James's — Public Patriarchy

> The dandies of society [. . .] were great frequenters of
> White's club, in St. James's Street, where, in the famous bay
> window, they mustered in force. [. . .] In the zenith of his
> popularity he [Beau Brummel] might be seen at the bay
> window of White's Club, surrounded by the lions of the day,
> laying down the law, and occasionally indulging in those
> witty remarks for which his was famous.[1]

> There seemed to be great difficulty in getting in; and we had
> to pass through several doors strongly barricaded before we
> came to the gambling room, which was in the front room
> upstairs.[2]

As one site in a larger network of 'male only' spaces in the west of
London, including bachelor chambers, hotels, shops, sporting venues,
clubs and gambling dens, the male-only club was, and still is, a place
defining male urban identity. In order to establish a superior position
for men, public patriarchy involves both a differentiation of men from
women (patriarchy) and men from other men (fratriarchy). Club architecture represents both the consolidation of bonds between public men
through the physical and ideological exclusion of women, as well as the
contestation of rivalries between certain male groups. Shared positions
of class and status, combined with allegiances formed through politics,
sport and gambling, operate to regulate exclusive policies regarding club
membership and define 'brotherhoods' of men between and within
clubs.

Existing simultaneously as both a public and a private space, the 'club'
collapses the separate spheres ideology of two distinct spaces, the male,
public city and the female, private home. Opposed to family homes,
clubs are arguably public spaces, but as proprietor-owned places with
specific rules regarding membership, clubs can be defined in terms of

Fig. 10 Robert Cruikshank, 'Exterior of Fishmongers-Hall, St James's Street, with a view of a Regular Break Down, showing "Portraits of the Master-Fishmonger and many well known *Greeks* and *Pigeons*"', Bernard Blackmantle, *The English Spy*

the private. The tensions between private and public in the club are articulated through architectural representations of domesticity, exclusivity and secrecy. Particular kinds of architectural spaces allow aspects of privacy to be enhanced or denied by controlling the distinction between what can be seen and what remains hidden, between what can be accessed and what is kept remote. On the one hand, ground-floor bow windows in clubs provide places to display exclusivity to the public street. On the other hand, the careful protection of subscription and gambling rooms and their physical remoteness from the street, suggest that exclusivity operates around notions of secrecy. Rambling tales represent this contradiction through the combination of images of exterior bow or bay windows – see, for example, the façade of Crockford's, St James's Street in figure 10 and views of the secluded interiors of gambling rooms – see, for example, Brooks's subscription room in figure 11.

The four most exclusive clubs of west London – Boodle's, Brooks's, White's and Crockford's – were in the early nineteenth century located at the top of St James's Street. Established in the seventeenth century, by the middle of the eighteenth century, Boodle's, Brooks's and White's had all moved into purpose-built club houses in St James's Street. Connected with tory politics, all-night gambling, high fashion

Fig. 11 Robert Cruikshank, 'The Great Subscription Room at Brooks's: Opposition Members engaged upon Hazardous Points', Bernard Blackmantle, *The English Spy*

and, in the early nineteenth century, dandy culture, White's was the oldest and most exclusive of the clubs of St James's Street.[3] The main rival to White's and connected with whig, or opposition, politics was Brooks's club, founded in 1764 under the management of William Brookes, a wine merchant and money lender.[4] In 1778, Brooks's club moved to new premises designed by Henry Holland at 60 St James's Street opposite White's.[5] Boodle's club, founded in 1762 at the same premises as Brooks's, moved to a new clubhouse in 1783 at 28 St James's Street, in a building next door to White's owned by Nicholas Kenney and designed in 1775 by John Crunden for the Savoir Vivre Club.[6]

In the early nineteenth century, a number of clubs, such as the Guards', the Union, the Roxborough, Watier's and the Oriental, followed suit and also acquired their own buildings in St James's, and still others, such as the Reform Club, the Travellers', the Oxford and Cambridge, the United Services and the Athenaeum, commissioned architect-designed buildings on prestigious sites situated along Pall Mall. At the same time, the district of St James's was notorious for an increasing number of gaming houses, or hells, established around King Street, St James's Street and Pall Mall, including a purpose-built gambling house constructed in the early nineteenth century. This was Crock-ford's, a private club and gambling house, built in 1828 at 50 St James's Street just to the north of Brooks's to the designs of Benjamin and Phillip Wyatt.[7] The whole of St James's was represented as a gambling district in the nineteenth century, but the most notorious places for gambling were Brooks's and Crockford's.[8]

THE CLUBHOUSE: MALE DOMESTICITY IN THE CITY

> the basement of a clubhouse [. . .] is usually sunk to a good depth so as to contain an additional floor within it, that is, an entresol between the lower most or kitchen floor and the apparent external ground floor. This economy of plan – which may be said to be particularly English – provides a complete habitation for the domestic and official part of the establishment, and an invisible one also[9]

The earliest clubs can be described as groups of male acquaintances with shared interests, who met periodically in public spaces, coffee houses or taverns, to eat, drink and gamble, or to discuss politics, art or litera-ture.[10] The first coffee house was established in 1650, but, by the end of the seventeenth century, there were over two thousand in London, many of them in the St James's area, catering for clientele who had moved west following the fire of London in 1666.[11] The perceived 'public' status of coffee houses and taverns varied. The publicness of coffee houses, arenas for debate, free speech and radical politics during and following the political reforms of 1688, suggested both autonomy and independence.[12] Inns and taverns were considered less politicized, more controlled and respectable; whereas alehouses and ginshops were thought of as disorderly and unregulated, of a lower social status. In order to segregate various grades of customer many houses were subdivided to provide certain clubs with private rooms.[13]

Club members paid a subscription to cover refreshments and the hire of a table or room for an evening in a house which rented out space to a number of different clubs. Venues in the St James's area, for example the Thatched House Tavern, home to the Literary Club, Dilettante Society and Pugilistic Society, and Almack's house in Pall Mall, a house where many club meetings took place, became known as subscription houses.[14] The restrictions exerted over entry through membership strictly differentiated these new 'Subscription or Club Houses to which the Members are elected by close ballot' from the taverns and coffee houses.[15] The 'club' as the table habitually occupied, or the room rented weekly by a group of men, also developed over time into another form of subscription house, a whole building rented, owned and sometimes designed, for the purposes of one club. From the late eighteenth century onwards clubs expressed preferences for buildings for their sole use; sometimes such a building was purchased by the club, but more commonly it was rented by the club proprietor and paid for through membership fees.

In the eighteenth century, clubs were traditionally proprietary, owned and managed by aspiring entrepreneurs. The proprietors were men with previous training in the service industry, servants to the aristocracy or proprietors of food and wine businesses, who came from lower classes than those of the members and ran clubs as a way of making profit. The role of the club manager, as property owner, money-lender and manager of club finance and profits, posed a social threat to members.[16] Certain club rules were established ostensibly to protect the manager from bankruptcy, potential debt or property loss, but such rules also represented members' concerns for their own money and property.[17] Many of these fears were indeed well founded; several club managers, including Nicholas Kenney of the Savoir Vivre, Raggett of White's and Crockford of Crockford's, made huge sums out of their members by funding loans for gambling debts and food bills.[18] In the early nineteenth century, proprietors were subject to an increasing pressure from the members who wished to control the management of the club and ownership of the clubhouse. Management committees composed of club members superseded the position of proprietors as club managers and challenged their roles as owners or lessees of clubhouses.[19] The first members' club, Arthur's, was established in 1811 and, from 1815, all the new clubhouses in St James's were owned and managed by their members.[20]

Initially clubhouses were conversions of family homes, but many of the new purpose-designed buildings modelled themselves on domestic dwellings. Boodle's was the first club to occupy its 'own house'. This was a building originally designed as a meeting place for the Savoir Vivre, a fashionable group of men who set standards of 'taste' in the arts.[21] The club had been meeting from 1772 at the Star and Garter, and in 1775 the proprietor, Nicholas Kenney, obtained the lease of three old houses in St James's Street and demolished them to build the first specially commissioned clubhouse.[22] Boodle's club took over the building in 1783. The design for the Savoir Vivre's clubhouse, consisting of a north section for the members and a southern one for 'a single man of fashion', resembled a town house, a private rather than a public building, both in terms of its elevation, a 'modest and domesticated front', and its asymmetric plan. The plan layout placed the main staircase to one side next to a series of rooms arranged in linear sequence from front to back.[23]

At Brooks's, internally the rooms were arranged around a central double-height space housing the staircase. As well as providing each room with access from a public hallway, this layout also gave all rooms equal status, creating a rather different social space to the sequential and intimate arrangement of Boodle's where one room had to be entered to reach another. But this design also followed a model adopted by domestic buildings, in this case the Palladian country villa. Only in the early nineteenth century, as clubs grew larger and their role changed from gathering places for the upper classes to drink and gamble, to centres of a public and more institutional nature did they require different kinds of buildings. It has been argued that the first club to break the 'domestic' tradition was Charles Barry's Travellers' Club of 1819. However, based on the Italian *palazzo*, the design still refers to a domestic, if not also civic, architectural typology as its model.[24] Subsequent club designs did move towards the erection of large free-standing buildings with plenty of space around them externally, while internally rooms on both floors were formally distributed around a central staircase.

Particularly in the proprietor-managed eighteenth-century clubhouse, based on a small and exclusive membership, the social hierarchy can be compared to the feudal domestic household.[25] While the relationship between members might be considered 'fraternal', that of members to the servants operated on a hierarchical basis. Here, certain social relations – the dominant role of the members and the subservient role of servants – were observed within the spatial organization of the club.

Domestic activities associated with the servants and the running of the club, such as cooking, cleaning and storage, were subjugated to places of the least importance in the attic or basement. Such places were generally considered unsightly and where possible kept hidden from view. Staff were confined to these distinct service zones within the club building, to basement kitchens, attic sleeping quarters and various places at the rear of the building.

Extreme lengths were taken to provide separate internal circulation, staircases and routes, for staff and members, in order to avoid contact unless for serving purposes. For example, when Boodle's added a new dining room in 1834, a new staircase connecting the kitchen and the dining room was also built to avoid members seeing staff carrying food.[26] Such strict spatial divisions reflect and reinforce clear class hierarchies. The relation of the proprietor (owner and/or manager) to members and servants was more complex. His role of dominant 'patriarch' within the space of the club 'family', was supported by his class relationship to the working-class staff but not to the upper-class members. It is not surprising therefore that the working- or middle-class proprietor/manager was considered a transgressive character, existing between social classes and moving, as only he could, between the different zones of the club.

Club rules codified the social relations between different occupants of the club – members and servants, proprietor and members, strangers and members – in spatial terms. Certain spaces were allocated to stated groups for particular times and specified activities.[27] Decisions about who could do what where were important in distinguishing members from non-members. For example, moneylenders who came to the clubs could not enter the main spaces of the buildings, but had to wait in the strangers' room on the ground floor near the entrance.[28] In both Brooks's and Boodle's, the most exclusive club activities, drinking alcohol, eating and gaming, took place in the members' suite of rooms upstairs; visitors could only be entertained in the ground-floor coffee or morning room.

A Member may admit a Friend or Friends on the ground Floor where they may have Tea or Coffee but no Wine. No Cards or Gaming to be allowed except in the rooms upstairs.[29]

Clubs are represented alternatively as the place in which bachelors might prepare for domestic life and as a married man's refuge from family life.[30] As in the home, day-to-day routines are important to the functioning of the clubs and times for meals, for supper and dinner, were set out in the club rules.[31] 'Club life' involved a large amount of time spent indulging in this kind of routinized behaviour with no purpose other than leisure. A typical day described a long breakfast at eleven o'clock, a walk down Bond Street, a look into a club in Pall Mall at four o'clock, a four-course dinner and a dessert at seven o'clock and two rubbers of cards from midnight until two o'clock.[32]

The streets around St James's also offered other domestic places for men in the form of chambers and hotels. Some were men returning to England from military or diplomatic service abroad, others were young bachelors, just moved to London from their family homes, who did not wish the financial burden of buying a large house and were not ready to marry.[33] The bachelor chamber is represented in the ramble, see for example figure 7, as the most important domestic space for men outside the family home at this time. This was the place where men dressed and groomed, met for breakfast and prepared themselves for a day in the city.[34] The Albany, where Bob Logic lived, consisted of a series of seventy bachelor chambers intended for men of the nobility and gentry. It was built off Piccadilly in 1803–4 by Alexander Copland to Henry Holland's designs. Each set of chambers was self-contained, but a dining room, bar and hot/cold communal baths were also provided. Despite rules limitating of the use of apartments to residential purposes, Henry Angelo had a fencing school in the Albany in 1804 and Gentleman Jackson held his pugilistic training rooms there in 1807.[35]

Hotels, such as Clarendon's, Limmer's, Ibbetson's, Fladong's, Stephen's and Grillon's, also provided spaces of male domesticity and intimacy in the city.[36] In general the only activities which took place in these venues were everyday ones, such as eating, drinking and sleeping. But some hotels were also known for their special features, for example, Fenton's medicinal baths, Parsloe's chess club, the Smyrna Coffee House's billiards and, for members of the sporting world, Limmer's, a 'midnight Tattersall's'.[37] Taverns too provided men with a social place outside the home and even public spaces such as streets were described as places for men to relax in.[38] Rambling texts represented certain streets in domestic terms: Bond Street was a 'fashionable lounge' and men were 'at home' in St James's Street.[39]

From a liberal rights perspective, we can argue that the club offers a space for the safeguarding of individuality. The clubhouse is a place of civil society, free from the coercive state, public morality, legal constraint and corporate interest.[40] At the same time, the club is set aside from the emotional pressures and social demands of the private familial realm. Lying between the political public and the social private, then, the club represents a domestic side to public patriarchy. By offering a private environment without the stresses of family life and a public realm without its political responsibilities, occupying a clubhouse suggests both the comfort and the freedom of being 'at home' but in the public spaces of the city.[41]

THE BOW WINDOW: DISPLAYING EXCLUSIVITY

> The dandies of society were [. . .] great frequenters of White's Club, in St. James's Street, where, in the famous bay window, they mustered in force.[42]

Clubs are male-only spaces in the city defined by the specific exclusion of women. These regulations are not written into club rules, but form part of club tradition. In the early nineteenth century, social events arranged by clubs which involved women such as masquerades, celebrations of military successes, coronations, royal birthdays could not take place in the clubhouse itself, but would use another space in the west of London, such as Almack's Assembly Rooms, the Pantheon or Vauxhall. Today, although some clubs allow women as visitors and associate members, they are still allocated specific spaces, times and routes in order to maintain parts of the clubs as male reserves. Although there were no regulations governing gender specifically, membership to clubs was and is restricted to men.

Club membership, however, not only excludes women, but also other men. In the eighteenth and early nineteenth centuries, members' rule books set out inter-club rivalries explicitly. For example, members of Boodle's could belong to all other clubs except Arthur's (White's).[43] Brooks's original rules forbade membership of any club except 'old'

Whites (this was repealed in 1772).[44] Only members of White's, Boodle's, Brooks's, Arthur's, the Cocoa Tree and the Travellers' were considered eligible at Crockford's.[45] In this way male identity was constructed through codes of exclusion and inclusion, distinction and emulation, through the patriarchal exclusion of all women to all clubs and through the fraternal inclusion of specific men in certain clubs.[46]

Political and party allegiances were particularly important in defining club fraternities. The clubhouses of White's and Brooks's were, in the late eighteenth century, sites of political friction. While White's welcomed tories, the whig opposition frequented Brooks's.[47] In the 1830s, the political opposition between the whigs and tories shifted to a rivalry between the conservatives at the Carlton Club and the liberals at the Reform, their respective clubhouses becoming institutionalized head-quarters of party politics.[48] Smaller-scale county affiliations were also connected to clubs, for example, Boodle's was associated with the country squirearchy, particularly men from Shropshire.[49]

The architecture of the clubhouse made a number of public state-ments about the values of different clubs. To be connected with a famous architect clearly gave a club a prestigious status, as did the formal style and spatial layout of the building. For example, in disagreements over the architect and the date of the design of Boodle's clubhouse, certain historians prefer to argue for Robert Adam's involvement for reasons of prestige.[50] It is suggested that the first-floor Venetian window on the elevation to St James's Street bears a formal similarity to Adam's Royal Society of Arts building in the Adelphi built a few years previously. Although claims for John Soane have also been staked, Adam has also been suggested as the architect of the suite of five apartments on the second floor, consisting of an antechamber, a back drawing room, a dining room, an oval room, as well as the drawing room or saloon with two adjoining side chambers.[51]

Brooks's clubhouse, erected opposite in 1776–8, is much grander than Boodle's in scale, style and layout. It has a centralized front façade with a pediment and two-storey Corinthian pilasters. Commonly attrib-uted to Henry Holland, as at Boodle's this well-known architect was not involved with the whole building, only the design of a prestigious suite of rooms on the first floor. These consisted of a subscription room running along St James's Street with a barrel-shaped roof and window facing south onto Park Place, an antechamber, eating room and a round smoking room.[52] As with Boodle's, it was important that the architecture publicly represented the values of the club. The adoption of classical and democratic Greek architecture at Brooks's was considered more suitable for a radical whig, rather than a country gentlemen's, club. At around the same time, 1787–9, White's was substantially altered to rival the new designs of Boodle's and Brooks's. In line with their political stance and in order to differentiate themselves from Brook's, White's rejected the flamboyant and enormous house designed for them by Adam, and instead opted for the more conservative designs of James Wyatt.[53]

The emergence of subscription houses as buildings designated as the property of one club, can be argued to coincide with a shift in the early nineteenth century from private patriarchy, centred on the containment of women in the home, to public patriarchy, focused on the control of women in public places of urban leisure. The creation of this new form of public masculinity required the combination of elements of both patriarchal and fratriarchal control. Fratriarchy, as a form of patriarchal civil society specifically created among men in the public, as opposed to the familial sphere, allowed bonds of allegiance to be created through struggles for power between men.[54] Fraternity was critical to the establishment of distinct and definable public masculine identities in new urban spaces of leisure and entertainment. The formation of male social clubs in the seventeenth century and their later manifestation as forms of architecture, signifies the emergence of these new rival forms of masculinity in public space, demonstrating that public patriarchy is not a homogeneous whole, but rather a set of heterogeneous and contested identities.

In the early nineteenth century an expansion took place in club life. White's and Brooks's were no longer the only clubs of importance in the West End. Boodle's and Arthur's were attracting numbers of country gentlemen, the Guards' had founded a club of their own, Watier's was attracting gamesters and Daubigne's and Graham's were frequented by men of fashion.[55] Subsequently the role of architecture became increasingly important in representing individual club identities to the public. From employing architects to design suites of rooms, clubs used competitions and hired architects to design new buildings on prestigious sites. The Travellers' Club, founded in 1819, 'to form a point of reunion for gentlemen who had travelled abroad', was the first clubhouse procured and designed through architectural competition.[56] A prime site on the south side of Pall Mall on the east and west corners of Waterloo Place was made available when Carlton House was pulled down in 1826. This became a scene of rivalry between the United Services and the Athenaeum over possible sites for their new buildings, exemplifying the significance of a good location and well-designed clubhouse for the status of a club.[57]

This increasing number of clubs and the popularization of club life lead to a tightening of control over entry in the most exclusive clubs. At White's, certain members, specifically the dandies, refused to give out new memberships in order to emphasize the principle of exclusiveness which was being undermined by the emergence of new clubs.[58] Changes to the building in 1811 enhanced the display of White's select membership to the outside world of St James's. The morning room was enlarged by taking over the space of the existing entrance hall, placed centrally in the front façade. The old front door was replaced with a new window, the famous 'Bow Window at Whites', which was built out over the entrance steps, creating a new focal point to the St James's Street elevation. The bow window provided a place for viewing the street, but also allowed the occupants of the club to display their 'conspicuous consumption' or their dress and leisure time to the public. The space in the morning room adjacent to this window was inhabited as a place of high fashion by a circle of dandies, including Beau Brummel.[59] The prestige of being a member of an exclusive club like White's was certainly a social achievement worth exhibiting to the public, especially in the case of a man like Brummel who had risen from a lower-class position — Brummel's father was a member of staff in the royal household.

The bow window in the centre of the front façade allowed men to show off their exclusivity to those in the surrounding rival clubs. A member of the Guards' Club opposite responded angrily to the 'dandies' in White's, criticizing them for being solely interested in their appearance: 'Damn those fellows; they are upstarts, and only fit for the society of tailors'.[60] Boodle's responded to the rivalrous environment by adding a bow window in 1821, giving the front façade a fully symmetrical elevation.[61] When Crockford's opened in 1828, the ground-floor rooms also possessed famous windows, as shown in figure 10. Rather than bow windows, these have been carefully described as 'bay' windows. This distinction is important, not so much in terms of their architectural construction, but in what such a difference represents in terms of the gaze. White's 'bow' window is represented as place for being looked at; whereas Crockford's 'bay' windows are considered observatories from which to look out and survey the street.[62] Whether this variation from being looked at to looking out can be explained as an historical change is hard to access since it is complicated by each author's relation to the clubs themselves. But, in any case, the emphasis on these St James's Street windows in representations of clubs in rambling texts indicates their importance as places for men to enjoy different aspects of visual pleasure – to see and be seen – to display exclusive masculine allegiances to each other and to the public in general.

A number of sites in St James's featured sequentially as key haunts in the typical rambler's daily routine. This consisted of midday rising and leisurely dressing followed by a late afternoon promenade around Bond Street, St James's Street and Pall Mall purchasing commodities and displaying self, dress, horse and carriage. As day moved into night, evening activities included suppers, card parties and routs held at family homes, visits to assembly rooms, theatres or operas and finally to the club for gambling and drinking till dawn.[63] Bond Street and St James's Street, with their gunmakers, booksellers, theatre ticket agents, sporting prints exhibitions, hatters, tailors, bootmakers, hairdressers, perfumers, jewellers and other expensive tradesmen, catered solely for the male consumer.[64] These fashionable shops, as well as the surrounding chambers, hotels, sporting venues, coffee houses, clubs and taverns, provided places where the exclusion of women meant that differences between men required public expression.

> Such was the costume in which he was destined to show off, and thus equipped, after a few minutes they emerged from the house in Piccadilly on the proposed ramble, and proceeded towards Bond Street.[65]

As we have already discussed in the previous chapter, obsessions with specific modes of dressing and talking reflected men's intense preoccupation with self-presentation. Establishing the correct aspects of display on the street or walking also played a critical part in the representation of public masculinity. Move in the wrong way, and young men on St James's Street might be considered street nuisances for their effeminacy, 'ladies men who scent thy mawkish way', or for their roughness, for example the fast and aggressive driving of wheeled vehicles.[66] However, the adoption of distinctive styles of urban street behaviour, such as walking on certain sides of the street, was not only an expression of male identity but also a result of the large amount of traffic, both vehicular and pedestrian.[67]

Centres for sport in the vicinity, such as Manton's shooting gallery in Davies Street, were important for establishing male bonds through the enjoyment of shared activities.[68] Coaching clubs, for example the Whip Club, the Benson and the Four-in-Hand, were very popular in the early nineteenth century. Members would meet at regular intervals and display themselves in certain London squares before setting off on a cross-country ride to dine.[69]

As shown in figure 12, young pugilists met at Gentleman Jackson's training rooms at 13 Bond Street to train and watch each other display physique and sporting skills.[70] Usually major pugilistic fights took place outside towns, or at the 'manly venue' of Fives Court, St Martin's Street, Leicester-Fields,[71] but on occasion the London homes of the nobility, domestic spaces usually associated with the family, would be used to stage special fights for an élite crowd.[72] Sporting clubs all met in taverns often owned by members of the sporting fraternity, for example Tom Cribb's tavern in Panton Street depicted in figure 13.[73] Such taverns, frequented by both working-class professional boxers and upper-class patrons, were the social centre of sport.

The basis for such shared male pursuits as drinking, sporting and gambling, originated at male-only education institutions, first at schools, such as Eton, and later at universities, such as Cambridge and Oxford.[74] Clubs formalized these male upper-class bonds in the form of cultural institutions, which linked specific sports to particular clubs, for example, fox-hunting at Boodle's and the Turf at White's.[75] As ways of communicating and exchanging information, clubs as well as magazines, maps and sporting calendars, were places from which to organize out of town activities and make bets.[76] But as commercial

Fig. 12 George and Robert Cruikshank, '*Art of Self-Defence*: *Tom* and *Jerry* receiving Instructions from Mr. Jackson, at his Rooms, in Bond-Street', Pierce Egan, *Life in London; or, the day and night scenes of Jerry Hawthorn, Esq., and his elegant friend Corinthian Tom, accompanied by Bob Logic, the Oxonian, in their Rambles and Sprees through the Metropolis*

Fig. 13 George and Robert Cruikshank, '*Cribb's Parlour*: *Tom* introducing *Jerry* and *Logic* to the Champion of England', Pierce Egan, *Life in London; or, the day and night scenes of Jerry Hawthorn, Esq., and his elegant friend Corinthian Tom, accompanied by Bob Logic, the Oxonian, in their Rambles and Sprees through the Metropolis*

forms of entertainment, sporting activities, characterized by competition, did not only create bonds between men but were used to establish dominance and determine hierarchies.[77] Clubs provided mechanisms for privileged groups to establish and control sporting legislation.[78]

'SANCTUM SANCTORIUM': THE SECRET SPACE OF GAMBLING

> The beautiful chandeliers, large pier glasses, in superb gilt frames, with curious designs, and the handsome side boards, loaded, with the costly glass and plate [. . .] his sight was quite dazzled by looking glasses, chandeliers, platecut glasses and decanters, all glittering with the glare of light emitted from an abundance of wax candles [. . .] some choice paintings, rich curtains, rare fruits, every delicacy in abundance [. . .] wine sparkling in the decanters – the whole formed a coup d'oeil of the most fascinating, dazzling and intoxicating appearance.[79]

One of the most popular and notorious forms of sporting activity for men in the early nineteenth century was gambling.[80] In the eighteenth century, White's was the place for gambling but, as club rules restricted certain kinds of game, Brooks's replaced White's as the club 'notorious for high play'.[81] In the early nineteenth century, St James's was the most fashionable gambling district with games taking place in exclusive clubs, such as Brooks's and Crockford's, as well as low gaming houses.[82] Gambling houses were referred to as 'hells', places of sin and evil where men made pacts with the devil, as well as 'temple[s] of ruin, indolence, and guile'.[83] These hells, removed from everyday life, were places of transgression. Not only did they represent hell but heaven as well, the extremities of good and evil.

> Hell is a title given to any well-known gaming house, and really appears to have been well chosen; for all the miseries that can fall to the lot of human nature, are to be found in those receptacles of idleness, duplicity and villainy.[84]

Rambling texts often compared the gambling system to a spider's web, clearly differentiating between those who benefited – gaming reptiles or sporting spiders, and those who lost – bleeding victims.[85] The frequenters of hells were known as 'greeks' and 'pigeons'; greeks made money while pigeons lost money.[86] Although the term 'greek' often represented desirable qualities of political democracy in the eighteenth and early nineteenth centuries, in this instance the reference is specifically to paganism and scenes of debauchery and cunning:

> Their familiar denominations are 'legs', 'greeks', 'sporting men', and 'of the ring'; terms synonymous with 'black legs', a set of titled and untitled well practised in all the secrets of leg-ism – a science of chicanery and fraud, by which its votaries are taught the mode of enriching themselves by impoverishing others.[87]

Pigeons, however, suggest naivety, a homing instinct and lack of autonomy. (Pigeons or unhappy gamblers have no choice but to return to hell, in the hope of recouping the debts they have incurred.) Rambles represented gambling as titillating but also as dangerous, as an exciting lure and a trap.[88] Social views on gambling reflected its two-sided status, both the heavenly promise of instant profit and the hellish entrapment of debt repayment.

The gambling room or the 'sanctum sanctorium', known as the saloon in Boodle's and the subscription room in Brooks's (see figure 11), was the place where these anxieties and ambitions were focused.[89] The importance of the 'sanctum sanctorium' was indicated by its generous size and location within a suite of rooms designed by well-known architects, the most ostentatious rooms of the club. At Crockford's, the 'sanctum sanctorium' was a small but 'handsomely' furnished room with a hazard table in the centre, located, as in Boodle's and Brooks's, on the upper floor running across the St James's Street elevation.[90] This room has been described as 'a scene of dazzling astonishment'.[91] It was an elaborate drawing room which could be divided by folding doors into a series of three gaming rooms, one used for playing cards.[92] These were furnished with a writing table for loans and demands for winnings, chairs, dice and counter bowls, small hand rakes for drawing counters and an oblong table with a green cloth — 'the all attractive hazard table'.[93] Downstairs, leading off the reading room, was a second gambling room for use when Parliament was in recess and the main gambling room was closed.[94]

> The drawing rooms, or real hell, consisted of four chambers: the first an anteroom, opening to a saloon embellished to a degree which baffles description; thence to a small curiously-formed cabinet or boudoir, which opens to the supper room. All these rooms are panelled in the most gorgeous manner; spaces are left to be filled up with murals and silks or gold ornaments; while the ceilings are as superb as the walls.[95]

Gambling was made illegal in coffee houses and public houses in the eighteenth century and laws controlled the kind of games played, the amount of money played for and the places in which gambling was allowed.[96] By the early nineteenth century, people playing unlawful games were charged under the Vagrancy Act as rogues and vagabonds.[97] The act of keeping a house or place for gambling and the act of playing a prohibited game within such a house was deemed disorderly.[98] Although their operations were as illegal as any other gambling venue, clubs were protected from the law by their élite, powerful and wealthy patronage.[99]

> of all the disgraceful scenes which deform the metropolis, the most vicious and ruinous is that of the fashionable hells, or rouge et noir gambling, and it is a matter of astonishment and reproachment that they have yet remained undisturbed by the law, and hitherto unnoticed by the public press.[100]

Given the illegal status of gambling, the 'sanctum sanctorium' was located in the most protected part of the house. It was separated from the street by a series of locked doors, often with circular peepholes for those guarding the rooms to survey potential visitors.[101] One representation of a gambling hell describes seven doors between the gambling room and the street.[102] In another description, there are three doors, one of which is iron.[103]

The houses are well fortified with strong iron-plated doors, to make an ingress into them a difficult and tardy matter. There is one at the bottom of the stairs, one near the top, and a third at the entrance into the room of play. These are opened and closed one after the other, as a person ascends or descends.[104]

The journey to the gambling room had the effect of dislocating the gambler from the world outside, creating an atmosphere of suspense and excitement conducive to gambling. On entry to the hell, the gambler had to surrender control, give himself up to the unexpected. Temporally as well as spatially, separation from everyday life was essential. Connections with diurnal cycles that could potentially shorten long gambling sessions had to be severed,[105] as shown in images of the interior of unspecified gambling rooms in both *The English Spy* (see figure 14), and *Life in London* (see figure 15). This isolation from the outside world was achieved by permanently drawing the curtains of the gambling room and lighting the rooms artificially with chandeliers and lamps.[106] Representing gambling as a night-time activity reinforced its transgressive status. The exact hours of opening depended on the type of the house: the more exclusive venues with the highest stakes opened until the early morning, whereas those with lower stakes shut at midnight.[107]

The usual location of gambling rooms on the first floor along the front

Fig. 14 Robert Cruikshank, 'The Interior of a Modern Hell. (Vide the affair of the cogged dice)', Bernard Blackmantle, *The English Spy*

Fig. 15 George and Robert Cruikshank, 'A Game at Whist, *Tom* and *Jerry* among the Swell "Broad Coves"', Pierce Egan, *Life in London; or the day and night scenes of Jerry Hawthorn, Esq., and his elegant friend Corinthian Tom, accompanied by Bob Logic, the Oxonian, in their Rambles and Sprees through the Metropolis*

façade of the club was paradoxical. Although this position gave these rooms a protected and special status within the internal architectural layout of the club, it contradicted the need for an illegal activity to be hidden. One can only suppose that to place such an internalized activity in such an exposed position was intentional. It represented another way of displaying the exclusivity of particular male fraternities to the public realm. Members of the most exclusive clubs were immune from legal interference. It was this privileged status that was displayed during the day via closed curtains to the street.

The representation of the gambling hell as an entrapping and web-like place was intensified by upper-class fears that the profits made by the working- and middle-class proprietors were at the expense of members of their own class. A number of rambles tell stories of young aristocrats loosing their inheritances to duplicitous gambling hell entrepreneurs.[108] Crockford, originally a fishmonger, apparently made a huge profit out of the upper classes through betting on fights, races, trotting and pigeon matches.[109] Gambling at his club in St James's Street, he was frequently represented in rambling tales at the centre of his web, trying to 'attract, entrap, and ruin the unwary'.[110] Aspects of entrapment were also associated with entry to the building itself. In one image, Crockford figures as a shark at the threshold of the front door to his club trying to lure John Bull into his St James's Street premises.[111]

> These dens have the appearance of private dwellings, with the exception, that the hall door of each is left ajar, during hours of play, like those of trap-cadgers, to catch the passing pigeons[112]

Enticement, duplicity and immorality were important themes in gambling. Anti-gambling texts spent much time describing the terms of gambling slang in great detail in order to demystify the sport and warn readers of the potential dangers involved.[113] In the early eighteenth century, the phrase 'to game' was used to describe card or dice games and a 'gamester' was someone who invited 'the unwary to game and to cheat them'.[114] The confusion between gambling hells, where the sole activity was gambling, and male clubs, where gambling activities often took place, was the focus of many contemporary texts on gambling, including rambles. The hell was considered a place of disrepute, the club a place of respected social status. The physical proximity of low gaming houses, found in obscure courts, to private clubs in the St James's area caused concern. Their spatial closeness meant that they might be mistaken for one another. This was a worry to middle- and upper-class commentators who feared that entering the wrong venue by mistake might result in upper-class men being sapped of money by gambling hell proprietors of a lower class.

Similar to the surface of the cyprian and dandy described in the previous chapter, fears of mistaken identity resulted in the representation of the hell as a place of false pretence. Low gambling houses were considered to 'masquerade' as male clubs, in order to create an aura of respectability. It was this element of 'masquerade' or 'disguise' in the confusion of low gaming hells and respectable clubs which was represented as the cause of the gamblers' entrapment. By 'imitating' social forms of club organization, in terms of committees, membership, balloting, entrance fee, annual subscription and its listing in the Court Guide, Crockford's was considered to be a common gaming house in disguise as a subscription house:[115]

in order to keep out those whom they have already plundered out of their last shilling, their houses assume every specious appearance. Thus the great 'hell' in St. James's Street is called 'Crockford's Club!', the 'hell' in Park Place is called the 'Melton Mowbray Club!' and the 'hell' in Waterloo Place, the 'Fox Hunting Club!!!'[116]

The class tensions in clubs around the ownership of money, as well as property, were most potent in the subscription room. This was the place in the club where the manager/proprietor in presiding over the gambling most diminished the members' sense of power and control. If the external surface of the building was associated with deceit so too was the interior decoration of these gambling rooms – represented as highly ornate. At Crockford's, the use of glass in mirrors and chandeliers, the careful arrangement of the lighting and the decorative embellishment of the interior, all contributed to the construction of a glittering atmosphere and a space of illusion.[117] This magical environment was interpreted by anti-gamblers as part of a conscious plan to seduce the gambler and produce in him the state of fantasy and delusion conducive to excessive gambling.[118] If the morality of gambling was connected to appearance and deception, then the interior architecture of the hell was a designed and duplicitous surface of seduction.

Concerns with the immorality of gambling were voiced by different classes for different reasons. Members of the upper classes, who feared losing their money to lower-class entrepreneurs, gave warnings against 'this most horrid vice gaming' which they suggested resulted in moral decline.[119] The rising middle classes also saw gambling as a problem, as extravagant and lazy. It was either represented as an upper-class vice, one which opposed values of stability, property, domesticity, family life and religion, or as an opportunity for the working classes to earn money without labouring, a concept entirely opposed to any sort of work ethic.[120] So, although in the eighteenth century taking extreme risks at gambling had been seen as a sign of virile masculinity, linked to political power, class and money, by the early nineteenth century, gambling had gained a disreputable status.[121] The tendency in rambling tales was to represent gambling as immoral.[122] This immoral status was frequently described in gendered terms in relation to deviant female sexuality. For example, a gambling hell might be described as 'an abandoned prostitution of every principle of hallow and virtue'.[123] Prostitutes and female gamblers were represented as synonymous – both robbed the public of money.[124] And female gamblers, as well as losing their fortunes, were considered to lose their virtue.[125] The wealthy male whose gambling had previously represented masculine power became increasingly associated with feminine immorality and with the weak and deceitful qualities of effeminate men, such as dandies.[126]

Unlike the usual conception of the city as the male space of work and institution, the club shows that public masculinity was constructed around notions of domesticity, leisure, intimacy and privacy. The allocation of certain clubs and spaces within clubs to specific groups of men gave club members the opportunity to define their masculine identity through the occupation and control of key places. In the ground-floor bow windows of their particular club, male members could display their social exclusiveness and leisure time to rival club members along the street. But gambling was perhaps the most exclusive leisure activity which occurred in the male clubs, especially those of St James's Street. The potential instability of class hierarchy indicated by gambling, resulted in its representation as an immoral and dangerous pastime, one which could only take place in the most secret, exclusive and private rooms of the clubs, on the upper floor behind a series of doors. The juxtaposition created here between the obvious display of the bow window and the deceitful surface of the gambling hell, sets up an interesting dialectic once again between revealing and covering, which the next chapters explore in relation to the surface or exchange value attached to the cyprian.

CHAPTER 4

Almack's Assembly Rooms — Exchanging Property

> But no matter what form it takes, whether direct or indirect,
> general or special, immediate or deferred, explicit or
> implicit, closed or open, concrete or symbolic, it is
> exchange, always exchange, that emerges as the fundamental
> and common basis of all modalities of the institution of
> marriage[1]

> The 'exchange of women' is a powerful and seductive con-
> cept. It is attractive in that it places the oppression of women
> within social systems rather than in biology. Moreover, it
> suggests that we look for the ultimate locus of women's
> oppression within the traffic in women, rather than within
> the traffic in merchandise.[2]

> Such assemblies always had one underlying feature: they
> formed a matrimonial market, where buyers and sellers
> were as eager, and sometimes the merchandise as unsuspect-
> ing and as passive, as in any other centre of commercial
> traffic.[3]

Described in contemporary guides as 'spectacles', urban spaces for leisure and public amusements for both the sexes were considered an
important aspect of early nineteenth-century London.[4] Almack's
Assembly Rooms and the Argyll Rooms figured as the ultimate destin-
ations for ramblers.[5] The interiors of both Almack's, see figure 5,[6] and
the Argyll Rooms, see figure 16,[7] are shown as luxuriant ballrooms filled
with men and women engaged in masquerades, dancing, gossiping and
flirting. They are clearly highly desirable spaces to be entertained in.
This chapter looks at how assembly rooms were represented in the

Fig. 16 Robert Cruickshank, 'The Cyprians' Ball at the Argyle Rooms', Bernard Blackmantle, *The English Spy*

ramble as marriage markets, both as places of respectable encounters between the sexes in terms of courtship and marriage rituals, such as dancing and dressing up, and as sites of more titillating and sexually charged forms of exchange.

Assembly rooms provided places of public gathering outside the family home for making marriage arrangements. At Almack's Assembly Rooms, King Street, St James's, activities of exchange, consumption and display articulated in relation to courtship and marriage were carefully controlled by the patrons. Concerns over the transgressions that conducting private aspects of family life in public company might produce created social tensions. The very 'publicness' of assembly rooms meant that entrants needed to be carefully selected in order to produce desirable marriage alliances. In effect, Almack's operated as a private club run by a number of female patrons, who controlled entry through subscriptions and enforced them through strict dress codes. As the most exclusive venue in London, Almack's status was reinforced by its position in the west at the heart of fashionable St James's. This location emphasized its connections with other sites of upper-class assembly and promenade, such as the Italian Opera

House and Nash's new Regent Street, while the architectural design displayed exclusivity through the grand scale of the rooms and the extravagant interior decoration.

Assemblies originated as events for dancing, entertainment, card games and refreshments, held in the country to celebrate the opening and closing of the hunt. From the early eighteenth century they spread over England as social events in which people could meet as potential marriage partners. At first they were held by private individuals in the best rooms of their country houses, later when such locations were not considered prestigious enough, groups of subscribers held assemblies in the public rooms of existing buildings, such as inns, hotels, grammar schools, town halls, shire halls, market halls and theatres. From the 1720s, specialized assembly rooms appeared, often uniting previously separated assemblies of different social classes in one independent building elaborate in decor. Between 1720 and 1820, seventy such assembly rooms were operating in England and Wales and by the early nineteenth century, assemblies in the form of masquerades, balls and concerts, took place on a regular basis in purpose-designed auditoria, concert and assembly rooms.

Assembly rooms followed a distinct architectural pattern. They always consisted of three spaces, each for a different activity: a ball room with musicians' gallery for dancing, a card room for playing cards and a room for refreshments.[8] The layouts varied, in some, for example Bath, the assembly rooms were on the first floor, whereas in others, for example York, the assembly rooms were on the ground floor.[9] Popular London assembly rooms in the eighteenth century included the Pantheon in Oxford Street and Carlisle House in Soho Square.[10] But the most exclusive and fashionable were Almack's Assembly Rooms, erected between May 1764 and February 1765, to the designs of architect Robert Mylne for a proprietor named William Almack.[11] The assembly rooms were used for balls and masquerades and reached the peak of their popularity in the second and third decades of the nineteenth century.[12]

At Almack's, with the exception of the ground-floor entrance, dressed with a pedimented Ionic doorcase, and six arch-headed windows expressing the ballroom along the King Street façade, the exterior of the building was plain brickwork.[13] The interior, however, consisting of 'three very elegant' rooms – cardroom, ballroom and tearoom – located on the first floor was described in lavish terms.[14] The other fashionable assembly rooms at this time were the Argyll Rooms, Little Argyll Street,[15] and the New Assembly Rooms, Hanover Square.[16] The Argyll Rooms were originally opened in 1806 by Henry Francis Greville but, in 1812, the management was handed over to Stephen Slade, who sold to the Regent Street Commissioners in 1819. The building reopened as a music shop in 1820 for the Royal Harmonic Institute, with a concert hall designed by Nash occupying the eastern part of the site and entertainment rooms located on the first floor.[17]

> Balls at Almack's, Willis's, and those at the Argyle Rooms, are particularly splendid, and numerously attended by the fashionable world: and the rooms themselves, at the latter, are in a style of non common magnificence.[18]

ASSEMBLY ROOMS: 'MATRIMONIAL BAZAARS'

> The economy – in both the narrow and the broad sense – that is in place in our societies thus requires women to lend themselves to alienation in consumption, and to exchanges in which they do not participate, that men be exempt from being used and circulated like commodities.[19]

> a matrimonial bazaar, where mothers met to carry on affairs of state; and often had the table, spread with tepid lemonade, weak tea, tasteless orgeat, stale cakes, and thin slices of bread and butter – the only refreshment allowed – been the scene of tender proposals.[20]

If we follow Irigaray's position set forth in chapter 1, then in patriarchy the exchange of women through marriage renders them commodities – objects of physical and metaphorical exchange among men.[21] In patriarchal society, marriage alliances operate as forms of gendered exchange, where women are moved between men as material and symbolic property. The relationship between women and property is a complex one, but simply put we can argue that in marriage women are both owned as private property and regarded as conduits for property.[22] In early nineteenth-century London, assembly rooms were sites where arrangments for the exchange of women through marriage took place.

The inheritance of property and the succession to titles in the early nineteenth century was a complicated affair. The prime factor affecting all property-owning families was the principle of primogeniture, where, in order to keep estates intact, titles and land were passed between men, from father to eldest son.[23] Restrictions were placed on the claims of younger sons and daughters on inheritance. The device of entail, for example, limited the heir's ability to sell or give away part of the estate. The inheritance of an intact estate played a crucial element in constructing male identity in the upper classes, where men's relationship to lineage was the basis of power and status.[24] The richer and more well-born the family, the more important primogeniture. And the key to primogeniture was marriage.[25] Marriage allowed the transmission and distribution of property in landed society between families. Through marriage, a significant amount of property could be transfered from the family of the bride to the family of the groom.[26] A contract of mutual concrete benefit between two families could ensure the continuity of the male line, the preservation of inherited property and the acquisition of further property, as well as set up useful political alliances.[27]

Although in patriarchy, descent and inheritance are transmitted from male to male, women make possible such exchanges between men.[28] Women are the conduits of property in the form of titles, money and land, but their own relation to property is curtailed by common and private laws.[29] In the early nineteenth century, in common law, after marriage, women's children and property – her portion and later earnings – with the exception of her freehold land, belonged to her husband.[30] The most wealthy brides might be the daughters of landed families with large portions, heiresses in families where the male line had come to an end, widows of landowners and daughters of rich bourgeoisie.[31] Women who were not landed heiresses were expected to bring large portions.[32] Nicknamed 'golden dollies',[33] these brides were highly desirable since men of the bourgeois class, less influenced by primogeniture, gave large portions to their daughters and cash contributions to the father of the groom.[34] These women, the daughters and also often widows of merchants, became targets for fortune hunters. By marrying bourgeois daughters with large portions, the younger sons of the gentry could become gentlemen of leisure.[35] In this way, city heiresses played an important part in alleviating financial problems of landed families.[36] But, as well as bringing money, rich wives were also useful for cementing political alliances.[37]

From another angle, the early nineteenth century also saw a rising proportion of marriages between London businessmen and the daughters of the gentry.[38] From 1780 to 1820, as many ancient families died out in the male lineage, an increasingly large number of heiresses appeared on the marriage market.[39] Since men could not take women's rank, such heiresses were only attractive if they owned land as well as titles.[40] They appealed to both the younger sons of the aristocracy with insubstantial inheritances of their own and to men with money but no land.[41] So despite the threat the newly wealthy bourgeoisie posed to older landowning families, alliances combining land and titles with money occurred through marriage. Offering money, social status and lineage, such unions benefited both sides, to form, from the 1820s, what has been described as a 'commercial aristocracy'.[42]

The development of a series of balls, assemblies and parties, which constituted the season and widened the pool of potentially satisfactory spouses, facilitated links between landed and commercial society across county boundaries.[43] The choice of marriage partners was greater at the national rather than the county level, and as a result a hierarchy developed between the regional short summer season at county assembly rooms and the longer national winter season held in London.[44] The London season provided the greatest series of opportunities for the urban bourgeoisie and the landed aristocracy to meet – 'a marriage market par excellence'.[45] Assembly rooms were key venues in facilitating such exchanges and alliances.[46]

At places like Almack's, young people met through the structured activities of card playing and dancing. Such pastimes went on in different spaces throughout the evening but, half-way through, there was a break for refreshments consisting of weak bohea, tea, lemonade, bread, butter and cake.[47] The disparaging comments made concerning these 'most wretched refreshments' suggest that the main purpose of the tearoom was not for enjoying fine food and drink but rather to facilitate another function – the arrangement of marriages. Indeed Almack's was represented as a place which had no purpose other than the establishment of good marriages.[48]

ALMACK'S: 'SEVENTH HEAVEN'

Commodities cannot themselves go to market and perform exchanges in their own right. We must, therefore, have recourse to their guardians, who are the possessors of commodities.[49]

Almack's balls in London are the resort of people of the highest rank during the season, which lasts from April to June; and five or six of the most intensely fashionable ladies (Princess L— among the number), who are called Patronesses, distribute the tickets.[50]

In order to create competition between buyers and control the price of commodities, it is in the interest of those who exchange commodities to exercise some form of social closure over their purchase by excluding new entrants.[51] In order to make the right connections through marriage, critical to the consolidation of an urban élite, entry to the assembly rooms had be restricted. Private ownership and management of the space was one way of maintaining exclusivity. In regional assembly rooms, subscribers contributed both to the balls and the ownership of the building.[52] In the case of Almack's Assembly Rooms, the built fabric was owned by Almack, a private entrepreneur, but the land the building stood on was leased from the crown. In order to pay the lease and manage the rooms, Almack was dependant on the private subscriptions of a small group of men and women of the upper classes.[53]

The 'exclusive principle' of subscription allowed patrons to regulate the potential range of marriageable men and women.[54] The subscription system excluded those of the wrong social connections through various mechanisms, such as the vetting of potential subscribers and the maintaining of prices at an artificially high level.[55] Constant fears were expressed concerning the invasion of middle-class interlopers, but codified social rituals defined and maintained the place as an exclusive space, as 'quality'.[56] When Almack's first opened on 12 February 1765, seven rules controlled entry to the new establishment.[57] A subscription book contained the names of 60 subscribers, each of whom paid ten guineas for twelve balls which took place on Wednesdays during the season. This degree of control over entry resembled a club. Indeed Almack's initial venture, which opened in September 1759 at 49 Pall Mall was synonymous with a 'club of both sexes'. This Ladies Club or Coterie, founded by six women, admitted through ballot ladies on equal terms with men, to play cards, eat and chat. This 'female' club differed very little from a male club and was indeed compared to White's.[58]

> The Ladies nominate and choose the gentlemen and, so that no lady can exclude a lady, or gentleman a gentleman.[59]

During Almack's heyday, directly after Waterloo and into the 1820s, entry was controlled by a number of fashionable patronesses. These females provided Almack with initial support for his venture, took charge of the subscription books and were given plenary power to accept or reject every application for tickets.[60] The selection procedure was represented as extremely complex. Each Monday from April onwards these seven patronesses sat at a long table with three baskets: one for applications from friends, relatives and near connections, another for acceptances and a third for rejections. Compiled from the third basket was a list of those who would never be admitted and those who could try their luck again.[61] The patronesses then distributed vouchers of admission:

> It is an immense favour to obtain one; and, for people who do not belong to the very highest or most modish world, very difficult.[62]

Like other places of upper-class entertainment in the west, further controls were exerted through strict rules governing appearance. Almack's observed a formal dress code. Men were only allowed entry in knee breeches, black tights, silk stockings, flat dancing slippers, a white cravat and a bicorne, while women were required to wear evening dress.[63] Such explicit restrictions reinforced social hierarchy ensuring that those of the 'wrong' class could not gain access. This suited the aristocracy, since it ensured that only those from the commercial world who conformed to their rules could gain access:[64]

> At the present time one can hardly conceive the importance which was attached to getting admission to Almack's, the seventh heaven of the fashionable world.[65]

Urban location could also ensure exclusivity and Almack's position in St James's substantiated its reputation.[66] This fashionable and upper-class neighbourhood, a short distance from the royal palace, the Houses of Parliament and various subscription houses, was considered to be the right location for the initial establishment of public assemblies in the late eighteenth century and their continued popularity in the early nineteenth century.[67] In London, places of social entertainment had a history of moving west, following the movement of the upper classes from the City, to Covent Garden and on to St James's – the more westerly the location, the higher the status of the establishment.[68]

Representations of assembly rooms in rambles reinforced the élitism of certain upper-class sites of leisure by contrasting them to places of a different class. For example, as we have seen in chapter 2, *Life in London* very carefully created a juxtaposition between Almack's and Allmax, a working-class tavern in the east.[69] Almack's was also connected through shared daily routines to places of a similar class. The ramble positioned assembly rooms in a temporal sequence, preceded by a trip to the opera and followed by parties at houses of the aristocracy.[70] The fact that Almack's assembly rooms stayed open until the early hours of the morning, in line with the late hours of fashionable and leisured society in the west of London, further highlighted its exclusive status:[71]

> It is believe me, like stepping upon classic ground: at every step you take, the ARTS not only stare you full in the face [. . .] It is the rallying point of *rank*, wealth, talents, and beauty: it is like wise, the meridian of fashion, style, elegance, and manners, from the *alpha* to the *omega* [. . .] The very air you inhale at Almack's is different from

the plebeian atmosphere, being scented with the evaporation of the essences and richest perfumes from all quarters of the globe.[72]

By controlling entry to the assembly rooms, the female patronesses took an important role in managing the exchange of women between men – daughters between husbands, fathers and sons. In rambling texts, such women are represented as 'mothers', or bawds in nineteenth-century slang.[73] In early nineteenth-century prostitution, the 'mothers' who controlled brothels and profited through the exchange of other women as sexual commodities were represented as business women who organized the exchange of goods.[74] By managing the exchange of women between men for their own benefit, such 'mothers' upset the laws of patriarchal exchange and property ownership. As female property owners and capitalists, making profits off the labour of prostitute workers, bawds posed a threat to patriarchy and were represented as the most evil figures in prostitution.[75] The relationship between the older bawd or 'charitable matron' and the younger prostitutes she hired was represented in rambles and other early nineteenth-century texts as highly suggestive of the mother–daughter bond.[76] But, while mothers care for daughters by providing housing and clothing, bawds kept prostitutes in debt and made profits through them.[77] Their relationship was closer to that of 'keeper and slave'.[78]

At Almack's, the marriageable daughters, or young virgins, were also represented in relation to prostitution and depictions of cyprians. For example, the well-known contemporary cyprian or courtesan, Harriette Wilson, was often present at assembly room balls visited by ramblers.[79] In confusing virginal daughters with cyprians, the ramble draws an analogy between two forms of exchange of women – the exchange of virgins through marriage and cyprians through prostitution. The assembly room was represented as a 'market', a public place in which, it was suggested, two forms of gendered exchange took place. Two types of female commodity – virgins and cyprians – could be circulated for exchange between men, each one with a different relation to her own exchangeability. Irigaray's discussion of the varying exchange values of virgin and prostitute described in chapter 1 is helpful here. Before marriage, in the public place of courtship, the virginal daughter may represent natural exchange value but, once confined within the private place of marriage, her exchange value is replaced by her use value as wife and mother. The cyprian, on the other hand, represents usable exchange value or exchangeable usage: even after sexual use, the cyprian remains in circulation on the public market. In representations of Almack's in rambling tales, the presence of cyprians alongside mothers and marriageable daughters or virgins suggested the role of the assembly rooms as a 'market' of female commodities where women were to be exchanged between men both as property – reproductive bodies – and as conduits for property – land and money.

WALTZING: 'AN OBSCENE DISPLAY'

One of leading absurdities which has now, for some years, prevailed amongst the English haut ton, is an avidity for crowded rooms. It is nothing short of this positive inconvenience that will satisfy our genuine fashionables.[80]

the indecent foreign dance called the Waltz was introduced (we believe for the first time) at the English court on Friday last [. . .] It was an obscene display [. . .] the novelty is one deserving of severe reprobation, and we trust it will never again be tolerated in any moral English society.[81]

In architecture, ornament may be added to a building to represent social status and communicate the purpose and value of an architectural place to the viewer and user. The role of public places as 'spectacles' indicates that, like a number of figures in the ramble, their status was defined through their surface, through forms of conspicuous consumption and display. The rivalry between entertainment establishments, such as assembly rooms, was expressed through the appearance of the venue, the scale and size of the rooms and the richness of the decor. For example, in anticipation of the arrival of Almack's as a competitor, Mrs Cornelys, the proprietor of Carlisle House in Soho Square improved the decoration of her establishment:[82]

enlarged her vast room, and hung it with blue satin, and another with yellow satin [. . .] but Almack's room which is to be 90 feet long, proposes to swallow up both hers.[83]

Almack's ballroom or 'great room', completed in 1767, was a vast size, capable of holding 17,000 people.[84] The social status of the ball-room was indicated by its position at the top of the grand staircase, preceded by a vestibule and flanked on either side by 'two other spacious apartments used occasionally for large suppers or dinners'.[85] The ball-room was also the most elaborately decorated space in the building, with crystal chandeliers, mirrors, fireplaces and a musicians' gallery.[86] As we see in figure 5, *Life in London* represents the ballroom at Almack's as a highly elaborate and lavish space, decorated with pairs of Corinthian pilasters, swagged draperies, rococo mirrors and two-tiered chandeliers. In descriptions, Almack's greatest early nineteenth-century rival, the Argyll Rooms, shown in figure 16, were also admired for their size and decor:

> These very splendid rooms consist of a suite of four: a ball room, between fifty and sixty feet long, hung with French crimson flock wall paper, figured with gold, and lighted by three rich chandeliers; a drawing-room and anti-room, hung with French green flock paper, with flowers of gold; each of the latter has a superb chandelier in the centre, and is richly carpetted and furnished; and the grand concert room is a parallelogram, elongated at one end by the orchestra, and at the other end by four tiers of boxes. The side walls of this saloon are decorated by fluted pilasters of the Corinthian order, and the aper-tures to the orchestra and boxes are terminated by four majestic columns of the same description. The cornice is ornamented by modilions, the ceiling arched, forming the segment of a circle, and enriched with octagonal Mosaic pannels, and with large embossed flowers in each pannel.[87]

Described by one commentator as 'nothing less than a market place for beauty',[88] it is clear from accounts of assembly ballrooms in numer-ous texts that the women occupying the space were considered to be on display.[89] As beautiful objects, desired and prized possessions, woman-as-commodity may 'stand for' something other than herself. As a sign or a signifier a woman is a floating image associated with surface and ornament, in the same way that femininity might be considered a spec-tacle to be looked at. Such forms of ornament adorn and communicate aspects of power and beauty, but can also be associated with masking or deceit.

In all representations of assembly rooms and masquerade balls in rambles (see, for example, figures 5 and 16), the women wear the low-cut dresses required of evening wear, displaying 'snowy orbs of nature undisguised heaved like the ocean with circling swell'.[90] As well as the addition of some elements – decorative feathers and jewellery for example – 'dressing up' in evening dress also required the reduction of clothing in order to display certain parts of the body. The event of 'dressing up' either in evening wear for balls or in the costumes required for masquerades suggested a degree of subversion through notions of display and disguise and women in low-cut evening dress were considered by ramblers to be cyprians. Crowded parties and new dances reduced the distances between people, reinforcing worries concerning mistaken identities. Although in the early nineteenth century, successful private routs or parties at upper-class locations, known as 'squeezers' and 'drums', were expected to be crowded,[91] and at venues as fashionable as Almack's they certainly were,[92] the close physical proximity of members of the opposite sex posed a threat to social order.[93]

Bringing strangers of different genders and possibly classes into close contact raised questions of public morality. Although 'publicness' could be promoted for political reasons as a sign of democracy and liberalism, the regulation of public space was also vital to the preservation and promotion of order.[94] Like the gallery of the theatre and the early coffee house, assemblies were intended to be public spaces governed by a shared philosophy of politeness. Crowds signified the potential loss of constraint and their presence was given as a reason to close certain assemblies, such as Carlisle House in Soho Square.[95]

Dancing, a popular activity in assembly rooms, particularly for the young, was also considered problematic in terms of public decorum.[96] At Almack's in 1814, Scotch reels and traditional English dances, such as minuets and country dances, were encouraged as polite, safe and secure.[97] Through their intricate rules and etiquette they expressed social control and hierarchy.[98] The introduction of the quadrille from Paris in 1815, followed a year later by the waltz, broke this routine.[99] The foreign origin, as well as the fast speed, of these two dances posed a threat to social and spatial order:

Before the minuet was banished from the ball-room, the carriage of both ladies and gentlemen was decidedly more refined than in the present day.[100]

The quadrille was considered to make 'people look ridiculous'.[101] The 'mazy waltz' was described as 'nothing short of a romp'.[102] The close physical proximity of non-family members in the intimate space created by a dance such as the waltz posed moral questions.[103] The main problem concerned the amount of intimate bodily contact between the male and female partners.[104] Women were discouraged from waltzing because male waltzers were considered too forward and because the dance itself was considered too fast and manly.[105] The graceful minuet was advocated instead as far more suitable 'to the slender form of the female'.[106]

Dancing performed an important role in the consolidation of marriage engagements, allowing the couple-to-be a chance for a moment of privacy and the audience an opportunity to view and judge them as a pair. As such, the picking of a dancing partner was represented as a choice of particular social significance.[107] While it was men's prerogative to choose the dancing partner, women were described as rivals for the attention of men with social status.[108] The novel *Almack's*, for example, satirized female society, both débutantes and matrons, as 'manoeuvring for husbands'.[109]

As well as an event in which to participate, dance at the assembly rooms was enjoyed as a form of visual pleasure.[110] As groups of dancers, for example performing quadrilles with headdresses of 'gold baskets full of fruit, flowers', young women provided 'a very interesting picture of symmetry [. . .] to the eye of the spectator'.[111] The link between dance and display was seen as a gendered and a moral issue and the display of the female dancer at assembly rooms balls was connected to the indecent exposure of the corps de ballet at the Italian Opera House described in detail in the following chapter.[112]

MASQUERADE: 'EVENTS IMMORAL'

'femininity' is a role, an image, a value, imposed upon women by male systems of representation. In this masquerade of femininity, the woman loses herself, by playing on her femininity.[113]

It is true, the dashing *Cyprian* here sometimes throws her bait to inveigle the gallants *flushed* with wine, tossing her head, and passing herself off as a woman of quality, to make a better bargain for her favours.[114]

Assemblies often took the form of masquerades, visual displays of conspicuous consumption on a lavish scale.[115] Established in Venice in the form of carnivals, by the beginning of the eighteenth century, the masquerade was adopted all over Europe. In Catholic countries, they were performed as part of carnival and elsewhere as court entertainment or in pleasure gardens or theatres.[116] Foreign entrepreneurs, such as Heidegger and Cornelys, introduced masquerades, masked balls and ridottos to the middle classes in England in the mid-eighteenth century.[117] Held at Ranelagh, Vauxhall and Marylebone gardens in the 1740s and 1750s, and at Carlisle House, Almack's and the Pantheon in the 1760s and 1770s, masquerades were at the height of their popularity from 1720 to 1790. In the early nineteenth century, Vauxhall, with its variety of walks, illuminations of coloured lamps, transparent paintings, musical exhibitions, fireworks, food and one-off spectacles was an important place for masquerades.[118] These pleasure gardens were a key destination for ramblers:[119]

a public garden, in the style of Tivoli at Paris, but on a far grander and more brilliant scale. The illumination with thousands of lamps of the most dazzling colours is uncommonly splendid.[120]

Masquerades have been described in terms of the 'carnivalesque', where an inversion of social norms takes place within the spaces of everyday life and codes of temporality and spatiality are transgressed.[121] Masquerades could also be considered liminal zones, where pleasure is permitted, but in a controlled and legitimate manner.[122] Masquerades epitomized the underground or clandestine life of the city; in eighteenth-century fiction, they were a popular setting for intrigue, seduction, adultery, rape and perversion.[123] Like rambling, the masquerade offered the pursuit of clandestine sexual adventure.[124]

English masquerades were associated with earlier entertainments of mumming or disguising.[125] The element of disguise in masquerade costume was described in terms of surface, artifice, travesty, self-alienation and phantasmagoria.[126] Many masquerade disguises had elements of fetishistic or aphrodisiac power.[127] The most famous carnival costume was the Venetian domino. This consisted of a voluminous hooded cloak worn with a three-cornered hat and a mask, either white, grotesque or of black velvet, a moreta, with a piece of black lace or silk bauta which covered the face.[128] Arguably it was the anonymity of such disguises which ensured the prolonged popularity of masquerades.[129] Certainly in rambling tales, elements of disguise and mistaken identity were central to the representation of the masquerade. At a masquerade at the Italian Opera House, shown in figure 17, Tom was fooled as to

Fig. 17 George and Robert Cruickshank, '*Tom* and *Jerry* larking at a Masquerade Supper at the Opera-House', Pierce Egan, *Life in London; or, the day and night scenes of Jerry Hawthorn, Esq., and his elegant friend Corinthian Tom, accompanied by Bob Logic, the Oxonian, in their Rambles and Sprees through the Metropolis*

Corinthian Kate's identity, while Jerry talked to a woman who appeared to be a nun, later revealed as Lady Wanton.[130]

Carnival costume provided rich possibilities for subverting identity through reversing dress. Men and women could wear the same, so the effect was androgynous, or appear in each other's clothes, in travesty.[131] As we have seen in the case of the cyprian and the gambling chamber, there is a tendency in early nineteenth-century rambling texts to connect surfaces with some kind of anxiety regarding identity. Surfaces may mask the 'real' identity of the person or place in terms of class, race or gender, allowing working classes to 'dress up' and, conversely, in this instance, the upper classes to 'dress down' so that class hierarchy is overturned.[132] The appeal of heterogeneity at masquerades – collective drinking, dancing, and gambling – was overshadowed by its transgressive aspects and dangerous morality.[133] Masquerades became thought of as mixed and vulgar and by 1800 had virtually disappeared as fashionable social events. They were replaced by 'fancy balls', which, in order to avoid 'the noise and confusion of a masked ball', were well regulated in terms of costume, behaviour, language and music.[134] Attempts were made to disconnect any connections between the fancy ball and the masquerade by removing the key elements such as the mask from the costumes and by associating dressing up with distinction and honesty rather than the deceit of disguise.[135]

A fancy ball has one peculiar attraction and advantage over balls in general, because it partakes of all the good of a masquerade, without having its exceptional qualities. The liberty, or rather the licentiousness, which the mask favours, is here excluded[136]

Rambling texts blamed women for much of the trouble and indecency connected with masquerades. For example, in *Fashion and Folly*, the immoral events at a masquerade ball are attributed to the presence of women.[137] In other contemporary accounts, writers describe them as promiscuous places unsuitable for married women.[138] While yet other representations warn women to stay away for their own safety, because of the potential violence which might be performed on them, specifically rape and seduction.[139]

Charles Right's masquerades and prime claret have been the ruin of more ladies in one night, than ancient history records as having fallen at the rape of the Sabines.[140]

While discouraging women from going to masquerades and blaming them for the indiscretions which were believed to take place there, rambling tales simultaneously suggested to their predominantly male readers that masquerades were ideal places to pick up women – 'to turn-up plenty of game'.[141] Scantily clad female bodies were presented visually and verbally as signifiers of sexual frisson. Rambles were especially fond of illustrating women in costumes which followed an oriental theme, with unstructured, low-cut and transparent dresses.[142] Equally the element of disguise also provided a form of titillation for the male reader, keeping him guessing about the secret identity of women who attended masquerades – were these women chaste wives or prostitutes picking up clients?[143] Not surprisingly women at masquerades, as well as at assembly room gatherings, were represented as cyprians. In *Life in London*, ramblers note the presence of women enagaged in prostitution, prostitutes as well as procuresses, at a masquerade ball held at the Italian Opera House.[144]

It is precisely because the masquerade makes overt the suggestion that men and women might subvert their own appearance, might 'masquerade', that these events are perceived as threatening to public patriarchal order, particularly to relations of looking between the sexes. For the rambler who wishes to control the ways in which he views the cyprian, or woman-as-commodity, the possibility that mimicry might be performed cannot be entertained. The tendency then is to limit the liberating potential of masquerades as places where women play with their own modes of display by presenting them as scenes of immorality and of deceptive female surfaces or cyprians. This is a trend which also features in a more complex way in representations of theatres and opera houses, architectural spaces whose key function is to provide places for visual pleasure.

CHAPTER 5

The Italian Opera House – Exchanging Looks

The Theatre [. . .] is a sort of enchanted island, where nothing appears as it really is, nor what it should be. In London, it
is a sort of time killer, or exchange of looks and smiles.[1]

To *look* and be *looked at*, to be superbly attired [. . .] it is most
certainly a brilliant spectacle.[2]

The location of the Italian Opera House in London's exclusive district of
St James's and its pivotal position in John Nash's plans for the development of the urban vicinity required that the architecture be beautiful to
look at.[3] The building was a place designed to enhance the pleasure of
looking. This occurred in a number of different ways. Certainly the
grand scale of the external elevations and their lavish decorative treat-
ment suggested the importance of the opera house as a spectacle within
the city – an object of visual delight. Internally, the spatial layout of the
foyers, lobbies, saloons, auditorium and green room provided a series of
places for public promenade and display. In rambles, although the Italian
Opera House was represented as a place where visual pleasure was
experienced through the exchange of looks between performers and
audience within the auditorium – boxes, gallery, pit and stage – it was in
the performer-only spaces, such as the green room shown in figure 18,
and audience-only spaces, such as the lobby and saloon shown in figure
19, where the most exciting visual exchanges took place. The green
room in particular, figured as a highly desirable destination for ramblers
in a number of texts.[4]

Fig. 18 Robert Cruikshank, 'The Green Room of the King's Theatre, or Noble Amateurs viewing Foreign Curiosities' (Portraits of ten noble and distinguished patrons of the opera, with those *certain* daughters of Terpsichore), Bernard Blackmantle, *The English Spy*

THE ITALIAN OPERA HOUSE: 'MODERN ORNAMENT TO THE METROPOLIS'

> This House was built upon a grand and extensive scale [. . .]
> It is altogether a master-piece of art, and an ornament to the Metropolis.[5]

> jeweller's shop of the nation[6]

The Italian Opera House is the name given to one of the many theatre buildings once located on the corner of Haymarket and Pall Mall. The first building, designed by John Vanbrugh in 1704 and altered by Robert Adam, was destroyed by fire on 17 June 1789. It was originally called 'The Queen's Theatre' and later, in 1714, renamed 'The King's Theatre'. The second theatre building to occupy the same site was designed by Michael Novosielski and opened on 3 April 1790. After destruction by fire in 1867, this building was replaced by a third theatre, 'His Majesty's Theatre', designed by Charles Lee in 1869. A fourth and final theatre was built on the site by C. J. Phipps in 1897. It is the second theatre building, known in the early nineteenth century as the Italian

Fig. 19 George and Robert Cruikshank, '*Tom* and *Jerry* in the Saloon of Covent-Garden Theatre', Pierce Egan, *Life in London; or, the day and night scenes of Jerry Hawthorn, Esq., and his elegant friend Corinthian Tom, accompanied by Bob Logic, the Oxonian, in their Rambles and Sprees through the Metropolis*

Opera House – the centre for Italian opera and French ballet in London – which is the architectural subject of this chapter. It is a building which, from its construction in 1790, underwent many changes internally and externally.[7] In 1818, the exterior was altered by Nash and G. S. Repton as part of the improvements to the area which accompanied the building of Regent Street.

The Italian Opera House was a place of public entertainment or 'winter spectacle' alongside many other theatres, assembly rooms and pleasure gardens.[8] Only a limited number of theatres in London could stage spoken dramas; this was controlled by licence or royal patent administered legally through the Theatres Act of 1737.[9] Drury Lane and Covent Garden, whose seasons ran from September to July, were the two winter 'patent' theatres; the Haymarket theatre, whose season ran from 15 May to 15 September, the only summer patent theatre. At the Italian Opera House, where the season ran from January to August, music and dancing were on the bill instead of spoken drama.[10] A typical evening lasted from 8 p.m. to 1 a.m. and included both an opera and a ballet, with a long interval between them.[11] From 1791, the Italian Opera House had a monopoly on the type of performance staged – it was the only place in London for Italian opera.[12]

The only way of accommodating the increasing size of London audiences while the patent existed was to increase the size of theatres.[13] At the Italian Opera House, Michael Novosielski's new horseshoe-shaped designs of 1790, based on Piermarini's La Scala, extended the size of the building, making the auditorium the largest in England.[14] In order to hold more people, the depth of the stage was reduced and the auditorium lengthened. In 1829, the total capacity was 2500: the pit held 800, the five tiers of boxes 900 and the gallery 800.[15]

The increasing size of theatres and the associated expansion of the distance between actor and audience had an impact on the kind of performances staged. In Restoration theatre, the close proximity of actor and audience had allowed the playwright to develop the complexity of actors' roles through wit and satire, whereas in larger theatres emphasis was placed on spectacular and scenic effects.[16] The acoustical problems created by the large volumes made the visual aspects of the performance especially important,[17] making 'theatres for spectators rather than playhouses for hearers'.[18] Accordingly performances whose design focused on visual appearance and sensation became more popular:

> the splendour of the scenes, the ingenuity of the machinist and the rich display of dresses, aided by the captivating charms of music [. . .] supersede the labours of the poet.[19]

The attitudes to the internal decoration of the Italian Opera House correspond to the increasing importance of visual spectacle. Although alterations to the interior were of pragmatic necessity since candles and later gas lighting brought about the quick deterioration of paintwork and fabrics, the frequency of redecoration also suggests that the appearance of the building was an important aspect of its public status.[20] Contemporary commentators expressed a concern that the constant focus on interior decoration might indicate a neglect of more serious architectural features, but they also considered that too little maintenance of the decor allowed a building to become 'dirty and degraded'.[21]

The kind of decoration chosen responded to changes in management and audience 'taste', as well as to technical innovations in materials and lighting. But probably the most critical attitude influencing the interior decoration of public buildings, such as the Italian Opera, was decorum. Public buildings were expected to be 'dignified' and 'clean'.[22] However, views on the 'appropriateness' of ornamentation varied according to fashion. For example, in 1821, a 'lighter and more classical' appearance was favoured,[23] whereas, in 1825, fanciful decoration was chosen with a preference for 'projecting ornaments, highly gilt, such as figures, crowns'.[24] Lighting was important for enhancing the decoration and a new chandelier added in 1824, made of a 'tapestry of transparent gems', was believed to add to the 'gorgeous appearance of the house' and display 'to beautiful advantage' the new decorations to the ceiling without dazzling the audience.[25]

The large volumes of theatre and opera buildings gave them a large enough presence in the city to represent the interests of royalty and aristocracy. They were ideal public monuments. The designs of Frederick the Great's theatre in Berlin (1741) and Victor Louis's Grand Theatre in Bordeaux (1773–80) strongly influenced English design. These buildings were designed to be free-standing objects exposed and decorated on all façades. Novosielski's design for the eastern Haymarket façade of the Italian Opera House attempted to follow these precedents, by formalizing the exterior of the existing building, positioning the entrances strategically within the façade, defining the corners with pavilions and running an arcade as a uniform element around the building at ground level.[26] Due to lack of funds, however, this design was only partly built, but the improvements of 1818, based on the designs of Nash and Repton, succeeded in transforming the theatre into a separately articulated urban block. A single-storey covered colonnade was wrapped around three sides of the existing theatre, becoming, on the fourth, western side, the Royal Opera Arcade.[27] The external detailing expanded on themes of grandeur and prestige, favouring expensive and enduring materials, such as stone, and impressive decorative features, such as the classical orders. A frieze in cement stucco representing the progress of music was located above the entrances off the Haymarket on the east façade.[28]

The role of the opera house as a spectacle in the city was further enhanced by its location in the fashionable west of London, as well as its pivotal role in the urban improvement schemes taking place in the immediate context. Nash's designs for the surrounding district were

orchestrated and scenic urban compositions, where individual buildings were given roles to play, but integrated into the scheme as a
whole. A concert room and a new chain of foyers along the north
side of the Italian Opera House were added to the building in order
to create an east–west axis linking the 'chair' entrance off the Royal
Opera Arcade to the principal entrances beneath the colonnade on the
Haymarket.[29]

The Italian Opera House's location in the western district of St
James's was important in defining its role as respectable and élite
opera house rather than a suspect and unstable theatre. From the early
seventeenth century, the ambiguous social status of theatres was
related to their spatial marginality – they were sited outside the City
of London. The area to the west of the City and to the east of St
James's became known as the theatre district. As well as housing
Covent Garden and Drury Lane theatres, St Giles and Seven Dials,
two of the worst rookeries in London, were also located there.[30] By
the late eighteenth century, this area had acquired a reputation for
prostitution.[31] Ramblers' visits to the theatres in this part of London
as seen in figure 20, described the 'spell' (prostitutes who waited
outside theatres for plays to finish) and the 'flash mollishers' (lower-
class prostitutes) on the streets and in the nearby brothels, bagnios,
coffee shops and gin shops.[32] In rambling tales, Covent Garden was
described as 'the seat of cyprian indulgence, the magnet of sensual
attraction'.[33] Slang terms for prostitution were associated with Covent
Garden, for example, 'Covent Garden Ague' meant venereal disease;
'Covent Garden Nun', a prostitute; and 'Covent Garden Abbess', a
bawd.[34]

The improvements to Regent Street in the early nineteenth century
established a boundary between this theatre district and the area further
west. The new street divided east from west, separated lower class from
upper class, and signified a distinction between immorality and morality. The location of the Italian Opera House to the west of this divide
gave it a social status distinct from the theatre district to the east, a
status that was *not* connected with the lower classes, immorality and
prostitution.

Fig. 20 George and Robert Cruikshank, '*Tom* and *Jerry* taking Blue Ruin after the Spell is Broke Up', Pierce Egan, *Life in London; or, the day and night scenes of Jerry Hawthorn, Esq., and his elegant friend Corinthian Tom, accompanied by Bob Logic, the Oxonian, in their Rambles and Sprees through the Metropolis*

FOYERS, LOBBIES, SALOONS: 'LADIES OF SALOON NOTORIETY'

> We are aware that fictitious names are assumed or given to the Ladies of Saloon notoriety [. . .] the *trading fair ones*, who began immediately to throw out their *lures*.[35]

> No doubt they [saloons] are found to answer well enough in bringing custom to the house, since it is not to be imagined that theatres would willingly incur the infamy of providing such profligate accommodation were there no gain attached to it. They stand accused upon 'bawd's plea' and no other.[36]

Increasing the size of theatre and opera house auditoria, meant increasing the number and size of the associated foyers, lobbies and saloons. Such rooms were located and designed as dynamic sequences which linked the entrances and the auditoria. Viewing possibilities between rooms were enhanced by orchestrating continuous and axial promenades. Staircases and other interior features, such as places to buy refreshment, were used as staging devices to create places of performance and spectacle to complement the auditorium. In Novosielski's design for the Italian Opera House, the two main entry points, from the Royal Opera Arcade to the east and from the Haymarket to the west, both opened onto an axis running east–west across the north of the auditorium. This axis was composed of a chain of grand staircases, foyers, an octagonal saloon and a round lobby. The round lobby served as an orientating device, from which one could enter the horseshoe-shaped corridor running behind the principal boxes at its apex.[37] This sequence of foyers, lobbies and saloons took the audience from the external colonnades and arcade to the interior of the auditorium, through a series of architectural spaces which maximized display.

At the start and end of the evening, as shown in figure 21, the entry points to the Italian Opera House on Haymarket suffered from overcrowding:

Fig. 21 George and Robert Cruikshank, '*Outside of the Opera-House at Night. Gallantry of Tom and Jerry*', Pierce Egan, *Life in London; or, the day and night scenes of Jerry Hawthorn, Esq., and his elegant friend Corinthian Tom, accompanied by Bob Logic, the Oxonian, in their Rambles and Sprees through the Metropolis*

such immense crowds I never saw collected before the doors of a theatre. The entrance to the boxes was crowded like a pit entrance. The ladies were nearly an hour making their way into a box they had secured places in.[38]

The close proximity of bodies at these entrances provided opportunities for intimate contact between strangers of different sexes and classes. Such crowds represented sites of potential deviancy. As a result, ways of entering the opera house became increasingly segregated, with a hierarchical range of separate entrances to differently priced seating areas. Those with more expensive seats got the prestigious entrances, with decoration, wider staircases and easier, more spacious access to the street. The opening to the entrance vestibule was enlarged in 1815 in order to facilitate the exit of people from boxes to carriages allowing them less of a chance to mingle.[39]

A series of private saloons or 'retiring rooms' intended for different classes of occupants, especially those of private boxes, were included in new theatre designs. Some considered these private saloons to be a 'positive nuisance', built specifically for the 'accommodation of most disreputable visitors', namely the reception and entertainment of prostitutes.[40] It is indeed possible that this was the case, since, although open encouragement of prostitution could result in the loss of licences, the presence of female prostitutes boosted takings. Managers therefore sought to retain prostitution within the theatres but to keep the 'rude and unseasonable interruptions of the "pretty girls"' which disturbed the performances out of sight and earshot of the auditorium.[41] John Ebers, the manager of the Italian Opera House, may have indicated just such an intention when he opened a new foyer for the gallery with direct passages from the pit and boxes. This displaced prostitutes from their visible position along Fop's Alley and the stage but still allowed them to be accessed by wealthy clients:

this Coffee Room will be an admirable resort for a lounge, and may be the means of reducing Fop's-alley, as well as the Stage, from half their nocturnal tenants. It is certain that, in this more remote haunt, the elegant Beau may indulge in his promenade with less interruption to the Audience, and fashionable badinage may be reconciled with decorum.[42]

It is interesting that it was the foyers, lobbies and saloons, those places where the most uncontrolled mixing of people occurred, which were considered synonymous with prostitution. If we return to the work of Irigaray and the assertion that the notion of exchange allows connections to be made between different systems, then we might discuss both theatrical performance and prostitution as situations where exchange takes place; in the former money is exchanged for visual pleasure, in the latter cash buys sex. On the stage and in the more public foyers, lobbies and saloons, only visual display and exchange took place; whereas the more private foyers, lobbies and saloons provided places for sexual exchanges to occur. At the beginning of the nineteenth century, sexual activity was also presumed to occur in the curtained boxes of the auditorium, whereas later, in the late nineteenth century, the sexual geography had shifted, and the stalls, promenade and dress circle lobby were thought to provide points of assignation for prostitutes and clients.[43] Simultaneous to the performance in the main auditorium, at interval breaks, and especially at the end of the evening, the foyers, lobbies and saloons also served as rendezvous points for excursions to nearby late-night venues of sexual exchange, such as brothels.

Saloon occupants represented in rambling tales included cyprians, potential male clients, male protectors or keepers of cyprians, bawds, procuresses, fruitwomen (who acted as go-betweens between cyprians and clients) and dress-hirers (who hired out dresses to cyprians on a nightly basis).[44] In the saloons, the cyprians or 'decked-out girls', were represented as seductive spectacles, painted and decorated with artificial flowers, muffs, feathers and jewellery. The display of the cyprian body involved both the addition of elements such as trinkets and subtraction of parts of clothing to reveal naked flesh.[45] Ramblers believed these trinkets to be payment for sexual favours. In various images and texts, such as figure 19, cyprians are represented clustering around the ramblers, throwing out their 'lures', lifting their already-revealing dresses to show off their ankles and leaning forward to display their breasts.[46] Such display represented an excessive and transgressive act – the cyprian as spectacle was an agent of seduction.

Between acts they fill the large and handsome 'foyers' and exhibit
their boundless effrontery in the most revolting manner.[47]

In the saloons represented in rambling texts everyone present is
engaged in watching the cyprians. Bawds and dress-hirers survey the
scene to ensure the prostitutes are working and not stealing costumes
rented for the night. Lecherous, drunken older men and fashionable
younger men look at the cyprians closely through glasses or spectacles.
In order to provide added pleasure for the reader, the visual exchange
between those looking and those being looked at, men with spectacles
and cyprians as spectacles, is conflated with another form of
exchange, prostitution. As well as describing the cyprian as an
exchangeable commodity circulated between sellers and buyers or
bawds and male clients, rambling also represents the cyprian as a seller
or someone in control of an economic transaction. At Covent Garden,
the ramblers are accosted by 'business like' cyprians.[48] At Drury
Lane, the cyprians are described as 'the trading fair ones'.[49] In
descriptions of the Italian Opera House, in the foyers, lobbies and
saloons, as well as in the auditorium, on stage and in the audience,
ramblers delight in watching cyprians.

THE AUDITORIUM: 'TO SEE AND BE SEEN'

The company seem to assemble only to see and be seen.[50]

> It is the resort equally of the lovers of music, the dance, and
> of those who care little for either, but who like to meet each
> other, and feast their eyes by gazing on all the most beautiful
> as well as best drest women resident in this country.[51]

The dominant activity in the Italian Opera House, both in the foyer and
auditorium spaces, was the exchange of looks, 'to see and be seen'.
Freud's theories of fetishism provide a model of looking where the male
spectator looks at the female fetish or spectacle. This suggests that the
display of females, as dancers on stage and as members of the audience
in boxes, is related to the viewing pleasures of the male patrons. But
although such a theoretical model is useful in the first instance to draw
our attention to the gendered aspects of active looking, the relationships

between spectators and spectacles in the Italian Opera House as described below indicate a far more complex series of visual exchanges.

Women's position in boxes framed them as objects of visual consumption for other members of the audience, but also gave them an excellent vantage point from which to look at other women and men. The preference of male patrons for positioning themselves in prominent places in the pit and in proscenium boxes on the stage, indicates that the Italian Opera House provided a setting where men displayed themselves to others. Representations in rambling tales of these male spectators with opera glasses allow us to interpret the male look as voyeuristic (a gaze which scrutinizes its object but is not returned) but also suggest that the act of looking is itself the subject of representation.

Within the auditorium of the Italian Opera House the internal spatial division of gallery, pit and boxes expressed social hierarchy. The upper classes occupied the pit and the boxes, with the lower classes in the gallery. Class segregation was regulated through price and dress restrictions. For example, in 1813 the price of box and pit at the Italian Opera House was 7s. compared to the gallery at 3s. 6d.[52] Full dress was required to enter the pit and boxes. There were also variations within the pit, boxes and gallery. For example, in the pit, cheaper seats were provided at first as resurrection boxes at the back, and later as two ranges of seats placed at the front next to the orchestra. Of the numerous tiers of boxes, the second tier was the most aristocratic, followed by the first and third, while those above were of a lower status, with the gallery occupying the central part of the top tier.[53]

Within the auditorium, the opportunities to see and hear the performance varied. A position in the pit provided the best position both to see and hear from.[54] Although the gallery provided the best panoramic views of the auditorium, the distance from the stage was too great to see detail and the reflection of sound from the ceiling made it hard to hear. In the boxes, the advantages of viewing the stage had to be balanced against viewing and being viewed by the rest of the auditorium. The horseshoe plan offered those in the boxes nearest the stage a poor view of the performance, but a position from which they could be most easily viewed by the rest of the auditorium.[55] In the Italian Opera House this situation was exaggerated by a long and narrow auditorium and a deep stage which protruded into the audience.[56]

the greater part of the persons in the boxes are not placed even at right angles to, but actually turned obliquely from, the stage. [. . .] the spectators in the boxes nearest the stage are better stationed for reconnoitring the audience, than for viewing the scenery or the performance.[57]

BOXES: 'SEDUCTIVE LURES'

The Earl of F— has a grand box on the ground tier, for the double purpose of admiring the chaste evolutions of the sylphic daughters of the Terpsichore, and of being observed himself by all the followers of the chameleon-like, capricious goddess, Fashion.[58]

A box at the opera is as indispensable as to the finished courtezan, who here spreads her seductive lures to catch the eye, and inveigle the heart of the inexperienced and unwary.[59]

In the early nineteenth century, the management and ownership of the Italian Opera House was a very complicated affair.[60] The opera was privately owned and managed by John Ebers, a bookseller of Old Bond Street from 1820 to 1827. It was economically dependent on private patronage and a subscription list. Opera house boxes in the auditorium could be owned, annually or seasonally subscribed to, sub-let or borrowed, often through opera booksellers for a commission. Special and controlled outlets existed, for example, at the Opera-office, Haymarket; at Ebers, 27 Old Bond Street; and at Sequin, Opera Office, 105 Quadrant, Regent Street. Since owning a property box or renting a subscription box gave a say in management, renting boxes and buying tickets also required the recommendation of one of the patrons of the opera, usually a leading society lady.

Owning a property box or renting a subscription box was seen as an indication of prestigious social status and fashionable position. The most affluent purchased boxes by the season, but as prices went up, some chose to share a box and others rented their boxes out for individual performances. Sharing and sub-letting boxes made them more affordable and allowed those of a lower class to occupy them.[61] As a result, an intricate social hierarchy associated with rank, deceit and snobbery, emerged between owners, renters and sub-letters, and between so-called private and public boxes.

The needs of the patrons had a great effect on the design and use of the building in general and specifically in relation to the design of the boxes.[62] The boxes played an important role in representing private wealth in public.[63] Partitions between boxes, first introduced from Europe at Covent Garden Theatre, denoted privately controlled property, as did curtains. Although these dividing partitions tended to make views of the stage difficult, they clearly indicated property ownership. Some theatres adopted half-height partitions, but to the aristocratic clientele of the opera, it was important that they were full-height.[64] Likewise, despite the disruptive effect an uneven surface had on acoustics, boxes were heavily decorated in order to express social status.

> every box forms a distinct room, furnished with curtains in front, and chairs, as in the Neapolitan theatres. Each box is constructed for the convenient accommodation of 6 persons, the width being four feet, and the depth about seven feet.[65]

Opera boxes provided safe and contained places from which to view or be viewed. Rambling tales represent such positions as favoured by men of the upper classes. They provided excellent vantage points for gazing at the stage or other parts of the auditorium:

> The OPERA, to the man of fashion, is the only *tolerable* place of public amusement, in which varied orders of society are permitted to participate. Here lolling at his ease, in a snug box on the first circle, in dignified security from the vulgar gaze, he surveys the congregated mass who fill the arena of the house, deigns occasionally a condescending nod of recognition to some less fortunate *roué*, or younger brother of a titled family, who is forcing his way through the well-united phalanx of vulgar faces that guard the entrance to *Fop's Alley;* or if he should be in a state of single blessedness, inclines his head a little forward to cast round an enquiring glance, a sort of preliminary overture, to some fascinating daughter

of fashion, whose attention wishes to engage for an amorous inter-
change of significant looks and melting expressions during the *last*
act of the opera.[66]

Boxes were described by both male and female authors as places in
which women were on display to male viewers.[67] But since, from the
late eighteenth century, a large number of box subscribers were women,
we might also suggest either that these women did not object to being
looked at or that the boxes provided other pleasures.[68] The boxes provided self-contained places protected from the rest of the auditorium
where visitors could be entertained. This opportunity for women to
exert control over public space and to display property ownership and
themselves may well have been perceived as a threat. Certainly opera
boxes were represented as places where wives were unfaithful to their
husbands, where mothers and marriageable daughters were involved in
female competition, jealousy and rivalry for male attention, and where
the women displaying themselves were described as cyprians.[69]
The boxes most commonly associated with cyprians were those which
provided the worst views of the stage and which had therefore been
rejected by 'serious' opera goers.[70]

'FOP'S ALLEY': 'MEETINGS AND GREETINGS'

From an entrance, occupying the centre of the lowest tier of
boxes, a few steps descended to the back of the pit, down to
the centre of which a broad space was left unencumbered to
within a few feet of the orchestra. This formed the
renowned 'Fop's Alley' [. . .] It was the practice of the day
for all the more 'exquisite' and fashionable of the male operatic patrons to quit their boxes or their scanty stalls during
various positions of the performance, and to fill the vacant
spaces in the centre and sides of the pit, where they could
laugh, lounge and chatter, eye the boxes from convenient
vantage points, and likewise criticise and applaud in common. The 'meetings and greetings' that took place in the pit
of the opera were looked upon as an essential portion of the
evening's entertainment.[71]

The pit of the Italian Opera House held 1000 people and was potentially the best place to watch and hear a performance. Providing an opportunity for the closest look at the legs of the performers on stage, the pit therefore gained a reputation as an unruly place where men commented on the physical merits and deficiencies of the female dancers' bodies, regularly interrupting ballets with cat calls and obscenities.[72]

With the audience in full dress, the visual effect of the pit was described as brilliant and to be present was to participate in a visual spectacle.[73] Down the centre ran a passage known as 'Fop's Alley'.[74] From this location, dandies could display themselves to the gallery and the boxes as well as enjoy watching others. Dressed in glamorous evening gowns and jewels, women were also present in the pit. Their experience, however, was described by female commentators as an unpleasant one, for three reasons: the rudeness of the predominantly male audience, the proximity of indecent dancers and the possible presence of prostitutes:

> If a female is young and pretty, every glass of every fop in the alley and pit is levelled at her; and the freedom with which her attractions are commented on, must be most offensive to delicacy; if she is ugly, or old, she is sure to be quizzed, laughed at, and stared at; and this our modern Dandies call good fun.[75]

When in 1828, four rows of stalls were installed in the pit of the Italian Opera House, their insertion created problems for the dandies.[76] In the past, only those with box tickets had been allowed entry to the pit. Although essential to the continuing operation of the opera house, the selling of separate tickets for the pit, as well as the sub-letting of box tickets, was not favoured since it allowed 'improper' company to the pit and resulted in the elimination of Fop's Alley.[77]

OMNIBUS BOXES: 'OPERATIC COGNOSCENTI'

> the boxes protrude to such a preposterous degree beyond
> the opening of the stage, as almost to drive the scenery from
> the boards, and to cause a very considerable portion of the

spectators themselves to form the background to the actors.[78]

The two proscenium boxes level the stage, are styled omnibus boxes [. . .] These boxes are occupied by the élite of Crockford's and White's and determine upon the pretensions of every new candidate for public applause.[79]

The ballet and opera operated as private enterprises where entrepreneurs and subscribers (a group of rich men of the upper classes, aristocrats and wealthy bourgeoisie) paid a substantial share of the costs.[80] Since these subscriptions were critical to the running of the opera, this sector of the audience was given certain privileges, such as special access to the pit and back stage, the first choice of seating and 'silver tickets'.[81] Two double omnibus boxes, named *loges infernales* after those in the Paris Opera, flanked the proscenium abutting the stage. The occupiers of these boxes were a 'distinguished group of operatic cognoscenti who form the circle of taste'.[82] Such a position provided them with a chance to display themselves to the audience along with the performers, but also a privileged vantage point from which to closely scrutinize the predominantly women dancers and singers.[83] In rambling tales, men in these boxes were represented holding spyglasses to their eyes, watching and discussing the different female dancers:

At this moment a whole army of young sylphides, more or less pretty came fluttering across the stage. My friend looked at them attentively with his 'lorgnette'.[84]

THE STAGE: 'WHAT A FOOT, LEG AND THIGH!'

Her great celebrity, however, rests on the beauty of her legs, which are become a standing article in the theatrical criticisms of the newspapers, and are often displayed by her in man's attire[85]

What a breast – what an eye! what a foot, leg and thigh!
What wonderful things she has shown us;
Round hips, swelling sides, and masculine strides –
Proclaim her an English Adonis.[86]

If the spaces of the opera house were designed for visual consumption and display, the stage was the public focus of such pleasure. The darkness and size of the auditorium produced a space in which a voyeur might control an unreturnable gaze. It has been argued that theatrical performances fetishized the dancer or actress positioning her as a spectacle to be viewed within a spectacle. If this is the case then, for example, in the *pas de deux* of classical ballet the body of the whole woman is fetishized, whereas in a female travesty dancer the legs alone are fetishized as erotic spectacles, creating 'a bazaar of legs'.[87]

In this context, an important effect of the increasing size of auditoria and the extended distance between pit and stage, was to diminish the appearance of the female body. It has been suggested that to compensate for a lack of scrutiny, numbers of female dancers were increased and/or dance styles were adapted to display more of the female body.[88] Technical refinements and developments in choreographic techniques, such as *pointe* work, introduced in Paris in 1828, and the *pirouette*, revealed the female body in new ways.[89] Changes in dress, such as the adoption of a shorter length and lighter fabric for dancers' skirts, as well as a lower décolletage and flesh coloured tights, also increased the eroticization of the female dancer. All these aspects enhanced the 'look' of the dancer maximizing feminine display. The availability of lithographs, souvenirs, prints and pictures of female dancers further increased opportunities for voyeuristic pleasure and the commodification of the female body.[90]

The early nineteenth century also saw the emergence of the travesty dancer, a female dancing a male role. Women's appearance in male dress opened up further possibilities for revealing the female body, through the adoption of a corseted midriff and skintight breeches.[91] Travesty dancers, such as Madame Vestris, 'attracted the most crowded houses' and provided a source of income for the theatres and opera houses, as well as a source of public fascination. Prints and song sheets carrying her picture were sold everywhere, the songs she performed were associated with her legs and plaster casts were made of them – *la jambe de Vestris*.[92]

In the early nineteenth century male patrons of the ballet were often connected with female dancers. For the patrons, following the patterns established at the Parisian ballet, 'owning' a dancer was a sign of wealth and prestige. The social prestige of supporting a dancer also increased if the woman was of foreign origin. For example, when Lord Fife secured Lisa Noblet, a Parisian, as the principal ballerina at the Italian Opera House in 1821,[93] and the Spanish Maria Mercandotti, 'the Andalusian Venus', in 1822,[94] it was considered most advantageous to his position.[95] Indeed rambling tales suggest that the patrons of the opera only appeared in their boxes to watch the dancers on stage and spent the rest of the evening behind the scenes in the green room.[96]

> There are a set of men in London, who from one year's end to the commencement of another, only eat, drink, sleep, and lounge away time at the theatres: a stage box is to them a paradise; and a trip behind the scenes and into the green-room, a perfect paradise.[97]

For the dancers, as ballet commercialized and the *corps de ballet* grew larger, wages dropped and money provided by patrons increased income.[98] But whether accepting this financial support and extra income from men, often in the form of meals and gifts, designates these dancers prostitutes is highly debatable. Certainly in rambling tales, female figures encountered both on stage and in the green room of the Italian Opera House were conflated with the cyprian, the archetypal prostitute.

GREEN ROOM: 'STUDYING NATURE'

> A division is necessary between theatre and the stage, and should be so characterised as to assist the idea of there being two separate and distinct places.[99]

> In this society I first made my appearance in the green room; a little, narrow, pink saloon at the back of the stage, where the dancers congregate and practice before an immense looking glass previous to their appearance in public.[100]

In theatres and opera houses the only place where performers and audience come together is the auditorium, the central space of performance and event. Outside the auditorium are other spaces which are used by either the audience (foyers, lobbies and saloons) or the actors (green room and dressing rooms). Violations of these social and spatial rules, actors in the lobbies or spectators backstage, are highly charged symbol-ically.[101] At the Italian Opera House, the doors which stopped the public from entering the region under the stage had been closed.[102] When Ebers re-opened these doors between the house and the stage in the early 1820s, it was to create a green room. Ebers argued this room would improve performances by providing a space for the dancers to limber up.[103] But apparently modelled on the *Foyer de la Danse* of the Paris Opéra, it provided the male patrons somewhere private to mix with the dancers and lounge after the performance. Access was a prized privilege and highly controlled.[104]

> Anxious as well to avoid an over-crowd behind the scenes, as not to refuse one gentlemen while another is admitted, it is thought right to state, that the admission behind the scenes will be strictly confined, as it is at Paris, to the annual Subscribers.[105]

In the etching of the green room at the Italian Opera House in a rambling text, see figure 18, the focus is on visual display.[106] The dancers display themselves in large mirrors, while the men watch and sketch them using eyeglasses.[107]

> Lord L— says that he has *seen, felt*, and (ap)*proved* them all – to be excellent *artistes* with very *finished movements*.[108]

In another image of a green room, this time at Drury Lane Theatre, see figure 22, three ramblers gather around to look closely at Madame Vestris dressed in travesty as Don Giovanni. Even at this intimate dis-tance, one rambler holds up an eyeglass to examine her.[109] With the increase in the size of theatre auditoria, positions which allowed the closest visual access to the female performers, such as Fop's Alley and the omnibus boxes, were associated with the highest social status. But it was in the green room, unobserved, that male patrons occupied their most intimate proximity to the women dancers. This is the place in the Italian Opera House represented in rambling tales as the most desirable site of private visual pleasure.

As cyprian, dancer and actress, the female figure in the auditorium and green room, as well as in the foyers, lobbies, saloons, features as an

Fig. 22 George and Robert Cruikshank, 'The Green-Room at Drury-Lane Theatre – *Tom* and *Jerry* introduced to the Characters in Don Giovanni', Pierce Egan, *Life in London; or, the day and night scenes of Jerry Hawthorn, Esq., and his elegant friend Corinthian Tom, accompanied by Bob Logic, the Oxonian, in their Rambles and Sprees through the Metropolis*

object of desire for the rambler. Within the auditorium, the focus is on the public display of females as fetish objects on stage and as spectacles in the boxes; whereas in the green room, it is the private display of women which offers the male patrons visual pleasure. In all these spaces, rambling tales make associations between the women present as actresses, dancers and members of the audience, and female sexual transgression. In some cases this is achieved by describing women's occupation of private spaces such as the boxes and green room as 'intriguing' and 'secretive'. In other instances, the public display of women's bodies on stage or in the foyers, lobbies and saloons is taken to be flaunting and indecent. At other times, the women in question are represented as cyprians. In connecting all women occupying the Italian Opera House with some form of immoral sexuality, two systems of exchange are conflated, the exchange of looks and the exchange of bodies. To look at the dancer is to possess the body of the cyprian – the visual stands for the sexual. It is through this connection of visual exchange with sexual pleasure in the rambler's desire for the cyprian, that it is possible to argue that the spaces of the Italian Opera House in London's St James's are gendered through looking and moving.

'On the market', in assembly rooms, theatres and opera houses alike, the women present are represented by ramblers as cyprians. Like the commodity with its dual values of use and exchange, the cyprian is both useful and exchangeable, she allows the exchange of sex for money. But as both seller and commodity in one, the cyprian also refuses patriarchal laws of exchange. In so doing, she is represented in rambling tales as a trangressive figure – an object desired, but also dreaded. The ambivalence of the rambler towards the cyprian indicates a patriarchal dis-ease at the heart of the ramble, a dis-ease with the presence of women in the public places of the city. It is the way in which *Finish*, the sequel to *Life in London*, represents this dis-ease by making connections between the cyprian body and the architectural spaces she occupies that I now explore in the concluding chapter.

CHAPTER 6

Life in and out of London

In 1828, following the success of *Life in London*, Pierce Egan and Robert Cruikshank published a sequel, *The Finish to the Adventures of Tom, Jerry and Logic in their Pursuits through Life in and out of London*. This final chapter considers this text in order to draw together some of the ideas concerning the gendering of space represented through the ramble.[1] As we have seen in previous chapters, *Life in London* represents a ramble which passes through places of cyprian display, such as Almack's Assembly Rooms and the Italian Opera House in the west of London. *Finish* maps a ramble, where prostitution features differently, including representations of spaces where sexual transactions actually took place, such as dress houses, bagnios, jelly houses, lodging houses and streets. These two rambles, or representations of gendered space, are separated by a decade, a period of time over which a marked shift in urban attitude appears to have taken place. The attitude to the city the ramble presents has changed from desire to disgust. Compare, for example, the frontispieces of the two books. The image shown in figure 2 from *Life in London* celebrates the pleasures of urban life, gambling, drinking, walking and pursuing women; the frontispiece of *Finish*, shown in figure 23, describes the effects of urban life in terms of debt, disease and moral corruption.

We have already discussed the tensions in early nineteenth-century spaces of leisure between consumer capitalism's need to extend the roles of women as cheap labourers and consumers in public spaces and patriarchal worries concerning the exposure of female property – mothers, wives, daughters. The control of women in such public spaces has been shown to be key in the choreography of both exclusionary and segregationist strategies of public patriarchy. *Finish* represents a further development – the early stages of re-establishing a private mode of patriarchy. This is indicated through representations which reject the city in favour of the country and celebrate domestic ideologies of family and stability as opposed to the pleasurable urban pursuits of the bachelor rambler.

Fig. 23 Robert Cruikshank, Pierce Egan, *The Finish to the Adventures of Tom, Jerry and Logic in their Pursuits through Life in and out of London* (frontispiece)

In *Finish*, the three heroes of *Life in London*, Corinthian Tom, Jerry Hawthorne and Bob Logic, suffer from their rambles and two of them perish. Only Jerry survives by leaving London, marrying Mary Rosebud and living in the country. Corinthian Kate, an object of desire in *Life in London*, also plays a key role in *Finish*. 'Unfaithful' to Tom, Corinthian Kate is ejected from her private home in the west and takes her own life in a lodging house in the east. Represented in *Finish* as a figure of disgust and pity, the decline of Corinthian Kate and her architectural surroundings signifies the rambler's increasing ambivalence towards the cyprian, as well as changing attitudes towards the public pleasures of city life.

Visual and verbal descriptions of the disintegration of the female body of the cyprian and the spaces of prostitution she is associated with in *Finish* highlight a tone which emphasizes the destructive elements of urban life. Similar metaphors are used to categorize both female bodies and architectural or urban spaces as disorderly. From *Life in London* to *Finish*, and within *Finish* itself, the kinds of spaces occupied by the cyprian, Corinthian Kate, shift from orderly to disorderly. While the cyprian body becomes increasingly more disorderly and porous, deformed by syphilis and alcohol, so do the unregulated places of prostitution she occupies. A comparison of the representation of Corinthian Kate's body, specifically her skin and clothes, and the decaying materiality of the room in the lodging house brothel where she finally dies (shown in figure 24) only serve to strengthen the analogy made between body and building.

Fig. 24 Robert Cruikshank, 'Melancholy End of *Corinthian Kate!* – One of those lamentable examples of dissipated LIFE IN LONDON', Pierce Egan, *The Finish to the Adventures of Tom, Jerry and Logic in their Pursuits through Life in and out of London*

The social decline of the cyprian is represented using a progression of different spatial metaphors which also describe changes from architectural order to disorder: from west to east, from private to public, from home to street, from closed to open and from contained to fluid. Corinthian Kate moves from private apartments paid for by Tom in the west, to lodgings in increasingly public brothels, to discovery by the ramblers in a state of drunken disorder under Covent Garden Piazza. A quick look at two visual representations, the first, shown in figure 3, a luxurious interior filled with beautiful objects and Corinthian Kate and Tom dancing, the second, shown in figure 25, a dirty street with an unrecognizable crumpled body (Corinthian Kate) lying on the ground, mark the transition clearly.

The category of 'disorderly' was used as a defining mechanism in the legislation used to control prostitution.[2] But although being disorderly was the only way a prostitute could be arrested, the term was open to

Fig. 25 Robert Cruikshank, 'One of those afflicting Occurrences in LIFE IN LONDON, *Tom, Jerry* and *Logic* arrested on their progress home by the melancholy Discovery of *Corinthian Kate*, in the last Stage of a Consumption, Disease and Inebriety', Pierce Egan, *The Finish to the Adventures of Tom, Jerry and Logic in their Pursuits through Life in and out of London*

interpretation.[3] Prostitution, defined as the payment of money by a client for sexual services, was not itself a criminal offence; but laws against soliciting, living off immoral earnings and running 'houses of ill-fame' were enforced selectively.[4] Two laws indirectly controlled prostitution. The first was the Disorderly Houses Act of 1752, passed for encouraging prosecutions against persons keeping bawdy houses and other spaces of illegal entertainment.[5] The second set were the various Vagrancy Acts which, by 1824, allowed the police to proceed against 'common prostitutes for behaving in a riotous or indecent manner'.[6]

Invariably the various solutions proposed to eradicate, suppress or contain prostitution involved ordering the female body through punishment and/or reform in highly regulated and controlled places. Reformist task forces set up to deal with 'street debauchery', such as the Society for the Reformation of Manners (1691–1738), the Society for Promoting Christian Knowledge (1698), the Proclamation Society (1787) and the Society for the Suppression of Vice (1802), peaked around the beginning of the nineteenth century in London. Their activities were largely concerned with maintaining public decorum and prosecuting brothels, among other illicit sexual activities.[7] For religious groups, such as the evangelicals, for whom the prostitute signified the immorality of urban society, the solution for such female deviants was moral reform through religious education.[8] All the built solutions to prostitution provided by the law and charities, including the Bridewells, the Lock Asylum (1787), the Magdalen Charity (1758), the London Female Penitentiary (1807) and the Guardian Society (1813), involved the physical confinement of women.[9]

DISORDERLY BODIES AND SPACES: MOBILITY

Openness permits exchange, ensures movement, prevents saturation in possession or consumption.[10]

But if we cannot altogether prevent the intercourse between buyers and sellers, let us, at least try to prevent the harmful commodity from being publicly exposed to view, and the infamous contract settled at the corner of every public street.[11]

As set out in chapter 1, it is possible to argue that in Irigaray's 'Women on the Market' the prostitute occupies a mimetic position. By taking herself to market and naming her price, the prostitute mimics male discourse, demonstrating how the exchange of women between men operates to structure patriarchy.[12] For the purposes of this argument, one can ask that the prostitute be understood as a self-perpetuating, moving subject, motivated by the desire to sell herself, who poses a threat to patriarchal ideologies concerning the circulation of women among men. If patriarchal capitalism controls the ownership and exchange of property by defining boundaries and identifying thresholds which are permanent, closed and fixed around women, then spatial metaphors of porosity, flow and openness, for example, represent a disease with female subjects and spaces, both of which operate within, but also escape, these controlling mechanisms. In rambles, such spatial thematics feature in representations of prostitution as bodies and spaces of disorderly exchange, consumption and display.

Previous chapters have discussed the way in which 'order' – social and spatial – operates in the ramble: to establish the public realm of the city as a place for men, the rambler emerges in the early nineteenth century as a representation of new kind of masculine urban identity connected with mobility and visibility. The rambler's mobility, his pursuit of pleasure in the form of cyprians or female sexual commodities, defines his urban masculinity and heterosexuality and is to be celebrated. And although moving is also a defining feature of the cyprian, her mobility is represented as cause for concern. *Finish* focuses on this worrying and disorderly aspect of female movement.

In a number of early nineteenth-century texts also concerned with the regulation of disorderly women or prostitutes, commentators describe the presence of prostitutes on the streets to be sufficient to overcrowd and block the flow of traffic.[13] The solution suggested is to 'push these scandalous scenes of lewdness and profligacy from the public eye' to give back the streets to the public at night.[14] The female body is represented here as out of place and out of control, a threat to public decorum:

because the public walks are glutted with prostitutes, who sometimes, like half-famished tigers, seize upon the new adventurers.[15]

Those concerned with public decency, such as the Vice Society responsible for the overhaul of the vagrancy laws between 1822–4, pointed to the prostitute as the cause of public disorder.[16] Discussions around the amendments to the Vagrancy Act of 1822 suggested that it was the distinction between public and private which needed to be more clearly defined in order to control public space. Here it was the prostitute's body which represented the encroachment of disorderly aspects of the 'private' into public space.[17]

Rising concern for disorderliness also appeared in discourse concerned with updating the Disorderly Houses Act of 1752.[18] In this piece of legislation, unregulated public places or public houses were considered to be the source of prostitution.[19] In the eighteenth and nineteenth centuries places of prostitution varied from the nunnery, or the closed residential private brothel, to the lodging house, or low and public brothel. In the early nineteenth century, brothels were located all over London, in Mayfair, Marylebone and Docklands, but the most exclusive houses were found to the west and the lowest to the east and in the slums of St Giles's in Covent Garden.[20] The more westerly its location, the more respectable the brothel and the more controlled it was considered to be. For example, the 'Nunneries' in King's Place, St James's, were thought to be the most exclusive and orderly in London.[21] In Mrs Hayes's brothel in King's Place, St James's, a surgeon was employed to inspect the prostitutes' bodies, while nearby in Mrs Fawkland's brothel in St James's Street, the cyprians were classified according to age and experience.[22] These nunneries were modelled on the French *maison close* where each brothel had a defined and controlled number of live-in prostitutes or 'boarders', giving the brothel keeper power over prostitutes and their earnings.[23]

Rambling texts represented women's careers in prostitution starting out in ordered and controlled places such as these brothels in St James's or in private houses rented for them by men in the west of London.[24] From here, the cyprian's path was always taken to follow a move downwards to increasingly more public brothels and finally to the street.[25] This is precisely the downward path described in *Finish*. As a result of her sexual infidelity, Corinthian Kate has to leave her apartments paid for by Tom in the west, relocating herself in a lodging-house further east, finally ending up on the street.[26] In the 1820s, prostitutes could rent rooms in lodging house brothels, but many preferred to take clients to an accommodation house where the client paid for the hire of a room.[27] Accommodation houses or houses of retreat, 'where the scenes of wickedness are acted in privacy and security', were also used by procuresses for introducing prostitutes and clients.[28] Other prostitutes or 'dress lodgers' would not live in brothels but go for a working day where they would also hire dresses.[29] *Finish* represents a number of these places, including in figure 26, the 'low brothel' where Jerry is robbed,[30] in figure 27, the public brothel which catches on fire during his visit,[31] and in figure 24, the lodging-house brothel where Corinthian Kate dies.[32]

Rambles also represent other places of late night resort where prostitutes were present; such as bagnios and jelly houses, where prostitutes could be sent for; and night houses and other late night venues, such as saloons, coffee rooms, cigar divans and chop houses, where rooms could be rented.[33] Such places are not focused on in *Life in London*, but in the

Fig. 26 Robert Cruikshank, '*Jerry up*, but not *dressed*! A miserable Brothel; his *Pal bolted* with the Togs; one of those unfortunate Dilemmas connected with LIFE IN LONDON arising from the effects of Inebriety', Pierce Egan, *The Finish to the Adventures of Tom, Jerry and Logic in their Pursuits through Life in and out of London*

Fig. 27 Robert Cruikshank, 'The "House of Accommodation" in Flames! The Inmates put to flight! Jerry narrowly escapes with his Life, and preserves *Ellen Prettyflower*, his Paramour, from an untimely Death', Pierce Egan, *The Finish to the Adventures of Tom, Jerry and Logic in their Pursuits through Life in and out of London*

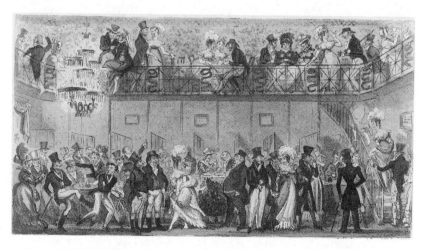

Fig. 28 Robert Cruikshank, 'The Royal Saloon in Piccadilly, or an Hour after the Opera', Bernard Blackmantle, *The English Spy*

English Spy and *Finish*, they feature as important rambling venues. In *The English Spy*, the Royal Saloon in Piccadilly, shown in figure 28, is described as a location where prostitutes and men gathered late at night to drink, smoke and gamble.[34] From the saloons, ramblers and cyprians visited flash-houses until the early hours of the morning, when they moved on to coffee shops.[35] The ramblers' favourite flash-house, the 'Finish', full of 'adversity and wickedness', was a popular place for an evening of rambling to end.[36] Another late-night option was the 'Cock and Hen Club', or the free-and-easy public-house concert, to which women were admitted.[37]

But last thing at night, the final resort was the street. Here drunk ramblers picked up cyprians and got involved in fights with the watchmen or Charleys. Early nineteenth-century records describing the policing of the streets of London, indicate a fairly systematic set of procedures, disturbed by incidents such as watchmen 'found sleeping or drunk and abandoning their beat to join prostitutes in nearby public houses'.[38] In *Life in London*, the street at night is represented as a boisterous and amusing place, populated with ineffectual comic watchmen as in figure 9.[39] In *Finish*, the picture has changed, instead the street at night as in figure 25 is represented as a place of dereliction and destruction, where cyprians, such as Corinthian Kate, are discovered drunk and disorderly on the brink of death.[40]

In the decline of the prostitute, her relationship to disorder is represented both in terms of the decreasing control over the places she occupies, but also in the increasing porosity of her own body. Female bodies are open, they can be entered in the act of love and when one is born one leaves them by passing across the threshold. From a feminist perspective, Irigaray has described this openness in positive terms as a place for the exchange of difference.[41] But the openness of the female body as a site of male desire is also potentially threatening. Pornographic tales in early nineteenth-century rambling magazines frequently used spatial metaphors, such as 'closet', 'slit' or 'catacomb', as forms of sexual innuendo in order to refer indirectly to the female body.[42] As well as a titillation, female openness was perceived as a problematic.[43] The open female body in the public realm, described as a 'deep hole', 'deep ditch' or 'deep pit', was considered both sexually immoral and a danger to the public:[44]

the unfortunate female is represented as a deep ditch, a narrow pit, of course eminently dangerous to the heedless passenger.[45]

The more promiscuous the woman, the deeper and more open the hole. An opened female body occupying the public realm formed a treacherous topography, a trap one could fall into.[46] Such a potentially dangerous terrain required regulation and male commentators expressed a desire for streets to be freed from what they described as 'serpentine allurements'.[47] A perforated body occupying the public realm was open to infection, disease and decay.[48] The final representations of the cyprian body in *Finish* are described visually and textually in exactly these terms, as over-consumed and over-penetrated. Corinthian Kate's is a ravaged body, the result of depravity in mind and character, only to end in early death.[49]

Spatial metaphors concerning openings were used to refer to architectural spaces as well as female bodies, but only places both desired and feared. The threshold or doorway of the brothel, the opening controlling movement in and out, was connected with moments of danger, suspense and intrigue. The exciting but potentially frightening transition from known exterior to unknown interior was a metaphor for the sexual act of penetration. For example, the two entrances of the seductive Fountain Tavern, a place of late-night refreshment, were represented as sexually enticing and obscure.[50] At the White House brothel in Soho Square, the more discreet side entrance was considered mysterious, but connected with immersion and death.[51]

In rambling tales, the procuress was often described at the threshold of the brothel or 'the mouth of her cavern'.[52] Representations of her purpose there shifted between threatening and titillating; either she was waiting to entice innocent young men or to 'procure' and 'ensnare' young women.[53] The attractive cyprian was also represented at the doorway. Her presence at the entrance was suggestive of the delights to follow,[54] 'the mysteries of the interior Cyprian Temple'.[55] Rambling texts indicated that she was positioned on the threshold in order to lure men inside to take a 'peep at the *Curiosities*'.[56] The visibility of cyprians at the entrance was not a simple matter. Their presence was not necessarily always obvious, indeed many texts described prostitutes as problematic because they tended to lurk in hidden places, 'beneath doorways and into blind alleys',[57] and to seek out 'the darkest and most unfrequented avenues'.[58] Hidden or tucked out of sight, such entrances were described by ramblers as covered holes into which men could be accosted or decoyed.[59]

DISORDERLY BODIES AND SPACES: VISUALITY

the duplicity of the veil's function [. . .] used to cover a lesser value and overvalue the fetish[60]

I was maintained in the utmost splendour by my keeper his vanity making him *shew me off* (as he called it) in all the extravagance of the modes.[61]

Acts and forms of display have featured in previous chapters as recurring sites for discussions of morality expressed though debates over the orderliness and disorderliness of surfaces. On the one hand, the act of 'revealing' could represent moral and honest revelation or immoral and flagrant exposure; on the other 'covering' might be interpreted as a moral and blushing modesty or an immoral and deceitful secrecy.[62] The surface also operated as a threshold or a space of transition, a place that mediated the relationship between private and public. 'Private' might be viewed as moral, safe and contained or as immoral, secretive and deceptive, 'public' as an honest display or a lewd and extravagant form of over-exposure, depending on context and the nature of the boundary or surface between them.

In the early nineteenth century, the surfaces of cyprian bodies and the spaces they occupied were categorized in terms of public and private, disorder and order, morality and immorality, depending on the class of commentator. For example, middle-class reformers interested in attacking the social habits of the upper classes, equated aspects of the private with property ownership. By describing the surface as deceitful and secret, privacy could be associated with moral disorder. In this way, private interiors like the 'snug private boudoirs' in the Royal Saloon in Piccadilly, as well as the gambling hells in St James's and the boxes at the Italian Opera House, were represented as places of intrigue and dishonesty.[63]

The female subject herself was a surface of critical concern. As we have discussed, correct amounts of display, decoration, exposure, revelation and covering in clothes worn by women, were related to time, place and activity and carefully regulated as 'fashion'.[64] The morality of the feminine surface depended on socially defined notions of appropriateness. According to some male writers, paying attention to the effect of the surface was praiseworthy when it was for the male gaze, but when it was for female self-interest it was represented as artifice and vanity.[65] Such a view makes for an interesting comparison with Irigaray's theory of mimicry which suggests that it is exactly in the area of female self-representation that a feminist criticism of the masquerade or the feminine surface lies.

The identity of a cyprian was believed to be determined by her 'gaudy' dress. Her interest in appearance was a problem linked to vanity and inappropriate desires for fine clothing.[66] The cyprian's clothed exterior indicated her moral status: the louder the clothes, the more debauched she was likely to be.[67] The most sly of cyprians, kept mistresses or 'jilts', were represented as deceitful enough to 'feign' passion in order to secure a settlement or a sum to live on.[68] In order to attract rich clients, cyprians were considered to 'dress-up' above their class, in other words, to disguise themselves. A cyprian, by wearing misleading clothing, might be mistaken for a virtuous women.[69] Evidence that some cyprians, dress-lodgers, did not own their clothes but rented them from brothels and that others would pawn their clothes in hard times seemed to substantiate the dishonest quality of cyprian dress.[70] In all these cases, the 'dress' of the cyprian is taken to be a deceptive surface, one able to mask what lies beneath. The surface as a sign of duplicity also featured in discussions of other women associated with prostitution. Procuresses and bawds, for example, were connected with disguise. Representations in rambling tales describe how, on the first meeting, bawds would remain 'muffled up' in front of ramblers, appearing 'genteel in person, address and conversation'.[71] Only later would their true identity be revealed – evil and cruel.[72]

Cyprians were associated with surface value and as kept mistresses they were supported financially more for *'empty shew* than *real use'*.[73] Men displayed their social status both through their cyprian mistresses and the houses they displayed them in.[74] Architectural decoration, elegant furnishings and tasteful displays of plate, lights and mirrors, were intended to act as a foil to the beauty of the cyprian and to enhance the pleasure of looking at her.[75] Like the imaginative interior saloons and lobbies of the theatres and opera houses, the Royal Saloon in Piccadilly was decorated in an exotic style as a Turkish kiosk. Here, as in other venues associated with gambling, large mirrors, a central chandelier, as well as vases of exotic shrubs and flowers, trellises and foliage, suggested the sensuality and luxury suitable for a place of pleasure.[76] Corinthian Kate's apartments, paid for by Tom, were equally attractive spaces, feminine and desirable, as were rooms described in exclusive brothels:

> This apartment is particularly calculated, from its elegant embellishments, to co-operate in setting-off to great advantage the charms of its female visitors; and to these regions of pleasure all the gay boys of the Town occasionally resort. *Mother* ***** is indefatigable in her selection, and keeping up her stock of beautiful females.[77]

The architectural interior operated as a seductive surface to complement and heighten the exchange or fetish value of the cyprian; while the cyprian, along with various fruits and wines, was also one of many consumable commodities on display. Setting up a relationship between a number of surfaces, organic and inorganic, the cyprian body and the architecture which contains her, is key in defining the seductive qualities in representations of a number of places connected with transgressive aspects of display; exclusive brothels, such as Charlotte Hayes',[78] the Fountain Tavern,[79] a gambling hell[80] and the Café Royal.[81] The recurring emphasis is on the play of ambiguous surfaces, those that both reveal and cover, mask and reflect, such as mirrors, glass and transparent fabrics.

The tension of the surface, between what is covered and what is revealed, also featured in descriptions of the exteriors of brothels. Discreet and respectable from the outside, brothels were unrecognizable from their street exteriors except to the initiated. These people understood the tell-tale signs, such as the blinds lowered over bedroom windows before nightfall, lights at the threshold and at the windows during the day.[82] Such inconspicuous fronts or surfaces were deceptively bland and therefore potentially dangerous, disguising any number of unexpected traps or snares. The common representations of exclusive brothels as nunneries, prostitutes as nuns and bawds as abbesses, are parodies of virtue which draw out the theme of the surface. Through 'taking the veil', the act of covering is emphasized, creating a secret place and suggesting a tension between what is hidden and what is revealed.[83]

FROM *LIFE IN LONDON* TO *FINISH . . . LIFE IN AND OUT OF LONDON*

From *Life in London* to *Finish . . . Life in and out of London* the emphasis of the ramble changes from delight and pleasure to fear and destruction. The representation of the cyprian shifts from an object of desire to one of disgust. Starting out in exclusive public venues in *Life in London* as alluring women in the company of admiring men, in *Finish* cyprians end life in back-alleys and filthy garret lodgings, solitary and secretive in dirty rags, their bodies covered in sores. I consider the deterioration of the cyprian between these two rambling tales to indicate a change in attitude to urban life. *Life in London* is a text primarily about the pleasures of being in the city rather than the country. *Finish*, subtitled *Life in and out of London*, rejects the destructive influences of the city – disease, debt and death – in favour of a return to country life and all that this implies.[84] *Finish*, in line with religious and moralizing tracts on prostitution published from the early-nineteenth century onward, represents the city as a site of disorder through the body of the degenerate cyprian.

Precursors to Benjamin's flâneur and prostitute of 1850s Paris, the dialectical relationship of male rambler and female cyprian is a gendered representation of the city. I have argued throughout *The Pursuit of Pleasure* that rambling emerges in early nineteenth-century London as a patriarchal construction of urban space representing male desire to control women in public places of leisure. This desire operates through tropes of mobility and visuality which locate men in controlling positions. The rambler is celebrated as an urban explorer, actively engaged in the pursuit of pleasure and women. The figure of the cyprian, on the other hand, is fixed by the rambler as visual spectacle and object of desire. The cyprian's relation with public space is represented as problematic. Her moving and visible body flouts patriarchal rules for the male occupation of public space. By representing her mobility as the cause of her eventual destruction, the ramble works morally and ideologically to contain all women in the city, placing them 'on the market', by conflating them with the cyprian, the public woman-as-commodity is only to be exchanged by men.

What has been presented here is a spatial story, one which has told of the rambler's pursuit of pleasure, but it is also an account of my own pursuit of pleasure, historical in the form of the ramble, theoretical in the work of Irigaray. Irigaray's work has throughout offered me 'a powerful and seductive concept' with which to mediate my reading of the ramble and follow men's pursuit of pleasure through early nineteenth-century London. 'Women on the Market' suggests to me both a critical and imaginative feminist perspective to the gendering of space, indicating that men and women traverse space, moving and looking, but in different ways.[85] The ramble represents gendered space in terms of dynamic and overlapping set of spatial practices rather than as a series of static architectural objects. These activities – consumption, display and exchange – both produce, and are produced by, the architectural and urban spaces they take place in. Depending on gendered identity and position, they are played out differently, creating the ever-changing topography of freedom and containment, display and concealment, desire and disgust that is *The Pursuit of Pleasure*.

Notes

CHAPTER 1

1. Aidan Andrew Dunn, *Vale Royal* (Uppingham: Goldmark, 1995), p. 9.
2. Hélène Cixous, *The Book of Promethea* (Lincoln: University of Nebraska Press, 1991), p. 7.
3. See, for example, Charles Baudelaire, *The Parisian Prowler* (London: The University of Georgia Press, 1997); Walter Benjamin, *Charles Baudelaire: a Lyric Poet in the Era of High Capitalism* (London: Verso, 1997); Louis Aragon, *Paris Peasant* (Boston: Exact Change, 1994); André Breton, *Mad Love* (London: University of Nebraska Press, 1987) and Guy Debord, 'Theory of the Dérive', *Internationale Situationniste* (December 1958), n. 2., republished in Ken Knabb (ed.) *Situationist International Anthology* (1989), pp. 50–4. For useful summaries of this work see, for example, Christel Hollevoet, 'Wandering in the City', *The Power of the City/The City of Power* (Whitney Museum of American Art, 1991–2). The most well-known anthology of critical texts on the flâneur is Keith Tester (ed.), *The Flâneur* (London: Routledge, 1994). Patrick Keiller's films *London* (1995) and *Robinson in Space* (1997) are good examples of contemporary flânerie, as is 'Topographics', the series of books about city wandering commissioned by Reaktion Press, including, for example, the work of artist Victor Burgin and writer/novelist Iain Sinclair.
4. Michael de Certeau, 'Spatial Stories', *The Practice of Everyday Life* (Berkeley: University of California Press, 1988), pp. 115–22.
5. See Iain Borden, Joe Kerr, Alicia Pivaro and Jane Rendell (eds.), *Strangely Familiar: Narratives of Architecture in the City* (London: Routledge, 1995) and Iain Borden, Joe Kerr, Jane Rendell (eds.) with Alicia Pivaro, *Unknown City: Contesting Architecture and Social Space* (Cambridge MA: The MIT Press, 2000).
6. Steve Pile, 'The Un(known)City . . . or, an urban geography of what lies buried below the surface', Borden *et al.* (eds.), *Unknown City*, pp. 263–79.
7. Luce Irigaray, 'Women on the Market', *This Sex Which Is Not One* (1977), trans. Catherine Porter with Carolyn Burke (Ithaca: Cornell University Press, 1985), pp. 170–91.
8. Thank you to Lynda Nead, who pointed me in the direction of the ramble.

9. Pierce Egan, *Life in London; or, the day and night scenes of Jerry Hawthorn, Esq., and his elegant friend Corinthian Tom, accompanied by Bob Logic, the Oxonian, in their Rambles and Sprees through the Metropolis* (London: Sherwood, Neely & Jones, 1820–1).

10. See also Amateur, *Real Life in London, or the Rambles and adventures of Bob Tallyho, Esq. and his cousin the Hon. Tom Dashall, through the metropolis; exhibiting a living picture of fashionable characters, manners and amusements in high and low life* (London: Jones and Co., 1821–2); Bernard Blackmantle, *The English Spy* (London: Sherwood, Jones & Co., 1825) and William Heath, *Fashion and Folly: The Bucks Pilgrimage* (London: William Sams, 1822).

11. General secondary histories of St James's are provided by the following: E. J. Burford, *Royal St. James's being a Story of Kings, Clubmen and Courtesans* (London: Robert Hale, 1988); Beresford E. Chancellor, *The Eighteenth Century in London: an Account of its Social Life and Arts* (London: B. T. Batsford, 1920); Beresford E. Chancellor, *Memorials of St. James's Street, together with the Annals of Almacks* (London: Grant Richards Ltd., 1922); Beresford E. Chancellor, *The Pleasure Haunts of London* (London: Constable,1925); Joan Glasheen, *St. James's London* (London: Phillimore, 1987); J. M. Scott, *The Book of Pall Mall* (London: Heinemann, 1965) and Edward Walford, *Old and New London* (London: Cassell, Petter and Galpin, 1873). A more detailed account of the architecture is provided by F. H. W. Shepperd (ed.), 'The Parish of St. James's Westminster, Part 1, South of Piccadilly', *The Survey of London* (London: The Athlone Press, University of London, 1960), v. 29; Shepperd (ed.), 'The Parish of St. James's Westminster, Part 2, South of Piccadilly', *Survey*, v. 30; Shepperd (ed.), 'The Parish of St. James's Westminster, Part 1, North of Piccadilly', *Survey*, v. 31; Shepperd (ed.), 'The Parish of St. James's Westminster, Part 2, North of Piccadilly', *Survey*, v. 32.

12. See, for example, P. J. Atkins, 'The Spatial Configuration of Class Solidarity in London's West End 1792–1939', *Urban History Year Book* (1990), v. 17, pp. 36–65, p. 38; Penelope J. Corfield, 'The Capital City', *The Impact of English Towns 1700–1800* (Oxford: Oxford University Press, 1982), pp. 66–81, p. 78 and Leonard D. Schwarz, 'Social Class and Social Geography: the Middle Classes in London at the End of the Eighteenth Century', *Social History* (1982), v. 7, n. 2, pp. 167–85, pp. 178 and 181.

13. Prince Puckler-Muskau, *Tour in England, Ireland, and France* (London: Effingham Wilson, 1832), (10 July 1827), v. 4, p. 49. See also Atkins, 'Spatial', pp. 43–4; Corfield, 'Capital', p. 75; Leonore Davidoff, *The Best Circles* (London: Croom Helm, 1986), p. 21; Schwarz, 'Social', p. 178 and Gareth Stedman Jones, *Outcast London: a Study in the Relationship Between Classes in Victorian Society* (Harmondsworth: Penguin, 1984), p. 34.

14. Irigaray, 'Women', p. 172.

15. See, for example, Linda Clarke (ed.), *Building Capitalism* (London: Routledge, 1992); Anthony D. King (ed.), *Buildings and Society: Essays on the Social Development of the Built Environment* (London: Routledge & Kegan Paul, 1980) and Thomas A. Markus, *Buildings and Power* (London: Routledge, 1993).

16. See, for example, Borden *et al.* (eds.), *Strangely Familiar* and Jonathan Hill (ed.), *Occupying Architecture: Between the Architect and the User* (London: Routlege, 1998).

17. See, for example, Beatriz Colomina (ed.), *Architectureproduction* (New York: Princeton Architectural Press, 1988).

18. See, for example, Sara Boutelle, 'Julia Morgan', Susana Torre (ed.), *Women in American Architecture: A Historic and Contemporary Perspective* (New York: Whitney Library of Design, 1977), pp. 79–87 and Lynne Walker, *British Women in Architecture 1671–1951* (London: Sorello Press, 1984).

19. See, for example, Lynne Walker, 'Women and Architecture', Judy Attfield and Pat Kirkham (eds.), *A View from the Interior: Feminism, Women and Design* (London: The Women's Press, 1989), pp. 90–110 and Gwendolyn Wright, 'On the Fringe of the Profession: Women in American Architecture', Spiro Kostof (ed.), *The Architect: Chapters in the History of the Profession* (Oxford: Oxford University Press, 1977), pp. 280–309.

20. See, for example, Diane Agrest, *Architecture From Without: Theoretical Framings for a Critical Practice*, (Cambridge, MA: The MIT Press, 1993); Denise Scott Brown, 'Room at the Top? Sexism and the Star System in Architecture', Ellen Perry Berkeley (ed.), *Architecture: a Place for Women* (London & Washington: Smithsonian Institution Press, 1989), pp. 237–46 and Leslie Kanes Weisman, *Discrimination by Design* (Chicago: University of Illinois Press, 1992).

21. See, for example, Dolores Hayden, *The Grand Domestic Revolution* (Cambridge, MA: The MIT Press, 1981); Dolores Hayden, *Redesigning the American Dream* (New York & London: Norton, 1986); Matrix, *Making Space: Women and the Man Made Environment* (London: Pluto Press, 1984) and Marion Roberts, *Living in Man-Made World: Gender Assumptions in Modern Housing Design* (London: Routledge, 1991).

22. See, for example, Frances Bradshaw, 'Working with Women', Matrix, *Making*, pp. 89–105; Karen A. Franck, 'A Feminist Approach to Architecture: Acknowledging Women's Ways of Knowing', Berkeley (ed.), *Architecture*, pp. 201–16; Magrit Kennedy, 'Seven Hypotheses on Male and Female Principles', 'Making Room: Women and Architecture', *Heresies: A Feminist Publication on Art and Politics* (1981), v. 3, n. 3, issue 11, pp. 12–13; Mimi Lobell, 'The Buried Treasure', Berkeley (ed.), *Architecture*, pp. 139–57; Susana Torre, 'The Pyramid and Labyrinth', Torre (ed.), *Women*, pp. 186–202 and Susana Torre, 'Space as Matrix', *Heresies*, pp. 51–2.

23. Beatriz Colomina (ed.), *Sexuality and Space* (New York: Princeton Architectural Press, 1992).

24. See, for example, Diane Agrest, Patricia Conway and Leslie Kanes Weisman (eds), *The Sex of Architecture* (New York: Abrams, 1997); Debra Coleman, Elizabeth Danze and Carol Henderson (eds.), *Architecture and Feminism* (New York: Princeton Architectural Press, 1996); Francesca Hughes (ed.), *The Architect: Reconstructing Her Practice* (Cambridge, MA: The MIT Press, 1996); Duncan McCorquodale, Katerina Ruedi and Sarah Wigglesworth (eds.), *Desiring Practices* (London: Black Dog Publishing Ltd, 1996); Jane Rendell, Barbara Penner and Iain Borden (eds.), *Gender, Space, Architecture: An Interdisciplinary Introduction* (London: Routledge, 1999), and Joel Sanders (ed.), *Stud: Architectures of Masculinity* (New York: Princeton Architectural Press, 1996).

25. See, for example, David Harvey, *The Condition of Postmodernity* (Oxford: Blackwell, 1989); Edward Soja, *Postmodern Geographies: the Reassertion of Space in Social Theory* (London: Verso, 1989) and Henri Lefebvre, *The Production of Space* (Oxford: Blackwell, 1991).

26. A number of feminist critiques of Harvey's and Soja's work appeared in 1990–1. See Rosalyn Deutsche, 'Men in Space', *Strategies* (1990), n. 3, pp. 130–7; Rosalyn Deutsche, 'Boys Town', *Environment and Planning D: Society and Space* (1991), v. 9, pp. 5–30; Doreen Massey, 'Flexible Sexism', *Environment and Planning D: Society and Space* (1991), v. 9, pp. 31–57 and Gillian Rose, 'Review of Edward Soja, *Postmodern Geographies* and David Harvey, *The Condition of Postmodernity*', *Journal of Historical Geography* (January 1991), v. 17, n. 1, pp. 118–21.

27. See the ground-breaking work produced in the mid-1990s by Liz Bondi, Linda McDowell, Doreen Massey and Gillian Rose. See, for example, Liz Bondi, 'Feminism, Postmodernism, and Geography: a Space for Women?', *Antipode* (August, 1990), v. 22, n. 2, pp. 156–67; Liz Bondi, 'Gender Symbols and Urban Landscapes', *Progress in Human Geography* (1992), v. 16, n. 2, pp. 157–70; Liz Bondi, 'Gender and Geography: Crossing Boundaries', *Progress in Human Geography* (1993), v. 17, n. 2, pp. 241–6; Doreen Massey, *Space, Place and Gender* (Cambridge: Polity Press, 1994); Linda McDowell, 'Space, Place and Gender Relations, Parts 1 and 2', *Progress in Human Geography* (1993), v. 17, n. 2, pp. 157–79 and v. 17, n. 3, pp. 305–18 and Gillian Rose, *Feminism and Geography: the Limits of Geographical Knowledge* (Cambridge: Polity Press, 1993).

28. See, for example, Shirley Ardener, 'Ground Rules and Social Maps for Women', Shirley Ardener (ed.), *Women and Space: Ground Rules and Social Maps* (Oxford: Berg, 1993), pp. 1–30 and Daphne Spain, *Gendered Spaces* (Chapel Hill: University of North Carolina Press, 1992).

29. See, for example, Anthony King, *The Bungalow* (Oxford: Oxford University

Press, 1995) and Steven Harris and Deborah Berke (eds.), *Architecture of the Everyday* (New York: Princeton Architectural Press), pp. 32–7.

30. Exceptions to this are, for example, Liz Bondi, 'Gender Symbols and Urban Landscapes', *Progress in Human Geography* (1992), v. 16, n. 2, pp. 157–70 and Gillian Rose, 'Making Space for the Female Subject of Feminism', Steve Pile and Nigel Thrift (eds), *Mapping the Subject* (London: Routledge, 1995), pp. 332–54.

31. In art history key texts include Lynda Nead, *Myths of Sexuality: Representations of Women in Victorian Britain* (Oxford: Blackwell, 1988); Linda Nochlin (ed.), *The Politics of Vision: Essays on Nineteenth-Century Art and Society* (London: Thames & Hudson, 1991) and Griselda Pollock, *Vision and Difference: Femininity, Feminism and the Histories of Art* (London: Routledge, 1988), pp. 5–26. In film studies see, for example, Ann E. Kaplan, *Women and Film: Both Sides of the Camera* (New York: Methuen, 1983); Annette Kuhn, *Women's Pictures; Feminism and Cinema* (London: Verso, 1994) and Laura Mulvey (ed.), *Visual and Other Pleasures* (London: Macmillan, 1989). In photography, a good example is Abigail Solomon-Godeau, 'The Legs of the Countess', *October* (Winter, 1986), pp. 65–108.

32. See, for example, Marina Warner, *Monuments and Maidens* (London: Picador, 1988).

33. See, for example, Catherine Hall, 'Feminism and Feminist History', *White, Male and Middle Class: Explorations in Feminism and History* (Cambridge: Polity Press, 1992), pp. 1–42 and Joan W. Scott, *Gender and the Politics of History* (New York: Columbia University Press, 1988), p. 6.

34. See, for example, Leonore Davidoff and Catherine Hall, *Family Fortunes* (Chicago: Chicago University Press, 1987).

35. See, for example, Mary Poovey, *Uneven Developments: the Ideological Work of Gender in mid-Victorian Britain* (Chicago: University of Chicago Press, 1988).

36. Jacqueline Rose, *Sexuality in the Field of Vision* (London: Verso, 1986).

37. Nancy Chodorow, *The Reproduction of Mothering: Psychoanalysis and the Sociology of Gender* (Berkeley, Los Angeles: University of California Press, 1978).

38. Carol Gilligan, *In a Different Voice: Psychological Theory and Women's Development* (Cambridge, MA: Harvard University Press, 1982).

39. For the most widely discussed examples of the work of Hélène Cixious and Julia Kristeva see, for example, Hélène Cixious, 'The Laugh of the Medusa', Elaine Marks and Isabelle de Courtivron (eds), *New French Feminisms: An Anthology* (London: Harvester, 1981), pp. 243–64 and Julia Kristeva, *Desire in Language: A Semiotic Approach to Literature and Art* (Oxford: Blackwell, 1980).

40. Luce Irigaray, *The Speculum of the Other Woman* (1974), trans. Gillian C. Gill (Ithaca: Cornell University Press, 1985); Irigaray, *This Sex*; Luce Irigaray, *Elemental Passions* (1982), trans. Joanne Collie and Judith Still (London: The

Athlone Press, 1992) and Luce Irigaray, *An Ethics of Sexual Difference* (1984), trans. Carolyn Burke and Gillian C. Burke (London: The Athlone Press, 1993).

41. Irigaray, 'Any Theory of the "Subject" has always been appropriated by the "Masculine"', *Speculum*, pp. 133–46.

42. Irigaray, 'This Sex Which Is Not One', *This Sex*, pp. 23–33.

43. See, in particular, Irigaray, *Elemental*, pp. 63–6 and Irigaray, *Speculum*, p. 229.

44. Luce Irigaray, *Thinking the Difference: For a Peaceful Revolution* (1989), trans. Karin Montin (London: The Athlone Press, 1994); Luce Irigaray, *Je, Tu, Nous: Towards a Culture of Difference* (1990), trans. Alison Martin (London: Routledge, 1993) and Luce Irigaray, *I Love to You: Sketches of a Possible Felicity in History*, trans. Alison Martin (London: Routledge, 1996).

45. The accounts of Irigaray given by Elizabeth Grosz, *Sexual Subversions* (London: Allen & Unwin, 1989); Toril Moi, *Sexual/Textual Politics: Feminist Literary Theory* (London: Methuen, 1985) and Margaret Whitford, *Luce Irigaray: Philosophy in the Feminine* (London: Routledge, 1991) are central to this debate.

46. See, for example, Donna Landry and Gerald Maclean, *Materialist Feminisms* (Oxford: Blackwell, 1993), p. 51.

47. Claude Lévi-Strauss, *The Elementary Structures of Kinship* (Boston: Beacon Press, 1969). I have drawn on the interesting feminist critiques of Lévi-Strauss's work by Elizabeth Cowie, 'Woman as Sign', Parveen Adams and Elizabeth Cowie (eds.), *The Woman in Question* (London: Verso, 1990), pp. 117–33; Rosalind Coward, *Patriarchal Precedents: Sexuality and Social Relations* (London: Routledge & Kegan Paul, 1983); Rosalind Coward and John Ellis, *Language and Materialism: Developments in Semiology and the Theory of the Subject* (London: Routledge & Kegan Paul, 1977) and Lon Fleming, 'Lévi-Strauss, Feminism and the Politics of Representation', *Block* (1983), v. 8, pp. 15–26.

48. Gayle Rubin, 'The Traffic in Women: Notes on the "Political Economy" of Sex', Rayna R. Reiter (ed.), *Toward an Anthropology of Women* (New York: Monthly Review Press, 1975), pp. 157–210, reprinted as Gayle Rubin, 'The Traffic in Women: Notes on the "Political Economy" of Sex', Joan W. Scott (ed.), *Feminism and History* (Oxford: Oxford University Press, 1996), pp. 105–51, p. 118. For commentaries on Rubin's work see Maggie Humm (ed.), *Feminisms: a Reader* (London: Harvester Wheatsheaf, 1992) and Rosemary Tong, *Feminist Thought: a Comprehensive Introduction* (London: Routledge, 1992).

49. Rubin, 'Traffic', pp. 105–51.

50. Irigaray, 'Women', p. 172.

51. Karl Marx, *Capital: the Process of Production of Capital* (Harmondsworth: Penguin, 1976), p. 138.

52. Marx, *Capital*, p. 126. It is worth noting that in making a distinction between the natural and exchangeable values of commodities, Marx uses the body of a

woman as exemplary of exchange. See Marx, *Capital*, p. 138. Furthur, quoting from a satirical poem, 'Dit du Lendit', by the medieval French poet Guillot de Paris, Marx describes 'femmes folles de leur corps' or wanton women, as one of the commodities to be found at a fair. See Marx, *Capital*, p. 178, footnote 1.

53. Irigaray, 'Women', p. 176.
54. Irigaray, 'Women', pp. 185–7.
55. Irigaray, 'Women', p. 186.
56. Irigaray, 'Women', p. 186.
57. Marx, *Capital*, p. 179.
58. Shannon Bell, *Reading, Writing and Rewriting the Prostitute Body* (Indianapolis: Indiana University Press, 1994), p. 91.
59. Solomon-Godeau, 'Legs', footnote 2.
60. Irigaray, 'Women', p. 174, footnote 3. These terms originated in the biological sciences: a homologous relationship refers to origins, whereas an analogous relationship is based on formal similarities.
61. Moi, *Sexual/Textual*, pp. 139–40.
62. Whitford, *Luce*, p. 197.
63. See, in particular, Irigaray, *Elemental*, pp. 14–17, 47, 67 and Irigaray, *Ethics*, p. 11.
64. Irigaray, *Ethics*, p. 15.
65. See, for example, Jane Flax, *Thinking Fragments: Psychoanalysis, Feminism and Postmodernism in the Contemporary West* (Berkeley, Los Angeles and Oxford: University of California Press, 1991), p. 232; Donna Haraway, 'Situated Knowledges: the Science Question in Feminism and the Privilege of Partial Knowledge', *Feminist Studies* (Fall 1988), v. 14, n. 3, pp. 575–603, especially, pp. 583–8 and Elspeth Probyn, 'Travels in the Postmodern: Making Sense of the Local', Linda Nicholson (ed.), *Feminism/Postmodernism* (London: Routledge, 1990), pp. 176–89, p. 178.
66. bell hooks, *Yearnings: Race, Gender, and Cultural Politics* (London: Turnaround Press, 1989).
67. Rosi Braidotti, *Nomadic Subjects* (New York: Columbia University Press, 1994).
68. See, for example, Liz Bondi and Mona Domosh, 'Other Figures in the Other Places: on Feminism, Postmodernism and Geography', *Environment and Planning D: Society and Space* (1992), v. 10, pp. 199–213 and Elizabeth Grosz, *Space, Time and Perversion* (London: Routledge, 1996).
69. See, for example, Daniel Miller (ed.), *Acknowledging Consumption* (London: Routledge, 1995); Rob Shields (ed.), *Lifestyle Shopping* (London: Routledge, 1992) and John Urry, *Consuming Places* (London: Routledge, 1995).
70. Pasi Falk, *The Consuming Body* (London: Sage, 1994), pp. 116–17 and 126–7.

71. Robert Bocock, *Consumption* (London: Routledge, 1993), pp. 69, 81–2 and 87.

72. Robyn Dowling, 'Femininity, Place and Commodities: a Retail Case Study', *Antipode* (October 1993), v. 25, n. 4, pp. 295–319.

73. Elizabeth Wilson, 'The Invisible Flâneur', *New Left Review* (1992), n. 191, pp. 90–110.

74. See, for example, Anne Friedberg, *Window Shopping* (Oxford: University of California Press, 1993); Jenny Ryan, 'Women, Modernity and the City', *Theory, Culture and Society* (November 1994), v. 11, n. 4, pp. 35–64; Gillian Swanson, 'Drunk with the Glitter: Consuming Spaces and Sexual Geographies', Sophie Watson and Katherine Gibson (eds.), *Postmodern Cities and Spaces* (Oxford: Blackwell, 1995), pp. 80–99; Elizabeth Wilson, 'The Rhetoric of Urban Space', *New Left Review* (1995), v. 209, pp. 146–60 and Hilary Winchester, 'The Construction and Deconstruction of Women's Roles in the Urban Landscape', Kay Anderson and Fay Gale (eds.), *Inventing Places* (Australia: Longman Cheshire, 1992), pp. 139–55.

75. Thorstein Veblen, *The Theory of the Leisure Class* (London: Penguin, 1979).

76. Winchester, 'Construction', pp. 148–9.

77. This is something that I have dealt with in depth in relation to women's roles as consumers and commodities in London's Burlington Arcade. See, for example, Jane Rendell, 'Subjective Space: an Architectural History of the Burlington Arcade', McCorquodale *et al.* (eds.), *Desiring Practices*, pp. 216–33; Jane Rendell, 'Thresholds, Passages and Surfaces: Touching, Passing and Seeing in the Burlington Arcade', Alex Cole (ed.), *The Optic of Walter Benjamin* (London: Black Dog Publishing Ltd, 1999), pp. 168–9, and Jane Rendell, '"Bazaar Beauties" or "Pleasure is our Pursuit": A Spatial Story of Exchange'; Borden *et al.* (eds.), *Unknown City*, pp. 105–22.

78. Rob Shields (ed.), *Lifestyle Shopping* (London: Routledge, 1992), p. 8.

79. Peter Stallybrass and Allon White, *The Politics and Poetics of Transgression* (London: Methuen, 1986).

80. Laura Mulvey, 'Visual Pleasure and Narrative Cinema', *Screen* (Autumn 1975), v. 16, n. 3, republished in Laura Mulvey, 'Visual Pleasure and Narrative Cinema', Laura Mulvey (ed.), *Visual and Other Pleasures* (London: Macmillan, 1989), pp. 14–26.

81. See, for example, Beatriz Colomina, 'The Split Wall: Domestic Voyeurism', Colomina (ed.), *Sexuality*, pp. 73–98 and Alice Friedman, 'Architecture, Authority and the Gaze: Planning and Representation in the Early Modern Country House', *Assemblage* (August 1992), v. 18, pp. 40–61.

82. Mulvey, 'Visual', pp. 14–26.

83. Rose, 'Making', p. 337.

84. Alice Friedman follows Kaja Silverman's, 'Fassbinder and Lacan: a

Reconsideration of Gaze, Look and Image', based on a close reading of Lacan's 'Four Fundamental Concepts of Psychoanalysis'. See Friedman, 'Architecture', pp. 42–3.

85. Irigaray, *Speculum*, pp. 113–17 and Irigaray, *This Sex*, p. 84.

86. Nathaniel S. Wheaton, *A Journal of a Residence During Several Months in London: including excursions through various parts of England and a short tour in France and Scotland in the years 1823 and 1824* (Hartford: H. & F. J. Huntingdon, 1830), p. 119.

87. The paradigm of the 'separate spheres' is an oppositional and a hierarchical system consisting of a dominant public male realm of production (the city) and a subordinate private female one of reproduction (the home). It is probably the most pervasive configuration of gendered space. As an ideological device, one which divides city from home, public from private, production from reproduction and men from women, the separate spheres is both patriarchal and capitalist. As such, it does not describe the lived experience of all urban dwellers, but rather sets up an ideology of gendered space. This is problematic for feminists, among others, because the assumptions regarding sex, gender and space contained within this binary hierarchy are considered to be natural rather than socially constructed and continually reproduced.

88. Judith Squires, 'Private Lives, Secluded Places: Privacy as Political Possibility', *Environment and Planning D: Society and Space* (1994), v. 12, pp. 387–410, p. 389.

89. Jeff Hearn, *Men in the Public Eye* (London: Routledge, 1991), pp. 25–6.

90. Mary P. Ryan, *Women in Public: Between Banners and Ballots, 1825–1880* (London: Johns Hopkins University Press, 1990), p. 4.

91. In general terms, patriarchy refers to the rule of the father or fathers and describes the social and political control of women by men. The exact definition of the term varies according to discipline. For example, for anthropologists, it is defined through property ownership, whereas for psychoanalysts, it is defined through relations within the patriarchal family. See Rosalind Coward, *Patriarchal Precedents: Sexuality and Social Relations* (London: Routledge & Kegan Paul, 1983), p. 7. Other similar concepts include viriarchy, androcracy, andrarchy and phallocracy. See Hearn, *Men*, p. 48.

92. Mary Anne Clawson, *Constructing Brotherhood: Gender/Class and Fraternity* (Princeton: Princeton University Press, 1989), pp. 49–50.

93. Sylvia Walby, *Theorising Patriarchy* (Oxford: Blackwell, 1990), pp. 178–9.

94. 'An Act for Consolidating into one Act and Amending the Laws relating to Idle and Disorderly Persons, Rogues and Vagabonds, Incorrigible Rogues and other Vagrants in England', 3 George IV, cap. 40 (1822), *Statutes at Large, 3*

NOTES TO PAGES 22-9

George IV (1822) (London: His Majesty's Statute and Law Printers, 1822), v. 62, pp. 133–42 and 'An Act for the Punishment of Idle and Disorderly Persons, and Rogues and Vagabonds, in that part of Great Britain called England', 5 George IV, cap. 83 (1824), *Statutes at Large, 5 George IV (1824)* (London: His Majesty's Printers, 1839), v. 64, pp. 281–9.

95. Elizabeth Wilson, *The Sphinx in the City: Urban life, the Control of Disorder, and Women* (London: Virago Press, 1991).

96. Janet Wolff, 'The Invisible Flâneuse: Women and the Literature of Modernity', *Theory, Culture and Society* (1985), v. 2, n. 3, pp. 36–46.

97. Lynda Nead, 'A Definition of Deviancy: Prostitution and High Art *c.*1860', *Block* (1985), n. 11, p. 41.

98. Pollock, *Vision*, p. 73.

99. Neil McKendrick, John Brewer and J. H. Plumb, *The Birth of a Consumer Society: The Commercialization of Eighteenth Century England* (London: Europa Publications, 1982), pp. 16 and 40.

100. John Brewer and Roy Porter (eds), *Consumption and the World of Goods* (London: Routledge, 1993).

101. Veblen, *Theory*.

102. Georg Simmel, 'Fashion', Donald Levine (ed.), *Georg Simmel: On Individuality and Social Forms* (Chicago: Chicago University Press, 1971), pp. 294–323.

103. Gilles Lipovestsky, *The Empire of Fashion: Dressing Modern Democracy* (Princeton: Princeton University Press, 1994), pp. 41–4.

104. David Cannadine, *Aspects of Aristocracy: Grandeur and Decline in Modern Britain* (New Haven & London: Yale University Press, 1994), p. 10.

105. Lipovestsky, *Empire*, pp. 41–4.

106. Colin Campbell, 'The Sociology of Consumption', Miller (ed.), *Acknowledging*, pp. 96–126, p. 109.

107. Pierre Bourdieu, *Distinction: a Social Critique of the Judgement of Taste* (London: Routledge & Kegan Paul, 1984).

108. Bocock, *Consumption*, pp. 17–18.

109. Richard Sennett, *The Fall of Public Man* (New York: First Vintage Books Edition, 1978). See also comments in Mike Featherstone, 'The Body in Consumer Culture', Mike Featherstone, Mike Hepworth and Bryan S. Turner (eds.), *The Body: Social Process and Cultural Theory* (London: Sage, 1991), pp. 170–96, p. 189.

110. For a discussion of language and dress as systems of meaning see, for example, Grant McCracken, *Culture and Consumption* (Bloomington: Indiana University Press, 1990), pp. 65–71.

111. McCracken, *Culture*, pp. 17–20.

112. Pierce Egan, *The Finish to the Adventures of Tom, Jerry and Logic in their Pursuits through Life in and out of London* (London: J. S. Virtue & Co., 1828).

CHAPTER 2

1. Griselda Pollock, *Vision and Difference: Femininity, Feminism and the Histories of Art* (London: Routledge, 1988), p. 79.

2. Amateur, *Real Life in London, or the Rambles and adventures of Bob Tallyho, Esq. and his cousin the Hon. Tom Dashall, through the metropolis; exhibiting a living picture of fashionable characters, manners and amusements in high and low life* (London: Jones & Co., 1821–2), pp. 198–9.

3. *Oxford English Dictionary*, CD ROM, 2nd edition (1989).

4. *OED*.

5. Pierce Egan, *Life in London; or, the day and night scenes of Jerry Hawthorn, Esq., and his elegant friend Corinthian Tom, accompanied by Bob Logic, the Oxonian, in their Rambles and Sprees through the Metropolis* (London: Sherwood, Neely & Jones, 1820–1).

6. 'The Rambler in London', *Rambler's Magazine or Fashionable Companion* (London: T. Holt, 1 April 1824), v. 1, n. 1.

7. Egan, *Life*, p. 75.

8. According to J. C. Reid, the tradition goes back to various sixteenth-century pamphlets, but the semi-narrative structure first appears in Edward Ward, *The London Spy* (London: J. Nutt & J. How, 1698–9). See J. C. Reid, *Bucks and Bruisers* (London: Routledge & Kegan Paul, 1971), p. 51.

9. See, for example, Anon., *Tricks of the Town laid open; or a companion for a Country Gentleman* (London: H. Slater & R. Adams, 1747); Anon., *The Country Spy or a Ramble through London* (London: n. p., 1750); Anon., *The Devil upon Crutches in England or Night Scenes in London* (London: Phillip Hodges, 1755); Anon., *The Midnight Spy or London from 10 in the Evening to 5 in the Morning, exhibiting a Great Variety of Scenes in High Life and Low Life* (London: J. Cooke, 1766); Anon., *A Sunday Ramble: or a modern Sabbath-day Journey in and about the Cities of London and Westminster* (London: n. p., 1776); Anon., *Tricks of the Town laid open; a true caution to both sexes in town and country* (London: Sabine, 1780); R. King, *The Complete London Spy for the present year 1781* (London: Alex Hogg, 1781); Anon., *London unmasked or the New Town Spy* (London, n. p., 1784) and G. A. Stevens, *The Adventures of a Speculist or, a Journey through London compiled from papers written by George Alexander Stevens (Author of a Lecture upon Heads)* (London: S. Bladon, 1788). See also J. C. Reid, *Bucks and Bruisers* (London: Routledge & Kegan Paul, 1971), p. 51.

10. *The Rambler's Magazine or Annals of Gallantry or Glee, Pleasure and Bon Ton; a delicious bouquet of amorous, bacchanalian, whimsical, humorous, theatrical and literary entertainment* (London: J. Mitford, 1828), v. 1, n. 5, p. 207.

11. See, for example, Anon., *A Fortnight's Ramble through London, or a complete display of all the Cheats and Frauds practised in that Great Metropolis with the best*

Methods for eluding them being a true and pleasing narrative of the Adventures of a farmer's son (London: Dean & Munday, 1817); George Andrewes, *The Stranger's Guide or the Frauds of London detected etc.* (London: J. Bailey, 1808); George Barrington, *Barrington's New London Spy for 1805, or the frauds of London detected, also a Treatise on the Art of Boxing by Mr. Belcher*, 4th edition (London: T. Tegg, 1805) and George Smeeton, *Doings in London; or Day and Night Scenes of the frauds, frolics, manners and depravities of the Metropolis* (London: Smeeton, 1828).

12. See Amateur, *Real*; Bernard Blackmantle, *The English Spy* (London: Sherwood, Jones & Co., 1825); Egan, *Life*; William Heath, *Fashion and Folly: or the Buck's Pilgrimage* (London: William Sams, 1822) and William Heath, *Fashion and Folly illustrated in a series of 23 Humorous Coloured Engravings* (London: William Sams, 1833). In the case of Egan, *Life*, the author and illustrators were equally well-known, but with Amateur, *Real* and Blackmantle, *English* there is some question over the identities of the authors. Amateur, *Real* has been attributed to Robert Dighton by the British Library, to Pierce Egan by the Guildhall Library and to Jonathan Badcock or William Combe by J. C. Reid. See Reid, *Bucks*, p. 74. The British Library Catalogue attributes Blackmantle, *English* to Charles Molloy Westmacott. Amateur, *Real* is so similar to Egan, *Life*, that it is arguably a copy using a different writer and illustrators. Although Blackmantle, *English* has the word 'spy' in its title, the tone of the work in both images and words so closely resembles Egan, *Life* and Amateur, *Real*, that I describe it as a ramble. Heath, *Fashion*, consists of a number of coloured engravings accompanied by verses, with no titles or plate numbers. In the 1833 edition the plates are each given titles. All four rambles describe a fairly consistent map of London, visiting similar sites and representing them in equivalent terms. For these reasons, I focus here primarily on Egan, *Life*, referring to the other texts for more details as relevant.

13. Egan, *Life*, pp. 23–4.

14. Egan, *Life*, p. 18.

15. Egan's nationality and date of death are debatable. See Reid, *Bucks*, pp. ix–x and 'Obituary – Pierce Egan', *The Gentleman's Magazine* (November 1849), v. 32, p. 548.

16. Typical guidebooks to the city in the early nineteenth century included, J. Britton, *The Original Picture of London enlarged and improved being a correct guide for the stranger as well as for the inhabitant of the Metropolis of the British Empire together with a description of the environs*, 26th edition (London: Longman, Rees, Orme, Brown & Green, 1827); William Carey, *The Strangers Guide through London: or a view of the British Metropolis in 1808* (London: James Cundee, 1808); John Corry, *The English Metropolis or London in the Year 1820* (London: Sherwood, Neely & Jones, 1820); John Corry, *The English Metropolis or London in the Year 1825* (London: Barnard & Farley, 1825); John Feltham, *Picture for*

London for 1818, 19th edition (London: Longman, Hurst, Rees, Orme, & Brown, 1818); John Feltham, *The Picture of London for 1821*, 22nd edition (London: Longman, Hurst, Rees, Orme, & Brown, 1821); James Grant, *The Great Metropolis* (London: Saunders & Otley, 1838); Samuel Leigh, *Leigh's New Picture of London* (London: Leigh, 1819); J. Britton and A. Pugin, *Illustrations of the Public Buildings of London* (London: John Wedle, 1838); Thomas Shepherd, 'Metropolitan Improvements or London in the Nineteenth Century . . . from the Original Drawings of Thomas H. Shepherd with notes by James Elmes', *London in the Nineteenth Century* (London: Jones & Co., 1 November 1829), v. 1 and Thomas Shepherd, 'London and its Environs in the Nineteenth Century from the Original Drawings by Thomas E. Shepherd', *London in the Nineteenth Century* (London: Jones & Co., 1 November 1829), v. 2.

17. There are a number of interesting accounts of journeys through London from the early nineteenth century. See, for example, M. D. Archenholz, *Picture of England containing a description of the laws, customs and manners of England interspersed with curious and interesting anecdotes* (Dublin: P. Byrne, 1791); Don Manuel Alvarez Espriella, *Letters from England* (London: Longman, Hurst, Rees, Orme, 1807); Erik Gustaf Geijer, *Impressions of England 1809–10*, (London: n. p., 1809–10); C. A. G. Goede, *The Stranger in England or Travels in Great Britain containing Remarks on the Politics, Laws, Manners, Customs, and Distinguished Characters of the Country and chiefly its Metropolis with Criticism on the Stage* (London: Mathews & Leigh, 1807); William Hutton, *A Journey to London* (London: William Hutton, 1818); Count Edouard de Melfort, *Impressions of England* (London: Richard Betley, 1836); Louis Simond, *Journal of a Tour and a Residence in Great Britain during the Years 1810 and 1811* (London: Longman, Hurst, Rees, Orme, & Brown, 1817); T. S. Surr, *A Winter in London or Sketches of Fashion* (London: Richard Phillips, 1806); Gebhardt Fredrich August Wendeborn, *A View of England towards the close of the Eighteenth Century* (Dublin: William Sleater for P. Wogan, 1791) and Nathaniel S. Wheaton, *A Journal of a Residence During Several Months in London: including excursions through various parts of England and a short tour in France and Scotland in the years 1823 and 1824* (Hartford: H. & F. J. Huntingdon, 1830).

18. Michael de Certeau, 'Spatial Stories', *The Practice of Everyday Life* (Berkeley: University of California Press, 1988), pp. 115–22.

19. Egan, *Life*, pp. 23–4.

20. Egan, *Life*, p. 22.

21. M. D. George, *London Life in the Eighteenth Century* (Harmondsworth: Penguin, 1992), pp. 116–45.

22. The population of London increased from 864,845 in 1801 to 1,225,964 in 1821, whereas the population of the City decreased from 87,000 in 1750 to 56,174 in 1821. See Smeeton, *Doings*, p. 3.

23. Egan, *Life*, p. 234.
24. See George Rudé, *Hanoverian London 1714–1808* (London: Secker and Warburg, 1971), pp. 4–11 and Donald A. Low, *Thieves Kitchen: The Regency Underworld* (Totowa, NJ: Biblio Distribution Centre, 1982), pp. 43–6.
25. George, *London*, pp. 11 and 75.
26. See, for example, Donald J. Olsen, *Town Planning in London: The Eighteenth and Nineteenth Centuries* (New Haven & London: Yale University Press, 1982), pp. 39–42; John Summerson, *Georgian London* (London: Pelican, 1962), pp. 31–54 and Steen Eiler Rasmussen, *London: The Unique City* (Cambridge, MA: The MIT Press, 1988), pp. 190–201.
27. Peter Borsay, 'Introduction', Peter Borsay (ed.), *The Eighteenth Century Town 1688–1820* (Harlow: Longman, 1990), pp. 1–38, pp. 33–6.
28. Louis James, *Print and the People 1819–51* (London: Allen Lane, 1976), p. 80.
29. According to the British Library Catalogue the text was written around the previously commissioned images.
30. Pierce Egan, *Walks through Bath* (London: Sherwood, Neely and Jones, 1819), p. iv.
31. Low, *Thieves*, p. 110.
32. Reid, *Bucks*, p. 55.
33. Kate represents the most famous courtesan of the early nineteenth century, Harriette Wilson. Harriette Wilson, along with her sister, Fanny, and friend, Julia Johnstone, were known as the three graces. Sue represents Mrs. Maples alias Mrs. Bertram alias Mother Bang. See Charles Hindley, *The True History of Tom and Jerry, or, the day and Night Scenes of Life in London, from the Start to the finish! With a key to the persons and places, together with a vocabulary and glossary of the flash and slang terms, occurring in the course of the work* (London: C. Hindley, 1890), glossary. For Harriette Wilson see, for example, Harriette Wilson, *Harriette Wilson's Memoirs of herself and others* (London: T. Douglas, 1825); Harriette Wilson, *The interesting memoirs and Amorous Adventures of Harriette Wilson one of the most Celebrated Women of the Present Day interspersed with numerous Anecdotes of Illustrious Persons* (London: W. Chubb, T. Blackfeter, T. Reed, 1825); Harriette Wilson, *Memoirs of Harriette Wilson written by herself* (London: J. J. Stockdale, 1825) and Harriette Wilson, *Memoirs of Herself and Others* (London: Peter Davies, 1829). See also secondary sources, Lesley Blanche, *The Game of Hearts: Harriette Wilson and her Memoirs* (London: Gryphon Books, 1957); Max Marquis, *Mistress of Many: Selections from the Memoirs of Harriette Wilson* (London: Bestseller Library, 1960) and Angela Thirkell, *The Fortunes of Harriette: the Surprising Career of Harriette Wilson* (London: Hamish Hamilton, 1936).
34. Reid, *Bucks*, p. 80.
35. *Cruikshank 200* (London: John Lordroper, 1992), p. 6 and Reid, *Bucks*, p. 81.

36. 'Peep o'Day Boys. A Street Row and the Author losing his reader. Tom and Jerry showing fight and Logic floored', Egan, *Life*, p. 219.

37. Egan, *Life*, p. 178. Blue ruin was one of the slang terms for gin.

38. Egan, *Life*, pp. 178–9 and 286–90.

39. My research has uncovered editions for 1823, 1870, 1900 and 1904; Pierce Egan, *Life in London; or, the day and night scenes of Jerry Hawthorn, Esq., and his elegant friend Corinthian Tom, accompanied by Bob Logic, the Oxonian, in their Rambles and Sprees through the Metropolis* (London: Sherwood, Neely & Jones, 1820–1); Pierce Egan, *Life in London; or, the day and night scenes of Jerry Hawthorn, Esq., and his elegant friend Corinthian Tom, accompanied by Bob Logic, the Oxonian, in their Rambles and Sprees through the Metropolis*, 2nd edition (London: Sherwood, Neely & Jones, 1821); Pierce Egan, *Life in London; or, the day and night scenes of Jerry Hawthorn, Esq., and his elegant friend Corinthian Tom, accompanied by Bob Logic, the Oxonian, in their Rambles and Sprees through the Metropolis* (London: Sherwood, Jones & Co., 1823); Pierce Egan, *Life in London; or, the day and night scenes of Jerry Hawthorn, Esq., and his elegant friend Corinthian Tom, accompanied by Bob Logic, the Oxonian, in their Rambles and Sprees through the Metropolis* (London: Chatto & Windus, 1870); Pierce Egan, *Life in London; or, the day and night scenes of Jerry Hawthorn, Esq., and his elegant friend Corinthian Tom, accompanied by Bob Logic, the Oxonian, in their Rambles and Sprees through the Metropolis* (London: Chatto and Windus, 1900) and Pierce Egan, *Life in London; or, the day and night scenes of Jerry Hawthorn, Esq., and his elegant friend Corinthian Tom, accompanied by Bob Logic, the Oxonian, in their Rambles and Sprees through the Metropolis* (London: Methuen, 1904). Reid also mentions editions for 1830 and 1841. See J. C. Reid, *Bucks*, pp. 73 and 224, footnotes 2, 3 and 5.

40. Jeremy Catnach, *Life in London, or the Sprees of Tom and Jerry, attempted in cuts and verse*, 5th edition (London: Jas. Catnach, 1822). Each broadside cost 2d. See Reid, *Bucks*, p. 76.

41. The first imitation was Amateur, *Real*. For translations, see Jean-Baptist-Balthazar Sauvan, *Diorama Anglais ou Promenades Pittoresque à Londres* (Paris: Didot, 1823) and for different locations, see David Carey, *Life in Paris; comprising the Rambles, Sprees and Amours of Dick Wildfire, of Corinthian Celebrity, and his Bang-up Companions, Squire Jenkins and Captain O' Shuffleton* (London: John Fairburn, 1822) and Brian Boru, esq., *Real Life in Ireland, or the Day and Night Scenes, Rovings, Rambles and Sprees, Bulls, Blunders, Bidderarions, and Blarney of Brian Boru, Esq. and his elegant friend Sir Shawn O'Dogherty, By a Real Paddy* (London: B. Bensley, 1821).

42. The first production took place on 17 September 1821 at the Royal Amphitheatre. By the summer of 1822 there were five versions running concurrently. See Reid, *Bucks*, pp. 77–87.

43. See, for example, Thomas Burke, *The Streets of London* (London: B. T. Batsford,

1940), p. 103 and John Rule, *Albion's People, English Society 1714–1815* (London: Longman, 1992), pp. 140–1. The first of the serial publications was *The Tour of Dr. Syntax in Search of the Picturesque* (London: Rudolf Ackermann, 1812). See Reid, *Bucks*, p. 52. See also Penelope Corfield, 'Walking the City Streets, an Eighteenth Century Odyssey', *Historical Perspectives* (1990), v. 16, pp. 132–74, p. 142.

44. Deborah Epstein Nord, 'The City as Theatre: From Georgians to Early Victorian London', *Victorian Studies* (1988), v. 31, n. 2, pp. 159–88, p. 159.

45. This new audience is specifically noted in the preface to Egan, *Life* (1870), p. 10. The increase in literacy rates was apparently most marked among men. See Clive Barker, 'A Theatre for the People', Kenneth Richards and Peter Thomas (eds.), *Nineteenth Century British Theatre* (London: Methuen, 1971), pp. 3–24, p. 18; James, *Print*, p. 146 and Louis James, *Fiction for the Working Man* (Oxford: Oxford University Press, 1963), p. 146.

46. See, for example, Lawrence Stone, *The Family, Sex and Marriage in England 1500–1800* (London: Penguin, 1990), pp. 37–8, 45 and 70.

47. The precise meaning of libertine has been debated. For Anna Clark it refers to the search for pleasure as life's primary goal. See Anna Clark, *The Struggle for Breeches* (Berkeley, Los Angeles & Oxford: University of California Press, 1995), p. 31. Elizabeth Wilson suggests that the word 'flâneur' derives from the Irish word for libertine. See Elizabeth Wilson, 'The Invisible Flâneur', *New Left Review* (1992), n. 191, pp. 90–110, p. 93.

48. See, for example, Mrs Arbuthnot's views quoted in M. D. George, *Hogarth to Cruikshank: Social Change in Graphic Satire* (London: The Penguin Press, 1967), p. 170.

49. See Pierce Egan, *The Finish to the Adventures of Tom, Jerry and Logic in their Pursuits through Life in and out of London* (London: J. S .Virtue & Co., 1828), p. iii.

50. See Frances Burney, *Evelina* (London: T. and W. Lowndes, 1779, 1784) and Frances Burney, *Evelina* (London: C. Dresden & F. Walther, 1788, 1794, 1795, 1808). In 1822 *Evelina* was retitled and published as Frances Burney, *Female Life in London, being the History of A Young Lady's Introduction to Fashionable Life and the Gay Scenes of the Metropolis Displaying A Highly Humorous, Satirical, and Entertaining Description of Fashionable Characters, Manners and Amusements in the Higher Circles of Metropolitan Society* (London: Jones & Co, 1822).

51. See, for example, *The History and Adventures of Miss Betsy Warwick the Female Rambler* (London: T. Sabine, 1825).

52. Amateur, *Real*, v. 1, p. 99.

53. Eric Partridge, *A Dictionary of Slang and Unconventional English* (London: Routledge & Kegan Paul, 1964), p. 958.

54. Francis Grose, *A Classical Dictionary of the Vulgar Tongue* (London: S. Hooper,

1788), n. p. and Pierce Egan, *Grose's Classical Dictionary of the Vulgar Tongue, revised and corrected, with the addition of numerous slang phrases, collected from tried authorities by Pierce Egan* (London: Sherwood, Neely & Jones, 1823), n. p.

55. Partridge, *Dictionary*, p. 959.

56. See, for example, *The Rambler's Magazine or the Annals of Gallantry, Glee, Pleasure, and the Bon Ton; calculated for the entertainment of the Polite World and to furnish a Man of Pleasure with a most delicious bouquet of amorous, bacchanalian, whimsical, humorous, theatrical and literary entertainment* (London: R. Randall, 1783–9); *The Ranger's Magazine or the Man of Fashion's Companion, being the XXXXX of the Month and general assemblage of Love, Gallantry, Wit, Pleasure, Harmony, Mirth, Glee, and Fancy, containing monthly List of Covent Garden Cyprians; or, the Man of Pleasures Vade Mecum* (London: J. Sudbury, 1795); *The Rambler's Magazine or Annals of Gallantry or Glee, Pleasure and Bon Ton* (London: J. Mitford, 1820); *The Rambler's Magazine or Fashionable Emporium of Polite Literature* (London: Benbow, 1822); *Rambler* (1824) and *Rambler's* (1828).

57. See, for example, Julia Johnstone, *Confessions of Julia Johnstone written by herself in contradiction to the fables of Harriett Wilson* (London: Benbow, 1825).

58. See, for example, *Covent Garden Magazine or Amorous Repository calculated solely for the Entertainment of the Polite World and the finishing of a Young Gentleman's Education* (London: G. Allen, January 1773); Harris, *Harris's List of Covent Garden Ladies or the Man of Pleasures Kalender, for the Year 1788, containing the histories and some curious anecdotes of the most celebrated Ladies now on the Town, or in keeping and also many of their keepers* (London: H. Ranger, 1788) and Harris, *Harris's List of Covent Garden Ladies or the Man of Pleasures Kalender, for the Year 1793, containing the histories and some curious anecdotes of the most celebrated Ladies now on the Town, or in keeping and also many of their keepers* (London: H. Ranger, 1793). Jack Harris kept a London tavern, the Shakepeare's Head, in Drury Lane, where under his 'Pimp Master General' the 'Whore's Club' met on Sundays. Harris published an annual register between 1760–1793 describing the faces, figures, manners and special talents of the Covent Garden Ladies who patronized his house. 8000 copies were printed and sold every year. See, for example, Archenholz, *Picture*, p. 196; Reay Tannihill, *Sex in History* (London: Abacus, 1992), p. 360; Nicky Roberts, *Whores in History* (London: HarperCollins, 1993), p. 175 and E. J. Burford, *Wits, Wenches, and Wantons* (London: Robert Hale, 1990), p. 210. See also *The Characters of the present most Celebrated Courtezans* (London: M. James, 1780), a text which claimed to be more truthful than Harris.

59. *OED* and Partridge, *Dictionary*, p. 284.

60. Walter Benjamin, *Charles Baudelaire: a Lyric Poet in the Era of High Capitalism* (London: Verso, 1973).

61. Egan, *Life*, pp. 179, 286 and 346.

62. Grose, *Classical* (1788), n. p. and Egan, *Grose's*, n. p. See also Partridge, *Dictionary*, p. 151.
63. Grose, *Classical* (1788), n. p. and Egan, *Grose's*, n. p.
64. Egan, *Life*, pp. 48–9.
65. Joseph Rykwert, *The Dancing Column: on Order in Architecture* (London: The MIT Press, 1996), pp. 317 and 320.
66. Egan, *Life*, p. 49 and Smeeton, *Doings*, pp. 85–92.
67. *La Belle Assemblée, or, Bell's Court and Fashionable Magazine addressed particularly to the Ladies. New Series* (London: J. Bell, 1819), (February 1819), p. 85.
68. Egan, *Life*, p. 95.
69. Egan, *Life*, p. 72.
70. See, for example, Grose, *Classical*, n. p.
71. Egan, *Life*, p. 291.
72. See Eileen Moers, *The Dandy: Brummel to Beerbohm* (Lincoln: University of Nebraska Press, 1978), p. 66.
73. Egan, *Grose's*, p. 168.
74. John Badcock, *Slang: a Dictionary of the turf, the ring, the chase, the pit, the bon-ton, and the varieties of life, forming the completest and most authentic lexicon balatronicum . . . of the sporting world* (London: T. Hughes, 1823), p. 57.
75. Badcock, *Slang*, p. 57.
76. Badcock, *Slang*, p. 168.
77. Hindley, *True*, glossary.
78. Badcock, *Slang*, p. 57.
79. Egan, *Life*, chapters 3 and 4, specifically pp. 43 and 53.
80. Classical architecture was at times used to represent theories of government by different political parties in contemporary cartoons. For example, Isaac Cruikshank used Palladian architecture to express the whig theory of government. See 'A Picture of Great Britain in the Year 1793' (1793). George Cruikshank adapted elements of his father's Constitutional Temple for the radicals to express a concept of representative government. See 'The House that Jack Built' (1819). The tories used classical imagery to express conservative theories of government in retaliation. See 'The House that Jack Built' (1819). See Egan's description of the frontispiece, Egan, *Life*, pp. xiii-xiv.
81. Egan, *Life*, pp. xiii-xiv and 22–4.
82. Egan, *Life*, preface, p. vi. George Cruikshank was also patriotic. See *Cruikshank 200*, p. 7 and Christopher North, 'On George Cruikshank', *Blackwoods Edinburgh Magazine* (July 1823), pp. 18–26, p. 18.
83. The London Lighting Act of 1761 systematized London street lighting to a certain extent by placing the responsibility for lighting streets and other public areas with municipalities and lighting commissions. See François

Bedarida and Anthony Sutcliffe, 'The Street in the Structure and the Life of the City: Reflections on Nineteenth Century London and Paris', *Journal of Urban History* (1980), v. 6, pp. 379–96, p. 381 and Corfield, 'Walking', p. 152.

84. The Westminster Paving Acts of 1761 replaced gravel and pebbles with granite blocks, the central drainage channel with kerbside gutters and provided a convex carriageway, underground drainage and the removal of rubbish and obstructions, such as old shop signs, all of which made pedestrian walking easier. In larger London estates in the west streets were maintained according to obligations written into the leases. See, for example, Dan Cruikshank and Neil Burton, *Life in the Georgian City* (London: Viking, 1990), p. 15; Nicola Johnson, *Eighteenth Century London* (London: HMSO, 1991), p. 20 and Roy Porter, *London* (London: Hamish Hamilton, 1994), p. 125.

85. The problems of poor quality oil lighting were not resolved, however, until gas lighting was used to light the whole of London. An Act of Parliament established the British Gas Company in 1810. See, for example, Alison Adburgham, *Shops and Shopping 1800–1914* (London: George Allen & Unwin, 1981), p. 7; Burke, *Streets*, p. 97 and Cruikshank and Burton, *Life*, pp. 24–5.

86. Regent Street ran between Regent's Park at the north end and Carlton House at the south end, connecting London's three east–west routes, Oxford Street, Piccadilly and the Strand. See, for example, Terence Davis, *John Nash* (Newton Abbot: David & Charles, 1966), p. 74; Terence Davis, *The Architecture of John Nash* (London: Studio, 1960), pp. 13–16; Hermione Hobhouse, *A History of Regent Street* (London: Queen Anne Press, 1975), pp. 72–3 and Dorothy Marshall, *English People in the Eighteenth Century* (London: Longmans 1956), pp. 74–5.

87. See, for example, Davis, *Architecture*, p. 17 and John Summerson, *John Nash: Architect to King George IV* (London: George Allen & Unwin, 1935), pp. 204–5.

88. Puckler-Muskau, *Tour in England*, v. 3 (5 October 1826), p. 47.

89. The most popular pugilistic journal in the early nineteenth century was the *Weekly Dispatch*. The tory *Blackwood's Edinburgh Magazine* printed eight articles in praise of pugilism from July 1819 to March 1821. See also Reid, *Bucks*, p. 17 and Robert W. Malcolmson, *Popular Recreations In British Society 1700–1850* (Cambridge: Cambridge University Press, 1973), p. 42.

90. Grose, *Classical* (1788), n. p.

91. George Smeeton, *The Flash Dictionary and The Art of Boxing* (London: G. Smeeton, 1821), preface.

92. Egan's history of pugilism, *Boxiana or Sketches of Pugilism by One of the Fancy* established him as a sporting authority. *Boxiana* was issued serially in 1812 and ran to five volumes by 1829. See Pierce Egan, *Boxiana* (London: George Smeeton, 1812); Pierce Egan, *Boxiana* (London: Sherwood, Neely & Jones,

1818) and Pierce Egan, *Boxiana* (New Series), (London: George Virtue, 1828–9).
93. Egan, *Boxiana* (1818), pp. 24–5.
94. Egan, *Boxiana* (1818), dedication, n. p.
95. Smeeton, *Flash*, preface.
96. See Dennis Brailsford, *Sport, Time and Society* (London: Routledge, 1991), p. 56. Drinking alcohol was widespread in England in the early nineteenth century. See, for example, Brian Harrison, *Drink and the Victorians: the Temperance Question in England 1815–72* (London: Faber, 1971), p. 37.
97. Egan, *Life*, title page.
98. Amateur, *Real*, v. 2, p. 250, footnote.
99. Egan, *Boxiana* (1818), p. 28 and Jacob Larwood, *The Story of the London Parks* (London: Francis Harvey, 1872), v. 8, p. 284.
100. See T. Rowlandson, 'Three Principal Requisites to form a Modern Man of Fashion' (London: n. d.).
101. Francis Grose, *Lexicon Balatronicum: a Dictionary of Buckish Slang, University Wit and Pickpocket Elegance* (London: C. Chappel, 1811), p. v.
102. See Porter, *London*, p. 179; Rob Shields, 'Fancy Footwork', Keith Tester (ed.), *The Flâneur* (London: Routledge, 1994), pp. 61–80, p. 61 and Peter Stalleybrass and Allon White, *The Politics and Poetics of Transgression* (London, Methuen & Co., 1986), p. 139.
103. Grose, *Classical* (1788), n. p.
104. Grose, *Classical* (1788), preface, pp. x–xv.
105. Samuel Pegge, *Anecdotes of the English Language chiefly regarding the area around London and its Environs – whence it will appear that the Natives of the Metropolis have not corrupted the language of their ancestors* (London: J. Nichols & Son, 1803).
106. Olivia Smith, *The Politics of Language* (Oxford: Clarendon Press, 1984), pp. 13 and 23–4.
107. Pegge, *Anecdotes*, p. iii.
108. John Badcock, *A Living Picture of London, for 1823, and Strangers guide through the streets of the metropolis shewing the frauds and wiles of all descriptions of rogues* (London: W. Clarke, 1828). See also Gareth Stedman Jones, 'The Cockney and the Nation 1780–1988', Gareth Stedman Jones (ed.), *Metropolis London: Representations and Histories since 1800* (London: Routledge, 1989), pp. 272–325.
109. Grose, *Classical* (1788), n. p.; Grose, *Lexicon*, n. p. and Egan, *Grose's*, n. p.
110. Badcock, *Slang*, p. 54.
111. Grose, *Lexicon*, preface, p. viii and Egan, *Grose's*, title page and preface, pp. xxv–xxviii.
112. See, for example, Andrewes, *Stranger's* and George Andrewes, *A Dictionary of the Slang and Other Cant Languages* (London: G. Smeeton, 1809); Badcock,

Slang and Badcock, *Living;* Amateur, *Real*; Egan, *Boxiana*, Egan, *Grose's* and Egan, *Life*; Smeeton, *Flash* and Smeeton, *Doings*. The two-volume sets include Smeeton, *Flash* and *The Art of Boxing* and Barrington, *Barrington's* and *the Art of Boxing by Mr. Belcher*, 4th edition (London: T. Tegg, 1805).

113. Egan, *Grose's*, p. xxii.
114. Grose, *Lexicon*, p. vi.
115. Egan, *Grose's*, title page.
116. Grose, *Lexicon*, p. vii.
117. *Sporting Ladies* (London), published in the 1770s was a list of prostitutes.
118. See Tannihill, *Sex*, p. 360; Roberts, *Whores*, p. 174 and Burford, *Wits*, p. 98.
119. See Brailsford, *Sport*, p. xi and Derek Birley, *Sport and the Making of Britain* (Manchester: Manchester University Press, 1993), p. 2.
120. Proscribed by law since 1750, boxing required the protection of influential patronage to deter magistrates from issuing warrants for arrest at illegal contests.
121. Wray Vamplew, 'Sport and Industrialisation: an Economic Interpretation of the Changes in Popular Sport in Nineteenth-Century England', J. A. Mangan (ed.), *Pleasure, Profit, Proselytism* (London: Frank Cass, 1988), pp. 7–20, p. 14.
122. Badcock, *Slang*, p. 168.
123. Badcock, *Slang*, p. 54.
124. Janet Wolff, 'The Invisible Flâneuse: Women and the Literature of Modernity', *Theory, Culture and Society* (1985), v. 2, n. 3, pp. 36–46.
125. Chapter 2 is entitled 'A Camera-Obscura View of the Metropolis, the Light and Shade attached to "seeing Life"', Egan, *Life*, p. 18.
126. 'TOM and JERRY *"masquerading it"* among the *cadgers* in the *Back Slums* in the Holy Land', Egan, *Life*, p. 346.
127. Egan, *Life*, p. 282.
128. See, for example, Summerson, *Georgian*, p. 178; Robert Altick, *The Shows of London* (Cambridge, MA: Harvard University Press, 1978) and George, *Hogarth*.
129. Arthur W. Frank, 'For a Sociology of the Body: An Analytic Overview', Mike Featherstone, Mike Hepworth and Bryan S. Turner (eds.), *The Body: Social Process and Cultural Theory* (London: Sage Publications, 1991), pp. 36–102, pp. 63 and 67.
130. Egan, *Life*, p. 20.
131. Davis, *Nash*, pp. 73–4.
132. The Royal Opera Arcade was a continuation of the colonnade around the Italian Opera House. It runs parallel to the Haymarket, between Charles II Street and Pall Mall. See chapter 5, footnote 27.
133. Quoted in Davis, *Nash*, p. 66 and Davis, *Architecture*, p. 66.

134. Amateur, *Real*, v. 1, p. 102.

135. Egan, *Life*, pp. 145–8.

136. See James Laver, *Dandies* (London: Weidenfeld & Nicolson, 1968), pp. 10 and 153.

137. Neil McKendrick, John Brewer and J. H. Plumb, *The Birth of a Consumer Society: the Commercialisation of Eighteenth Century England* (London: Europa Publications, 1982), p. 43 and Faired Chevianne, *A History of Men's Fashion* (Paris: Flammarin, 1993), p. 9.

138. Chevianne, *History*, p. 22.

139. The word dandy may stem from the Scottish term 'jack-a-dandy' used to describe a person dressing up at a fair, or from the French verb to waddle. According to Grose it was used in the late eighteenth century to mean 'the ton, or the clever thing'. See Grose, *Classical* (1788), n. p. Badcock dates the origin at 1816. See Badcock, *Slang*, p. 63. Egan dates it at 1820. See Egan, *Grose's*, n. p. and Egan, *Life*, p. 42, footnote 5. The *OED* states that from 1813, dandy meant swell, later, from 1817 to 1820, the term was applied to wasp-waisted and heavily whiskered men.

140. Smeeton, *Doings*, p. 48.

141. Moers, *Dandy*, pp. 17–38 and George, *Hogarth*, p. 166.

142. Egan, *Grose's*, n.p.

143. Dorothy George outlines three main types of print-shop dandy: caricatures of social notorieties; absurd, languid and effeminate dandies; and dandies imitating the catchphrases, dress and manners of their model. See George, *Hogarth*, pp. 163–4. See, for example, the following caricatures of dandies: Robert Cruikshank, 'Dandies Dressing' (1818); Richard Dighton, 'The Dandy Club' (1818); George Cruikshank, 'The Dandies Coat of Arms', (1819); George Cruikshank, 'Monstrosities' (1822) and a caricatured account of a day in the life of a dandy in Felix MacDonogh, 'The Exquisite's Diary', *The Hermit in London*, 5 volumes in 3 (London: Henry Colburn 1819), v. 3, pp. 79–86. See also Jessica R. Feldman, *Gender on the Divide: The Dandy in Modernist Literature* (New York: Cornell University Press, 1993), p. 43.

144. MacDonogh, *Hermit* (1819), v. 5, p. 34.

145. MacDonogh, *Hermit* (1819), v. 5, p. 34 and Elizabeth Wilson, *Adorned in Dreams* (London: Virago Press, 1985), p. 180.

146. See, for example, Chevianne, *History*, p. 16 and Aileen Ribeiro, *Dress and Morality* (London: B. T. Batsford, 1986), pp. 118–20.

147. Badcock, *Slang*, p. 63.

148. Laver, *Dandies*, p. 10.

149. The art of cutting is illustrated in a set of plates by M. Egerton, 'The Cut Celestial', 'The Cut Infernal' and 'The Cut Direct' (1827). In each a dandy

NOTES TO PAGES 54–5

NOTES TO PAGES 54-5

walking or riding in London meets a friend or acquaintance and stares at the sky, then at the ground.

150. Moers, *Dandy*, p. 66.

151. Soho was a breeding ground for cholera in 1832. The houses were without drains or sewers, subdivided and sub-let with an average of twenty-four per house, many of them Irish immigrants. See for example, Borsay, 'Introduction', p. 19; Leonard D. Schwarz, 'Social Class and Social Geography: The Middle Classes in London at the End of the Nineteenth Century', Borsay (ed.), *Eighteenth*, pp. 315–37; Davis, *Architecture*, p. 15 and Geoffrey Tyack, 'James Pennithorne and the London Street Improvements 1838–55', *London Journal* (1990), v. 15, n. 1, pp. 38–56, pp. 42–3.

152. Borsay, 'Introduction', p. 15.

153. *Report from the Select Committee on the Office of Works* (1828), p. 74, quoted in Dana Arnold, 'George IV and the Metropolitan Improvements: The Creation of a Royal Image', Dana Arnold (ed.), *Squanderous and Lavish Profession: George IV, his image and patronage of the arts* (London: The Georgian Group, 1995), pp. 51–6.

154. Smeeton, *Doings*, p. 91.

155. William Tait, *Magdelinism* (Edinburgh: P. Rickard, 1840), p. 4.

156. Incomes in traditional forms of female employment, dressmaking and millinery for example, were low and infrequent as a result of both foreign competition and the shortness of the London season which provided only a small peak of employment from April to June. See, for example, Schwarz, 'Social', pp. 17–18 and P. J. Corfield, 'The Capital City', P. J. Corfield (ed.), *The Impact of English towns 1700–1800* (Oxford: Oxford University Press, 1982), pp. 66–81, p. 75.

157. *Memoirs of the Life of Madame Vestris of the Theatre Royal Drury Lane and Covent Garden* (London: privately printed, 1830), p. 69 and *Memoirs of the Life Public and Private Adventures of Madame Vestris* (London: John Duncombe, 1836), p. 50. According to the British Library Catalogue, the 1830 edition appeared in 1839 under the name Molloy Westmacott, who, under the pseudonym of Bernard Blackmantle, was the author of the *Spy*. The author of the 1836 version, under the pseudonym of Arthur Griffenhoofe, was George Coleman. The name 'T. Duncombe' is written on the British Library copy of the text. For biographies of Madame Vestris, see William W. Appleton, *Madame Vestris and the London Stage* (New York: Columbia University Press, 1974); Charles Pearce, *Madame Vestris and Her Times* (London: Stanley Paul, 1923) and Clifford John Wiliams, *Madame Vestris: a Theatrical Biography* (London: Sidgwick & Jackson, 1973).

158. *Belle* (July 1806), p. 314.

159. *Belle* (July 1806), p. 314.

160. Blackmantle, *Spy*, v. 2, pp. 18–19.
161. Grose, *Classical* (1788), n. p. and Egan, *Grose's*, n. p.
162. 'An Act for Consolidating into one Act and Amending the Laws relating to Idle and Disorderly Persons, Rogues and Vagabonds, Incorrigible Rogues and other Vagrants in England', 3 George IV cap. 40 (1822), *Statutes at Large, 3 George IV (1822)* (London: His Majesty's Statute and Law Printers, 1822), v. 62, pp. 133–42 .
163. 'An Act for the Punishment of Idle and Disorderly Persons, and Rogues and Vagabonds, in that part of Great Britain called England', 5 George IV, cap. 83 (1824), *Statutes at Large, 5 George IV (1824)* (London: His Majesty's Printers, 1839), v. 64, pp. 281–9.
164. *Rambler's* (March 1822), v. 1, n. 3, p. 109.
165. Adburgham, *Shops*, pp. 1–2.
166. *Belle* (February 1806), p. 64.
167. *Belle* (February 1806), p. 20.
168. *Belle* (February 1806), pp. 16 and 20.
169. *Belle* (July 1809), p. 43 and *Belle* (October 1810), p. 213.
170. *Belle* (July 1809), p. 43.
171. *Belle* (July 1806), p. 231.
172. *Belle* (February 1806), p. 20.
173. M. J. D. Roberts, 'Public and Private in Early Nineteenth Century London: the Vagrant Act of 1822 and its Enforcement', *Social History* (1988), v. 13, n. 3, pp. 273–94.
174. MacDonogh, *Hermit* (1819), v. 2, p. 186 and Amateur, *Real*, v. 2, p. 26.
175. Egan, *Life*, p. 173.
176. William Hale, *Considerations on the Causes and the Prevalence of Female Prostitution: and on the Most Practicable and Efficient Means of Abating and Preventing that, and, all other crimes against the virtue and safety of the community* (London: E. Justing, 1812), p. 4 and Michael Ryan, *Prostitution in London* (London: H. Bailliere, 1839), p. 170.
177. See, for example, *Memoirs* (1830) and *Memoirs* (1836).
178. *Memoirs* (1836), pp. 7–8.
179. Luce Irigaray, *An Ethics of Sexual Difference* (London: The Athlone Press, 1993), p. 11.

CHAPTER 3

1. Captain Gronow, *Reminiscences of Captain Gronow formerly of the Grenadier Guards and M.P. for Stafford being Anecdotes of the Camp, the Court and the Clubs at the close of the last War with France related by himself* (London: Smith, Elder, 1862), pp. 46 and 62.

2. W. M. Weare, *The Fatal Effects of Gambling* (London: T. Kelly, 1824), pp. 409–10.

3. White's was founded at White's Chocolate House in 1693 and in 1787 moved to a building designed by James Wyatt and owned by John Arthur at 37–8 St James's Street. See, for example, Arthur T. Bolton, 'Eighteenth Century Club-Houses – White's', *Country Life* (3 June 1916), pp. 10–14; Algernon Bourke, *History of White's Club* (London: Algernon Bourke, n. d.); Percy Colson, *White's 1693–1950* (London: Heinemann, 1951); Anthony Lejeune, *White's The First Three Hundred Years* (London: A. & C. Black, 1993) and F. H. W. Shepperd (ed.), 'The Parish of St. James's Westminster, Part 2, South of Piccadilly', *The Survey of London* (London: The Athlone Press, University of London, 1960), v. 30, pp. 450–8. See also J. B. Papworth, *Designs for Alterations and Decorations to the Interior, White's Club, 37–8 St. James's St., London* (1842–3), ref. PAP 122 (2), Royal Institute of British Architects Drawings Collection, London.

4. The spelling varies, Brook's, Brooks's, Brookes's. For consistency I have chosen to use Brooks's, unless directly quoting. See for example, *Memorials of Brooks's: From the Foundation of the Club 1764 to the Close of the Nineteenth Century Compiled from the Records of the Club* (London: Ballantyne, 1907); Henry S. Eeles and Earl Spencer, *Brooks: 1764–1964* (London: Country Life, 1964); Philip Ziegler and Desmond Seward, *Brooks's: A Social History* (London: Constable, 1991); James Lees-Milne, 'Brooks's Club, St. James's Street', *Country Life* (14 September 1978), pp. 710–13; Gordon Nares, 'Two Centuries at Brooks's' *Country Life* (1 February 1952), pp. 290–4 and Stanley C. Ramsey, 'London Clubs II – Brooks's', *Architectural Review* (1913), v. 34, pp. 7–11. The club archives are uncatalogued at the Greater London Records Office and include documents of Brooks's, Fox's, St James's and the Dilettante Club, including the Subscription Books from 1764–74, 1779–82, 1794–8, 1799–1805, 1806–13, 1814–21, 1822–8. For an architectural account of the club-house, see J. Mordaunt Crook, 'The Clubhouse', Philip Ziegler and Desmond Seward (eds.), *Brooks's: A Social History* (London: Constable, 1991), pp. 153–60. The most detailed history of the club before it moved to St James's Street is F. H. W. Shepperd (ed.), 'The Parish of St. James's Westminster, Part 1, South of Piccadilly', *The Survey of London* (London: The Athlone Press, University of London, 1960), v. 29, pp. 327–35.

5. The drawings contained in the archives at the Greater London Records Office were returned to Brooks's in 1975. These drawings were unavailable to me, but personal correspondence with Joseph Mordaunt Crook has persuaded me that there are no remaining drawings of the clubhouse from the eighteenth or nineteenth century in the club's possession.

6. See, for example, Roger Fulford, *Boodle's* (London: privately printed for

Members of the Club, 1962); Arthur T. Bolton, 'London Clubs: Boodle's', *Country Life* (9 December 1916), pp. 12–20; Christopher Hussey, 'Famous Clubs and Their Story – Boodle's Club London', *Country Life* (24 December 1932), pp. 716–20; Stanley C. Ramsey, 'London Clubs V – Boodle's Clubs', *Architectural Review* (October 1913), v. 34, pp. 71–6 and Shepperd (ed.), *Survey*, v. 30, pp. 441–9. Contemporary accounts of the building include, *Particulars of a Valuable Leasehold Estate called the Sçavoir Vivre, St James's Street, November 1802* (Boodle's Club Archives); a sketch of the exterior in T. Malton, *A Picturesque Tour through the Cities of London and Westminster* (London, 1792) and a plan of the building from 1804 (part of a series of drawings of the club by John Papworth for alterations carried out in 1821 and 1834). See J. B. Papworth, 'Designs for Alterations to the Morning Room and to the Façade, Boodle's Club, 28 St. James's St., London' (1821), ref. PAP 93 (33), 2–16 and 'Addition of a Kitchen and Dining Room, Boodle's Club, 28 St. James's St., London' (1834), ref. PAP 93 (33), 17–21, Royal Institute of British Architects Drawings Collection, London. Among the more useful items in Boodle's uncatalogued archives are 'Rules and List of Members for Boodle's Club 1762–4'; 'Boodle's Rules' (n. d.); 'Rules and List of Members for Boodle's Club 1762–93'; 'Rules and List of Members for Boodle's Club 1787–9'; 'Boodle's Club Rules 1857–80'; 'Names of the Managers from 1766 –1896'; 'Members Signatures' (commencing 1782); 'Boodle's Membership Book from 1814 –1820' and 'Betting Book' (1783–1855).

7. See, for example, Henry Blyth, *Hell and Hazard or William Crockford versus the Gentlemen of England* (London: Weidenfeld & Nicolson, 1969); Deale, *Crockfords or Life in the West* (London: Saunders & Otley, 1828); Denys Forrest, *Foursome in St. James's: the Story of the East India, Devonshire, Sports and Public Schools Club* (Brighton: Dolphin Ltd, 1982); A. L. Humphreys, *Crockfords, or the Goddess of Chance in St. James's 1828–1844* (London: Hutchinson, 1953); Henry Luttrell, *Crockford-House: a Rhapsody in 2 Cantos* (London: Murray, 1827) and H. T. Waddy, *The Devonshire Club and Crockfords* (London: Eveleigh Nash, 1919).

8. See, for example, Amateur, *Real Life in London, or the Rambles and adventures of Bob Tallyho, Esq. and his cousin the Hon. Tom Dashall, through the metropolis; exhibiting a living picture of fashionable characters, manners and amusements in high and low life* (London: Jones & Co., 1821–2), v. 1, pp. 290–314 and Bernard Blackmantle, *The English Spy* (London: Sherwood, Jones and Co., 1825), v. 1, pp. 372–7 and v. 2, pp. 247–52. For Brooks's see, in particular, Robert Cruikshank, 'The Great Subscription Room at Brooks's: Opposition Members engaged upon Hazard-ous Points', Blackmantle, *English*, v. 2, p. 252, plate 20; T. Rowlandson, 'The Great Subscription Room' (London: 1808) and T. Rowlandson, 'Gaming at Brooks Club, 60 St. James's St.' (*c.* 1810–15).

9. J. M. Scott, *The Book of Pall Mall* (London: Heinemann, 1965), p. 102.
10. Maginn, *The Clubs of London with Anecdotes of their Members, Sketches of Character and Conversations in Two Volumes* (London: Henry Colburn, 1828), v. 1, p. 2.
11. Shepperd (ed.), *Survey*, v. 30, p. 432.
12. See Judith Squires, 'Private Lives, Secluded Places, Privacy as Political Possibility', *Environment and Planning D: Society and Space* (1994), v. 12, pp. 387–410, p. 389 and Peter Stallybrass and Allon White, *The Politics and Poetics of Transgression* (London: Methuen, 1986), p. 98.
13. Brian Harrison, *Drink and the Victorians: the Temperance Question in England 1815–72* (London: Faber, 1971).
14. See, for example, Bryant Lillywhite, *London Coffee Houses* (London: George Allen & Unwin, 1963), p. 26. The Thatched House Tavern was established in 1704 or 1705. See Shepperd (ed.), *Survey*, v. 30, p. 466. For the Pugilistic Society, see Pierce Egan, *Boxiana* (London: Sherwood, Neely & Jones, 1818), p. 27. For Almack's, see, for example Scott, *Book*, pp. 70–1 and Shepperd (ed.), *Survey*, v. 29, pp. 327–35.
15. John Feltham, *Picture for London for 1818*, 19th edition (London: Longman, Hurst, Rees, Orme & Brown, 1818), pp. 411 and 414–15.
16. Shepperd (ed.), *Survey*, v. 30, p. 443.
17. See 'Subscription Book' (1779–82), Brooks's Club Archives, n. p., rules 8–11, 36–7 and 39. These rules remained in 'Subscription Book' (1794–98), 'Subscription Book' (1799–1805) and 'Subscription Book' (1806–13). See also 'Subscription Book' (1814–21), Brooks's Club Archives, n. p., rules 8–11 and 27–9. See 'Original Rules and List of Members & C. Boodle's Club 1787–91', London, Boodle's Club Archives, n. p., rule 3.
18. Captain Gronow, *Captain Gronow's last Recollections being the Fourth and Final Series of the Reminiscences and anecdotes with a portrait* (London: Smith, Elder, 1866), pp. 137–8; Blackmantle, *Spy*, v. 1, p. 375; Deale, *Crockfords*, v. 1, pp. 172–92 and Andrew Steinmetz, *The Gaming Table: Its votaries and victims in all time and countries especially in England and in France* (London: Tinsley Brothers, 1870), pp. 189–90.
19. For example, in Boodle's there had been managers from 1762; see 'Original Rules and List of Members & C. Boodle's Club 1762', Boodle's Club Archives. In Brooks's a managers' group from among the members was formed in 1795. See 'Subscription Book' (1794–8), 14 June 1795, rule 34. In White's the election of three managers was recommended in 1791. See Bourke, *History*, pp. 167–8.
20. Ralph Nevill, *London Clubs: their History and Treasures* (London: Chatto & Windus, 1969), p. 69 and Anon., 'Arthur's: the End of a Famous London Club', *Country Life* (1 June 1940), pp. 546–9, p. 547.

21. *The Macaroni and Theatrical magazine* changed its name to *The Macaroni Savoir Vivre and Theatrical magazine*. See Shepperd (ed.), *Survey*, v. 29, pp. 442–3.

22. See Shepperd (ed.), *Survey*, v. 29, pp. 333–4 and 'Particulars of a Valuable Leasehold Estate called the Sçavoir Vivre, St James's Street' (November 1802), Boodle's Club Archives, London. Only half the document remains.

23. 'Particulars' (November 1802).

24. Peter Fleetwood-Hesketh, 'The Travellers' Club, London', *Country Life* (17 November 1966), pp. 1270–4, pp. 1271 and 1273.

25. Walford, *Old*, p. 143.

26. The drawings for this addition are interesting in that they colour code the separate circulation of members and staff, clearly indicating their social separation in the mind of the architect. See J. B. Papworth, 'Addition of a Kitchen and Dining Room, Boodle's Club, 28 St. James's St., London' (1834), ref. PAP 93 (33), 17–21, Royal Institute of British Architects Drawings Collection, London.

27. 'Original Rules and List of Members & C. Boodle's Club 1787–91', Boodle's Club Archives, n. p., rules 5 and 10.

28. See, for example, Percy Rudolph Broemel, *Paris and London in 1815* (London: Murray & Co., 1929), p. 114; Gronow, *Reminiscences* (1862), pp. 78 and 183–6 and Weare, *Fatal*, p. 269.

29. 'Original Rules and List of Members & C. Boodle's Club 1787–91', Boodle's Club Archives, n. p., rule 6.

30. See Edward Walford, *Old and New London* (London: Cassell, Petter & Galpin, 1873), p. 140 and Scott, *Book*, p. 61.

31. See 'Subscription Book for 1764–74' and 'Subscription Book for 1779–82', Brooks's Club Archives, n. p., rules 7, 22 and 23; 'Subscription Book for 1794–8', Subscription Book for 1799–1805', 'Subscription Book for 1806–13' and 'Subscription Book for 1814–21', Brooks's Club Archives, n. p., rules 7, 21 and 22. See 'Original Rules and List of Members & C, Boodle's Club 1857–80,' Boodle's Club Archives, n. p., rule 10.

32. Felix MacDonogh, 'Vacant Hours', *The Hermit in London* (London: Henry Colburn, 1819), v. 2, pp. 143–53. This account describes the Oriental, founded in 1824 by members of the East India Club who found they did not fit in well to English society. The Oriental Club was built at the west end of Hanover Square by Benjamin Wyatt in 1828. See Forrest, *The Oriental*, p. 23. Another account describes the Nabob Club. See MacDonogh, 'The Nabob Club', *Hermit* (1819), v. 2, pp. 211–16.

33. Feltham, *Picture* (1818), pp. 412–16.

34. Pierce Egan, *Life in London; or, the day and night scenes of Jerry Hawthorn, Esq., and his elegant friend Corinthian Tom, accompanied by Bob Logic, the Oxonian, in their Rambles and Sprees through the Metropolis* (London: Sherwood, Neely & Jones,

1820–1), p. 145–8; William Heath, *Fashion and Folly: or the Buck's Pilgrimage* (London: William Sams, 1822), plate 3; Amateur, *Real*, v. 1, pp. 101–2; MacDonogh, 'A Morning's Ride in a Noble-Man's Curricle', *Hermit* (1819), v. 2, pp. 35–8 'An Exquisite's Diary', v. 3, pp. 79–86.

35. See, for example, F. H. W. Shepperd (ed.), 'The Parish of St. James's Westminster, Part 2, North of Piccadilly', *The Survey of London* (London: The Athlone Press, University of London, 1963), v. 32, pp. 44–5, 98–9, 111–20, 258–9 and 367–89 and Dorothy Stroud, *Henry Holland: His Life and Architecture* (London: Country Life, 1966).

36. Feltham, *Picture* (1818), pp. 286, 412.

37. Gronow, *Reminiscences* (1862), pp. 74–5.

38. Harrison, *Drink*, pp. 39–40.

39. Amateur, *Real*, v. 2, p. 365 and Egan, *Life*, p. 8.

40. Squires, 'Private', p. 393.

41. Scott, *Book*, p. 100.

42. Gronow, *Reminiscences* (1862), p. 46.

43. 'Original Rules and List of Members & C. Boodle's Club 1762–4', Boodle's Club Archives, n. p., rule 12.

44. 'Subscription Book' (1779–82), Brooks's Club Archives, n. p., rule 38.

45. Blackmantle, *Spy*, v. 1, p. 376.

46. See John Philips, 'Characteristic Sketches of the London Club Houses' (London: G. Humphrey, 1829). This is a series of thirteen etchings, of which only four remain, which characterize the clubs through animals; elephants (the Athenaeum), amphibians (the United Services), cheetahs (unnamed but probably Crockford's) and tigers (the Oriental).

47. Bourke, *History*, pp. 151–9. This political rivalry was the subject of much satire. See, for example, J. Gilray, 'Promised Horrors of the French Revolution' (London: H. Humphrey, 1793).

48. For histories of the Reform and Carlton clubs, see Charles Petrie, *The Carlton Club* (London: Eyre & Spottiswoode, 1955); Barry Phelps, *The Power and the Party* (London: Macmillan, 1984); Stanley C. Ramsey, 'London Clubs I – The Reform Club', *Architectural Review* (1913), v. 33, pp. 87–90; Waddy, *Devonshire* and George Woodbridge, *The Reform Club 1836–1978: a History from the Club's Records* (1978).

49. Nevill, *London*, p. 64. Drawings of the club focus on the country-based residency of the membership. See for example, I. Cruikshank, 'A Whist – er at Boodles – or – A Choice Piece of Double Milled Yorkshire Broad Cloth' (London: Fowes, 1820) and J. Gilray, 'Standing Dish at Boodles' (London: H. Humphrey, 28 May 1800).

50. Stanley C. Ramsey states it was built by John Crunden in 1765 to the designs of Robert Adam. See Ramsey, 'London', p. 71. Christopher Hussey asserts

that it was designed and built in 1775 by John Crunden. See Hussey, 'Famous', p. 718. See also Beresford E. Chancellor, *Memorials of St. James's Street, together with the Annals of Almacks* (London: Grant Richards, 1922); Howard M. Colvin, *A Biographical Dictionary of British Architects, 1660–1840* (New Haven & London: Yale University Press, 1995), p. 242 and T. Malton, *A Picturesque Tour through the Cities of London and Westminster* (London: n. p., 1792).

51. The main saloon at Boodle's has also been compared to Soane's Assembly Rooms in Brighton. See Arthur T. Bolton (ed.), *Portrait of Sir John Soane* (London: Soane Museum Publications, 1927), p. 182. For a summary of the spaces, see 'Particulars' (November 1802) and Nevill, *London*, p. 64.

52. See H. Holland, 'Two Alternative Plans and a Perspective for Brooks's Club, St. James's St., London' (1776), (London: Sir John Soane Museum). Anthony Richardson, biographer of the Scottish architect Robert Mylne, asserts that Holland's designs for Brooks's are based on Mylne's for Almack's clubhouse in Pall Mall and that the subscription room is based on Mylne's design for Almack's Assembly Rooms in King Street. See Anthony Richardson, *Robert Mylne, Architect* (London: B. T. Batsford, 1955), pp. 22 and 25. Dorothy Stroud also mentions Henry Holland's involvement with Almack's Assembly Rooms. See Stroud, *Henry*, p. 10. See also Eeles and Spencer, *Brooks*, p. 52; Lees-Milne, 'Brooks's', pp. 712–13 and Mordaunt Crook, 'The Clubhouse', p. 159.

53. Damie Stillman, *English Neo-Classical Architecture* (London: A. Zwemmer, 1988), pp. 462–4.

54. If patriarchy is based on the social metaphor of fatherhood and hierarchical domination by men; fratriarchy is based on the social metaphor of brotherhood and collective domination by men. See Mary Anne Clawson, *Constructing Brotherhood, Gender / Class and Fraternity* (Princeton: Princeton University Press, 1989), pp. 4–5. See also Jeff Hearn, *Men in the Public Eye* (London: Routledge, 1991), p. 67 and Carole Pateman, *The Disorder of Women* (Cambridge: Polity Press, 1989), pp. 35, 39 and 42.

55. Gronow, *Reminiscences* (1862), p. 79.

56. Almeric Fitzroy, *History of the Travellers Club* (London: George Allen & Unwin, 1927); Peter Fleetwood-Hesketh, 'Travellers', pp. 1270–4, p. 1271 and Shepperd (ed.), *Survey*, v. 29, p. 399.

57. Shepperd (ed.), *Survey*, v. 29, pp. 386–99.

58. Bourke, *History*, pp. 205–6.

59. Bourke, *History*, p. 189.

60. Gronow, *Captain* (1866), p. 143.

61. See J. B. Papworth, 'Designs for Alterations to the Morning Room and to the Façade' (1821) and 'Addition of a Kitchen and Dining Room' (1834), Boodle's Club, 28 St James's St., London, Ref. PAP 93 (33), 2–21, Royal Institute of

British Architects Drawing Collection, London. See also Fulford, *Boodle's*, p. 21.

62. See Robert Cruikshank, 'Exterior of Fishmongers-Hall, St James's Street, with a view of a Regular Break down', showing "Portraits of the Master-Fishmonger and many well known *Greeks* and *Pigeons*"', Blackmantle, *English*, v. 1, p. 373, plate 24. See also Humphreys, *Crockfords*, p. 23 and Blyth, *Hell*, p. 106.

63. See, for example, Amateur, *Real*, v. 1, p. 102; Blackmantle, *Spy*, v. 2, p. 253; Egan, *Life*, p. 213; Gronow, *Reminiscences* (1862), pp. 74–9 and Felix Mac-Donogh, 'A Morning Ride in a Noble-Man's Curricle', *Hermit* (1819), v. 2, pp. 35–42, especially pp. 40–1.

64. Captain Gronow describes the bootmaker, Hoby, next to the Guards' Club, and the fashionable 'coiffeur', Rowland next to the Thatched House in St James's Street. See Captain Gronow, *Recollections and Anecdotes being a Second Series of Reminiscences of the Camp, the Court and the Clubs by Captain R. H. Gronow (formerly of the Grenadier Guards and M. P. for Stafford)* (London: Smith, Elder, 1863), pp. 136–7. See also Alison Adburgham, *Shopping in Style* (London: Thames & Hudson, 1979), pp. 76–7; Alison Adburgham, *Shops and Shopping 1800–1914* (London: George Allen & Unwin, 1981), p. 7 and Thomas Burke, *The Streets of London* (London: B. T. Batsford, 1940), p. 109.

65. Amateur, *Real*, v. 1, p. 102.

66. A plate from William Heath features St James's Street and some associated verses, *Fashion* (1822), plate 14 and MacDonogh, *Hermit* (1819), v. 5, pp. 36–8.

67. John Badcock, *A Living Picture of London, for 1823, and Strangers guide thro' the streets of the metropolis shewing the frauds and wiles of all descriptions of rogues* (London: W. Clarke, 1828), pp. 47–8. See also Burke, *Streets*, p. 107; Penelope Corfield, 'Walking the City Streets, an Eighteenth Century Odyssey', *Historical Perspectives* (1990), v. 16, pp. 132–74, p. 147 and A. E. Richardson, *Georgian England* (London: B. T. Batsford, 1931), p. 81.

68. Gronow, *Reminiscences* (1862), pp. 210–11.

69. See Gronow, *Captain* (1866), p. 97 and Jacob Larwood, *The Story of the London Parks* (London: Francis Harvey, 1872), v. 8, pp. 283–4. See also Derek Birley, *Sport and the Making of Britain* (Manchester: Manchester University Press, 1993), p. 31.

70. Gentleman Jackson was a figure central to early nineteenth-century boxing. Jackson's Rooms were formerly called D'Angelo's Rooms and belonged to a family who had been running a riding school and fencing academy for 30 years. See Pierce Egan, *Boxiana (Boximania, or Sketches of Ancient and Modern Pugilism)* (London: G. Smeeton, 1812), p. 289; Egan, *Boxiana* (1818) and Pierce Egan, *Boxiana* (London: Sherwood, Neely & Jones, 1821), p. 13. See also Dennis Brailsford, *Bareknuckles: a Social History of Prize Fighting*

(Cambridge: Lutterworth Press, 1988), pp. 70–1. See George and Robert Cruikshank, '*Art of Self-Defence*: *Tom* and *Jerry* receiving Instructions from Mr. Jackson, at his Rooms, in Bond-Street', Egan, *Life*, p. 217.

71. For a description of a typical journey to get to a fight, including the type of transport used, the role of the patrons/nobility and the placing of bets, see Amateur, *Real*, v. 1, pp. 604–20. See also Pierce Egan and Robert Cruikshank, *The Road to a Fight or Going to a Fight at Musley Hurst or a Picture of the Fancy* (1814). This is a continuous strip of pictures, 14 ft by 2.5 inches, wound on a spindle and enclosed in a cylindrical box, with an illustration of a boxing match on the lid. See also Egan, *Boxiana* (1818), pp. 14–15.

72. H. Alken, 'A Private Turn-up in the Drawing Room of a Noble Marquis' (London: Jones & Co., 21 July 1821), Amateur, *Real*, v. 1, p. 620.

73. See George and Robert Cruikshank, '*Cribb's Parlour*: *Tom* introducing *Jerry* and *Logic* to the Champion of England', Egan, *Life*, p. 220. *Boxiana* listed houses kept by pugilists and other people connected with the sporting world around the country and in London. See Egan, *Boxiana* (1821), p. 20. Tom Cribb was a retired Champion of England, beating Tom Molineaux at Thistleton Gap on 28 September 1811. See Egan, *Life*, p. 219.

74. See, for example, Blackmantle, *Spy*, v. 1, p. 57. The links between male-only private education and sporting rituals have been explored by Derek Birley. See Derek Birley, 'Bonaparte and the Squire: Chauvinism, Virility and Sport in the Period of the French Wars', J. A. Mangan (ed.), *Pleasure, Profit, Proselytism* (London: Frank Cass, 1988), pp. 21–41.

75. See Shepperd (ed.), *Survey*, v. 29, pp. 334–5 and 419–24.

76. Dennis Brailsford, *British Sport: a Social History* (Cambridge: The Lutterworth Press, 1992), p. 53. See, for example, E. and J. Weatherby, *The Racing Calendar* (1794–1830); *The Sporting Magazine or Monthly Calendar of the Transactions of the Turf, The Chase, and every other Pleasure interesting to the Man of Pleasure and Enterprise* (1793); John Lawrence, *The Sportsman's Repository*, (1820) and Yorkshire Gentleman, *The Sporting Almanack and Olympic Ephermeris* (London: Knight & Lacey & C. Stocking, 1826).

77. Dennis Brailsford, *Sport, Time and Society* (London: Routledge, 1991), p. xi and Birley, *Sport*, pp. 2 and 4–6.

78. Interview with Mr Edmunds, Secretary of Boodle's Club, July 1995.

79. Deale, *Crockfords*, v. 2, p. 253.

80. The increasing popularity of gambling after 1815 has been attributed to the prolonged war with France, where money received from tours abroad, the lax system of credit and the dominance of paper currency made possible the deferral of payment of debts. See, for example, Birley, *Sport*, p. 129; Mark Clapson, *A Bit of a Flutter: Gambling and English Society 1823–1961* (Manchester: Manchester University Press, 1992), pp. 1–11 and Donald A. Low, *Thieves*

Kitchen: The Regency Underworld (Totowa, NJ: Biblio Distribution Center, 1982), pp. 134–5.

81. See, for example, Gronow, Reminiscences (1862), pp. 76–7 and Steinmetz, Gaming, pp. 180–2.

82. Deale notes the gambling houses in the neighbourhood in 1828, the games played, the stakes placed, the kind of bank and the opening hours. See Deale, Crockfords, v. 2, p. 78. Weare lists the gambling houses in the neighbourhood. See Weare, Fatal, p. 348. Amateur notes the gambling houses and proprietors in the St James's area. See Amateur, Real. v. 1, pp. 290–315.

83. John Badcock, Slang. A dictionary of the Turf, the ring, the chase, the pit, the bon-ton, and the varieties of life, forming the completest and most authentic lexicon balatroni-cum . . . of the sporting world (London: T. Hughes, 1823), p. 291.

84. Amateur, Real, v. 1, p. 291.

85. Deale, Crockfords, v. 1, p. 122.

86. See George Cruikshank's illustrations to verses called the 'Greeks and the Pigeons' (1817), George, Hogarth, p. 170. See, for example, Amateur, Real, v. 1, p. 292; Blackmantle, Spy, v. 2, pp. 247–8 and Deale, Crockfords, v. 1, p. 43.

87. Deale, Crockfords, v. 1, p. 43.

88. Amateur, Real, v. 1, p. 290.

89. The subscription room was so-called because an extra sum had to be paid by members in order to pay the gambling staff. Interview with Mr Edmund, Secretary of Boodle's Club (July 1995). I can find no evidence for this but, as with much club history, it is part of an oral tradition. It may be the case that originally when Brooks's was a club at Almack's house in Pall Mall, the club subscription paid for the hire of the room, food, drink and gambling staff, and that this tradition has continued.

90. Deale, Crockfords, v. 1, p. 225.

91. Amateur, Real, v. 1, p. 196.

92. Bentley's Miscellany, quoted in Waddy, Devonshire, pp. 125–6.

93. Low, Thieves, p. 150.

94. Humphreys, Crockfords, p. 57.

95. Waddy, Devonshire, p. 121.

96. See, for example, Charles Dunne, The Academicans of 1823, or, the Greeks of the Palais Royal, and the Clubs of St. James's (London: Lawler & Quick, 1823), pp. 99–114. The Academicians of 1823 was also published as Rouge et Noir, with French extracts in both and dedicated to his 'Royal Highness the Duke of XXXX and XXXXXX Bishop of XXXXXXXXX Commander in CCCCC' [sic].

97. See, for example, 'An Act for Consolidating into one Act and Amending the Laws relating to Idle and Disorderly Persons, Rogues and Vagabonds, Incor-rigible Rogues and other Vagrants in England', 3 George IV cap. 40 (1822),

Statutes at Large, 3 George IV (1822) (London: His Majesty's Statute and Law Printers, 1822), v. 62, pp. 133–42, ss. 3 and 5.

98. See, for example, 'An Act for the Better preventing Thefts and Robberies, and for regulating Places of Publick Entertainment, and Punishing Persons Keeping Disorderly Houses', 25 George II, cap. 36, n. 4 (1752), *Statutes at Large, 23 George II – 26 George II (1750–2)* (Cambridge: Charles Bathurst, 1765), v. 20, pp. 375–80. This was updated in 'An Act for Making Perpetual an Act passed in the twenty-fifth year of the Reign of His present Majesty, for the better preventing Thefts and Robberies, and for regulating Places of Publick Entertainment, and punishing Persons Keeping Disorderly Houses, for the further punishing persons selling Ale or other liquors without license', 28 George II, cap. 19 (1755), *Statutes at Large, 26 George II – 30 George II (1753–6)* (Cambridge: Charles Bathurst, 1765), v. 21, pp. 290–2.

99. Weare, *Fatal*, p. 405.

100. 'Scene in a Gaming Room', Weare, *Fatal*, pp. 344–5.

101. Weare, *Fatal*, pp. 82–3.

102. Weare, *Fatal*, p. 356.

103. H. Alken, 'A Modern Hell or Fashionable Gaming House', Amateur, *Real*, p. 300.

104. Deale, *Crockfords*, v. 2, pp. 82–3.

105. A Brooks's club anecdote tells of a gaming binge which ran from a Tuesday to a Thursday night. See, for example, Griffiths, *Clubs*, p. 235.

106. Amateur, *Real*, v. 1, p. 290.

107. Weare, *Fatal*, p. 366.

108. Blackmantle, *Spy*, v. 1, pp. 372–7.

109. Deale, *Crockfords*, v. 1, p. 225.

110. Badcock, *Slang*, n. p.

111. See for example, W. Heath, 'Another Unsafe House' (London: Tom McLean, 1829) and John Philips, 'Characteristic Sketches of the London Club Houses' (London: G. Humphrey, 1829).

112. Weare, *Fatal*, p. 354.

113. See, for example, Deale, *Crockfords*; Dunne, *Academicans*; Weare, *Fatal* and Steinmetz, *Gaming*, pp. 260–72.

114. *Oxford English Dictionary*, CD ROM, 2nd edition (1989).

115. Deale, *Crockfords*, v. 1, p. 72.

116. Deale, *Crockfords* , v. 1, p. 65.

117. Blackmantle, *English*, v. 1, p. 377.

118. Letter to *The Times* (22 July 1824), quoted in Deale, *Crockfords*, v. 1, pp. 85–6, footnote.

119. *Sporting Magazine* (April 1819), pp. 5–6.

120. Dunne, *Academicans*, p. 55; Weare, *Fatal*, p. 384 and *Sporting Magazine*

(September 1821), p. 257. See also Low, *Thieves*, p. 127 and Munting, 'Betting', p. 68.
121. See Lejeune, *White's*, p. 229.
122. Amateur, *Real*, v. 1, p. 292.
123. Heath, *Fashion*, plate 21. This plate is untitled in the 1822 edition but accompanied by verse. It is given the title 'Losing their Tippery, at Trent et Un', William Heath, *Fashion and Folly illustrated in a series of 23 Humorous Coloured Engravings* (London: William Sams, 1833), plate 14.
124. In Isaac Cruikshank's 'Dividing the Spoil' (1796) one half of the etching shows working-class prostitutes in St Giles dividing the spoils of their robbery, in the other half, upper-class women in the west divide money won in gambling.
125. Broemel, *Paris*, p. 123.
126. MacDonogh, *Hermit* (1819), v. 3, p. 198.

CHAPTER 4

1. Claude Lévi-Strauss, *The Elementary Structures of Kinship* (Boston: Beacon Press, 1969), pp. 479–80.
2. Gayle Rubin, 'The Traffic in Women: Notes on the "Political Economy" of Sex', in Joan W. Scott (ed.), *Feminism and History* (Oxford: Oxford University Press, 1996), pp. 105–51, p. 118.
3. Beresford E. Chancellor, *Memorials of St. James's Street, together with the Annals of Almacks* (London: Grant Richards, 1922), p. 195.
4. See, for example, descriptions in William Carey, *The Strangers Guide through London: or a view of the British Metropolis in 1808* (London: James Cundee, 1808); John Corry, *The English Metropolis or London in the Year 1820* (London: Sherwood, Neely and Jones, 1820); John Corry, *The English Metropolis or London in the Year 1825* (London: Barnard & Farley, 1825); John Feltham, *Picture of London for 1818*, 19th edition (London: Longman, Hurst, Rees, Orme & Brown, 1818); John Feltham, *The Picture of London for 1821*, 22nd edition (London: Longman, Hurst, Rees, Orme & Brown, 1821); James Grant, *The Great Metropolis* (London: Saunders & Otley, 1838); Samuel Leigh, *Leigh's New Picture of London* (London: Leigh, 1819); J. Britton and A. Pugin, *Illustrations of the Public Buildings of London* (London: John Wedle, 1838); Thomas Shepherd, 'Metropolitan Improvements or London in the Nineteenth Century . . . from the Original Drawings of Thomas H. Shepherd with notes by James Elmes', *London in the Nineteenth Century* (London: Jones & Co., 1 November 1829), v. 1 and Thomas Shepherd, 'London and its Environs in the Nineteenth Century from the Original Drawings by Thomas E.

Shepherd', *London in the Nineteenth Century* (London: Jones & Co., 1 November 1829), v. 2.

5. Amateur, *Real Life in London, or the Rambles and adventures of Bob Tallyho, Esq. and his cousin the Hon. Tom Dashall, through the metropolis; exhibiting a living picture of fashionable characters, manners and amusements in high and low life* (London: Jones and Co., 1821–2); Bernard Blackmantle, *The English Spy* (London: Sherwood, Jones & Co., 1825); Pierce Egan, *Life in London; or, the day and night scenes of Jerry Hawthorn, Esq., and his elegant friend Corinthian Tom, accompanied by Bob Logic, the Oxonian, in their Rambles and Sprees through the Metropolis* (London: Sherwood, Neely and Jones, 1820–1) and William Heath, *Fashion and Folly: The Bucks Pilgrimage* (London: William Sams, 1822).

6. See George and Robert Cruikshank, 'Highest "Life In London" – Tom and Jerry "sporting a Toe" among the Corinthians, at ALMACK'S, in the West', Egan, *Life*, pp. 290–311 and p. 310; H. Alken, 'Almack's: Tom and Bob sporting their figures at a Fancy Dress Ball', Amateur, *Real*, v. 2, pp. 229–41 and pp. 232–3 and Heath, *Fashion*, plate 12. This plate is untitled in the 1822 edition but given the title 'Almack's, a swell evening', William Heath, *Fashion and Folly illustrated in a series of 23 Humorous Coloured Engravings* (London: William Sams, 1833), plate 7.

7. See Blackmantle, 'The Cyprians' Ball or Sketches of Characters at the Venetian Carnival,' *English Spy*, v. 2, p. 48, plate 4 and pp. 39–63 and Heath, *Fashion*, plate 15. This plate is untitled in the 1822 edition but given the title 'Masquerading at the Argyll Rooms', Heath, *Fashion* (1833), plate 8.

8. The architectural history of assembly rooms is not well documented. For an account of eighteenth-century assembly rooms as a neo-classical type, see Damie Stillman, *English Neo-Classical Architecture* (London: A. Zwemmer, 1988), pp. 469–77. For a description of the social life and architecture of provincial eighteenth-century assembly rooms, see Mark Girouard, 'Moonlit Matchmaking: Assembly Rooms of the Eighteenth Century', *Country Life*, v. 180, ns. 4644, 4647 and 4650 (1978), pp. 540–4, 766–8 and 1057–9. For an analysis which links the spatial layout of assembly rooms to social relations of class and power, see Thomas A. Markus, *Buildings and Power* (London: Routledge, 1993). For an examination of concert rooms and assembly rooms in London, see Robert Elkin, *The Old Concert Rooms of London* (London: Edward Arnold, 1955), pp. 74–8.

9. Girouard, 'Moonlit', n. 4650, p. 1058 and n. 4647, p. 767.

10. The Pantheon was designed by James Wyatt and opened in 1772. In January 1794 it burnt down and was rebuilt in 1795 for masquerades and music. The second Pantheon was demolished in 1812 and a third Pantheon rebuilt by Sidney Smirke as a bazaar. See, for example, F. H. W. Shepperd (ed.), 'The Parish of St. James's Westminster, Part 2, North of Piccadilly', *The Survey*

of London (London: The Athlone Press, University of London, 1960), v. 31, pp. 268–83; Beresford E. Chancellor, *The Eighteeenth Century in London: An Account of its Social Life and Arts* (London: B. T. Batsford, 1920), figs. 94 and 95 and Elkin, *Old*, pp. 66 and 70. For descriptions of Carlisle House see, for example, J. R. Smith, 'The Promenade at Carlisle House' (London: J. R. Smith, 1 December 1781); Chancellor, *Memorials*, p. 198 and Simon McVeigh, *Concert Life in London from Mozart to Haydn* (Cambridge: Cambridge University Press, 1993), p. 67.

11. There is very little architectural information about Almack's, no architectural plans, sections or elevations exist. For a brief contemporary description, see an advertisement for Almack's Assembly Rooms addressed to the 'Ladies and Gentlemen, Subscribers to the Assembly in King street St. James's' that appeared in the *Public Advertiser* (15 November 1765) in Robert Mylne's Diary entry for 14 November 1765, quoted in Anthony Richardson, *Robert Mylne, Architect* (London: B. T. Batsford, 1955), p. 65 and F. H. W. Shepperd (ed.), 'The Parish of St. James's Westminster, Part 1, South of Piccadilly', *The Survey of London* (London: The Athlone Press, University of London, 1960), v. 29, p. 305. For other general descriptions of the accommodation at Almack's see E. J. Burford, *Royal St. James's being a Story of Kings, Clubmen and Courtesans* (London: Robert Hale, 1988), p. 197; Elkin, *Old*, p. 80; Richardson, *Robert*, pp. 63–4; Shepperd (ed.), *Survey*, v. 29, pp. 304–7 and Edward Walford, *Old and New London* (London: Cassell, Petter & Galpin, 1873), p. 193.

12. Accounts of Almack's can be found in contemporary diaries and novels. See, for example: Captain Gronow, *Reminiscences of Captain Gronow formerly of the Grenadier Guards and M. P. for Stafford being Anecdotes of the Camp, the Court and the Clubs at the close of the last War with France related by himself* (London: Smith, Elder & Co., 1862); Captain Gronow, *Recollections and Anecdotes being a Second Series of Reminiscences of the Camp, the Court and the Clubs by Captian R. H. Gronow (formerly of the Grenadier Guards and M. P. for Stafford)* (London: Smith, Elder, 1863); Captain Gronow, *Celebrities of London and Paris being a Third Series of Reminiscences and Anecdotes of the Camp, the Court and the Clubs containing a correct account of the Coup D'etat by Captain R. H. Gronow formerly of the Grenadier Guards and M. P. for Stafford* (London: Smith, Elder, 1865); Captain Gronow, *Captian Gronow's last Recollections being the Fourth and Final Series of the Reminiscences and anecdotes with a portrait* (London: Smith, Elder, 1866); Prince Puckler-Muskau, *Tour in England, Ireland, and France* (London: Effingham Wilson, 1832); Marianne Spencer Stanhope, *Almack's: A Novel in three volumes* (London: Saunders & Otley, 1826); Charles White, *Almack's Revisited* (London: 1828) and G. Yates, *The Ball or a Glance at Almack's in 1829* (London: Henry Colburn). There was another Almack's in Brighton, described by Prince Puckler-Muskau, and a series of magazines, *Almack's 1827–8* (Brighton: Taylor & Son, 1827). A

number of secondary social histories of London which deal specifically with St James's mention Almack's: for example, Burford, *Royal*, pp. 117–18 and 195–269 and Chancellor, 'The Annals of Almack's', *Memorials*, part 2, pp. 195–269.

13. For exterior views of Almack's, see, for example, Burford, *Royal*, p. 197; 'Willis's Rooms, King Street', Elkin, *Old*, p. 80 and Shepperd (ed.), *Survey*, v. 30, plate 51a.

14. For accounts of Almack's interiors, see letter from Gilly Williams to George Selwyn (22 February 1765) quoted in Stephen Turner, 'Almack's and Society', *History Today*, v. 26, n. 4 (April 1976), pp. 241–9, p. 242. See also letter from Walpole to Lord Hertford (14 February 1765), quoted in Chancellor, *Memorials*, p. 199; Burford, *Royal*, p. 117 and Shepperd (ed.), *Survey*, v. 29, p. 306. For interior views. See, for example, 'London: Almack's Ballroom', Richardson, *Robert*, p. 24, fig. 10 and 'The Ball Room, Willis' Rooms', Walford, *Old*, p. 19. For satirical etchings of Almack's, see G. Cruikshank, 'Longitude and Lattitude of St Petersburgh' (1813).

15. The building was burned down in 1830. See Elkin, *Old*, pp. 115–22; David Reynolds (ed.), *Weber in London 1826* (London: Oswald Wolff, 1976), p. 38; John Summerson, *John Nash: Architect to King Geoge IV* (London: George Allen & Unwin, 1935), pp. 224–5 and M. Wilson Disher, *Pleasures of London* (London: Robert Hale, 1950), p. 173.

16. Elkin, *Old*, pp. 92–104.

17. Reynolds (ed.), *Weber*, p. 38.

18. J. Britton, *The Original Picture of London enlarged and improved being a correct guide for the stranger as well as for the inhabitant of the Metropolis of the British Empire together with a description of the environs*, 26th edition (London: Longman, Rees, Orme, Brown & Green, 1827), p. 363.

19. Luce Irigaray, 'Women on the Market', *This Sex which is not One* (Ithaca: Cornell University Press, 1985), pp. 170–91, p. 172.

20. Chancellor, *Memorials*, p. 216.

21. Irigaray, 'Women', p. 172.

22. For a discussion of the relationship between women and property from a theoretical and anthropological perspective, see, for example, René Hirschon, *Women and Property – Women as Property* (London: Croom Helm, 1984), pp. 1–20.

23. Sybil Wolfram, *In-Laws and Out-Laws: Kinship and Marriage in England* (London: Croom Helm, 1987), p. 75, footnote 11 and Lawrence Stone, *The Family, Sex and Marriage in England 1500–1800* (London: Penguin, 1990), p. 70.

24. Leonore Davidoff and Catherine Hall, *Family Fortunes* (Chicago: Chicago University Press, 1987), pp. 205–6.

25. Joan Perkin, *Women and Marriage in Nineteenth-Century England* (London: Routledge, 1989), p. 5.

26. Davidoff and Hall, *Family*, p. 209.
27. Stone, *Family*, p. 414.
28. Susan Staves, *Married Women's Separate Property in England, 1660–1833* (London: Harvard University Press, 1990), p. 4.
29. Staves, *Married*, p. 6.
30. Perkin, *Women*, p. 53 and Wolfram, *In-Laws*, p. 74.
31. John Habakkuk, *Marriage, Debt, and the Estates System: English Landownership 1650–1950* (Oxford: Clarendon Press, 1994), pp. 171–2.
32. Stone, *Family*, p. 72.
33. Alison Adburgham, *Shopping in Style* (London: Thames and Hudson, 1979), p. 40.
34. Habakkuk, *Marriage*, p. 172.
35. See Davidoff and Hall, *Family*, p. 210 and Rogers, 'Money', p. 278.
36. Habakkuk, *Marriage*, p. 199. There is considerable debate over the exact relations between the aristocracy and the bourgeoisie in terms of principles of mobility and exclusivity in marriage patterns. Nicholas Rogers bases his argument on the typical example of the city aldermen. See Nicholas Rogers, 'Money, Land and Lineage: the Big Bourgeoisie of Hanoverian London', Peter Borsay (ed.), *The Eighteenth Century Town 1688–1820* (Harlow: Longman, 1990), pp. 268–314, p. 207. Donna Andrew argues however that aldermen are not typical of London's big bourgeoisie. See Donna Andrew, 'Alderman and the Big Bourgeoisie of London reconsidered', *Social History* (1981), v. 6, n. 3, pp. 359–64.
37. Stone, *Family*, pp. 72–3.
38. Rogers, 'Money', p. 281.
39. David Cannadine, *Aspects of Aristocracy: Grandeur and Decline in Modern Britain* (New Haven & London: Yale University Press, 1994), pp. 10–11 and 209.
40. Wolfram, *In-Laws*, p. 72.
41. Habakkuk, *Marriage*, pp. 205–11.
42. See, for example, Penelope J. Corfield (ed.), *The Impact of English Towns 1700–1800* (Oxford: Oxford University Press, 1982), pp. 27–31 and Rogers, 'Money', p. 279.
43. Leonore Davidoff, *The Best Circles* (London: Croom Helm, 1986), p. 21.
44. Girouard, 'Moonlit', n. 4644, p. 544 and Stone, *Family*, pp. 50–1 and 213.
45. Corfield (ed.), *Impact*, p. 30.
46. Girouard, 'Moonlit', n. 4650, p. 1059.
47. Girouard, 'Moonlit', n. 4644, p. 542.
48. Stanhope, *Almack's*.
49. Karl Marx, *Capital: the Process of Production of Capital* (Harmondsworth, Middlesex: Penguin, 1976), p. 178.
50. Puckler-Muskau, *Tour* (10 February 1827), v. 6, p. 325.

51. C. C. Harris, *Kinship* (Milton Keynes: Open University, 1990), p. 93.
52. Girouard, 'Moonlit', n. 4644, pp. 543–4 and 767.
53. After Almack's death in 1792, the management passed to James Willis, the proprietor of the Thatched House Tavern in St James's Street. See Shepperd (ed.), *Survey*, v. 29, p. 306.
54. William Jackson quoted in McVeigh, *Concert*, p. 12.
55. Priestley, *Prince*, p. 45.
56. Puckler-Muskau, *Tour* (15 April 1827), v. 4, p. 16.
57. Almack was granted the lease on four small houses on the south side of King Street abutting Bingham's Yard from September 1764 to March 1765. See Shepperd (ed.), *Survey*, v. 29, pp. 304–5.
58. This 'female' club consisted of Mrs Fitzroy, Lady Pembroke, Mrs Meynell, Lady Molyneux, Miss Pelham, and Miss Lloyd. See letter from Horace Walpole to Montagu. See Shepperd (ed.), *Survey*, v. 29, p. 334, footnotes 85–7.
59. Letter from Mrs Boscawen to Mrs Delaney, quoted in Turner, 'Almack's', p. 242.
60. This group consisted of the Countess of Jersey, the Countess of Sefton, the Countess Cowper, the Viscountess Castlereagh, Mrs Drummond-Burrell, later Lady Willoughby, Princess Lieven (wife of the Russian ambassador) and Princess Esterházy (wife of the Austrian ambassador). See Gronow, *Reminiscences* (1862), p. 43.
61. 'A Board of Red Cloth' (London: S. W. Fores, 18 February 1827). See Alison Adburgham, *Silver Fork Society: Fashionable Life and Literature* (London: Constable, 1983), p. 104.
62. Puckler-Muskau, *Tour* (10 February 1827), v. 6, p. 325.
63. Eileen Moers, *The Dandy: Brummel to Beerbohm* (Lincoln: University of Nebraska Press, 1978), p. 45.
64. McVeigh, *Concert*, pp. 11–12.
65. Gronow, *Reminiscences* (1862), p. 43.
66. Yates, *Ball*, p. 65.
67. Places of public entertainment in the parish of St James's included an early concert hall (1775–1800), a casino in Great Marlborough Street (1778–81), the Great Room in Piccadilly (1778–1817), the Assembly Rooms, Oxford Street (1772) and the Argyll Rooms, Little Argyle Street (1806–30). See Shepperd (ed.), *Survey*, v. 31, p. 12.
68. See, for example, George Rudé, *Hanoverian London 1714–1808* (London: Secker & Warburg, 1971), p. 72; Adburgham, *Shopping*, p. 74 and P. J. Atkins, 'The Spatial Configuration of Class Solidarity in London's West End 1792–1939', *Urban History Year Book* (1990), v. 17, pp. 36–65, pp. 37–8.
69. Egan, *Life*, pp. 286 and 310.

70. Richard Rush, *A Residence at the Court of London* (London: Century, 1987), (16 April 1818), pp. 93–4.

71. For example, in 1819 Thomas Moore stayed till 3 a.m. See *Thomas Moore's Diary* (May 1919), quoted in Chancellor, *Memorials*, p. 219.

72. Egan, *Life*, pp. 293–4.

73. Francis Grose, *A Classical Dictionary of the Vulgar Tongue* (London: S. Hooper, 1788), n. p.

74. Egan, *Life*, p. 167.

75. George Andrewes, *The Stranger's Guide or the Frauds of London detected etc.* (London: J. Bailey, 1808), pp. 23–4.

76. Phebe Philips, *The Woman of the Town* (London: J. Roe & Ann Lemoine, 1809), p. 18.

77. George Smeeton, *Doings in London; or Day and Night Scenes of the frauds, frolics, manners and depravities of the Metropolis* (London, Southwark: Smeeton, 1828), p. 85.

78. Guardian Society, *Report of the Provisional Committee of the Guardian Society for the Preservation of Public Morals providing Temporary Asylums for Prostitutes Removed by the Operation of the Laws from the Public Streets and Affording to such as Them as are Destitute Employment and Relief Submitted to a General Meeting held at the City of London Tavern on Wednesday 13th December 1815* (London: James Low, 1816), p. 17.

79. Blackmantle, *English*, v. 2, pp. 54–8, plate 4. Stella Margetson argues that Cyprians would not have been allowed at Almack's. See Margetson, *Leisure*, p. 27.

80. Yates, *Ball*, p. 49.

81. *The Times*, quoted in M. D. George, *Hogarth to Cruikshank: Social Change in Graphic Satire* (Harmondsworth: Penguin, 1967), p. 172.

82. Shepperd (ed.), *Survey*, v. 29, p. 305.

83. Walpole (16 Dec 1764), quoted in Chancellor, *Memorials*, p. 198.

84. Shepperd (ed.), *Survey*, v. 29, p. 306 and Girouard, 'Moonlit', n. 4644, p. 543.

85. Walford, *Old*, pp. 196–200 and Elkin, *Old*, p. 75.

86. Girouard, 'Moonlit', n. 4644, p. 543.

87. John Summerson, *John Nash: Architect to King Geoge IV* (London: George Allen & Unwin, 1935), p. 225.

88. E. W. Bulwer, *Godolphin*, quoted in George, *Hogarth*, p. 163.

89. Amateur, *Real*, v. 2, p. 234.

90. Blackmantle, *English*, v. 2, p. 62.

91. Puckler-Muskau, *Tour* (7 June 1827), v. 4, p. 28.

92. Yates, *Ball*, p. 53.

93. Yates, *Ball*, p. 51.

94. R. S. Neale, *Bath: a Social History 1680–1800* (London: Routledge & Kegan Paul, 1981), p. 225.

95. George, *Hogarth*, p. 66 and McVeigh, *Concert*, p. 14.
96. Rush, *Residence* (16 April 1818), p. 93.
97. Gronow, *Reminiscences* (1862), pp. 44–5.
98. Girouard, 'Moonlit', n. 4644, p. 543.
99. Turner, 'Almack's, p. 244. There is disagreement over the date of introduction of the quadrille. Raikes gives the date as 1813, see Walford, *Old*, p. 197. Gronow gives the date as 1811, see Gronow, *Reminiscences* (1862), p. 45. The etching 'First Quadrille Danced at Almack's' is dated 1812.
100. Yates, *Ball*, p. 6.
101. Quoted in Walford, *Old*, p. 198.
102. Gronow, *Reminiscences* (1862), p. 45 and Yates, *Ball*, p. 55.
103. Felix MacDonogh, *Hermit in London or Sketches of English Manners*, 3 volumes in 2 (London: H. Colburn & Co., 1822), v. 2, p. 126.
104. For satirical etchings of dances as indecent, see Burney, 'Waltz' (London: n.d.) and Bunbury, 'The Long Minuet as danced at Bath' (1787).
105. MacDonogh, *Hermit* (1822), v. 2, p. 127.
106. Yates, *Ball*, pp. 76–7.
107. Mrs Calvert's Journal (10 April 1818), quoted in Turner, 'Almack's', p. 246.
108. MacDonogh, *Hermit* (1822), v. 2, p. 125.
109. Anon., 'Review of Marianne Hudson, *Almack's 1827–8*' (Brighton: Taylor & Son, 1827), p. 15.
110. Yates, *Ball*, pp. 46–7.
111. See Tom Moore's Diary entries of May and June 1826, quoted in Chancellor, *Memorials*, pp. 219–20. See also Yates, *Ball*, p. 58.
112. Yates, *Ball*, pp. 4 and 35–6.
113. Irigaray, *This*, p. 84.
114. Egan, *Life*, p. 194.
115. Celina Fox and Aileen Ribeiro, *Masquerade* (London: Museum of London, 1983), p. 2.
116. Fox and Ribeiro, *Masquerade*, p. 8.
117. Terry Castle, *The Female Thermometer: Eighteenth Century Culture and The Invention of the Uncanny* (Stanford: Stanford University, 1994), p. 84.
118. Britton, *Original*, p. 360 and Feltham, *Picture* (1821), pp. 295–6.
119. Amateur, *Real*, v. 1, pp. 626–42 and v. 2, pp. 513–16; Blackmantle, *English*, v. 2, pp. 626–7 and Egan, *Life*, p. 338.
120. Puckler-Muskau, *Tour* (10 July 1827), v. 4, p. 7.
121. Peter Stallybrass and Allon White, *The Politics and Poetics of Transgression* (London: Methuen, 1986).
122. Rob Shields (ed.), *Lifestyle Shopping* (London: Routledge, 1992), pp. 7–8.
123. Castle, *Female*, p. 83.

124. H. Alken, 'Masquerade: Tom and Bob keeping it up in Real Character', Amateur, *Real* (London: Jones and Co., 1822), v. 1, pp. 626–42 and 632; Blackmantle, *English*, v. 2, p. 642; George and Robert Cruikshank, '*Tom* and *Jerry* larking at a Masquerade Supper at the Opera-House', Egan, *Life*, pp. 191–212 and 192 and Heath, *Fashion* (1822), plate 15. This plate is untitled in the 1822 edition but given the title 'Masquerading at the Argyll Rooms', Heath, *Fashion* (1833), plate 8. See also Theodore Lane, 'Masquerade, Argyle Room' (London: Proprietor of Argyll Rooms, 1826). According to the British Museum Catalogue 1820–7 this etching shows one of C. Wright's masquerades.
125. By the beginning of the sixteenth century the word masque replaced mumming and disguising. See F. S. Forrester, *Ballet In England: A Bibliography and Survey c. 1700 – June 1966* (London: The Library Association, 1968), pp. 60–1.
126. Castle, *Female*, p. 82.
127. Castle, *Female*, p. 88.
128. Fox and Ribeiro, *Masquerade*, p. 7 and Forrester, *Ballet*, p. 61.
129. *Masquerade: Catalogue to an Exhibition* (2 July – 2 October 1983), Museum of London, London.
130. Egan, *Life*, pp. 194 and 201–2.
131. Fox and Ribeiro, *Masquerade*, pp. 7–8 and Castle, *Female*, p. 96.
132. Blackmantle, *English*, v. 2, pp. 628–9.
133. Castle, *Female*, p. 86.
134. MacDonogh, *Hermit* (1822), v. 2, pp. 92–3.
135. MacDonogh, *Hermit* (1822), v. 2, p. 96.
136. MacDonogh, *Hermit* (1822), v. 2, pp. 91–2.
137. See Heath, *Fashion* (1822), plate 15 and Heath, *Fashion* (1833), plate 8.
138. MacDonogh, *Hermit* (1822), v. 3, p. 195.
139. For fights after masquerades, see, for example, Thomas Kelly, 'Scene at the Breaking Up of a Fashionable Rout', A. Thornton, *Don Juan* (London: T. Kelly, 6 July 1822), v. 1, n. 20 and H. Alken, 'A Touch at the Fine Arts – A Striking Effect – the Handling by no means good, or pleasant to the eye', Thomas McLean, *Repository of Wit and Humour* (London, 1824). See also Burford, *Royal*, p. 146.
140. *Memoirs of the Life Public and Private Adventures of Madame Vestris* (London: John Duncombe, 1836), p. 51.
141. Egan, *Life*, p. 192, footnote unnumbered.
142. Fox and Ribeiro, *Masquerade*, p. 11.
143. Castle, *Female*, pp. 91–2.
144. Egan, *Life*, p. 194.

CHAPTER 5

1. Amateur, *Real Life in London, or the Rambles and adventures of Bob Tallyho, Esq. and his cousin the Hon. Tom Dashall, through the metropolis; exhibiting a living picture of fashionable characters, manners and amusements in high and low life* (London: Jones & Co., 1821–2), p. 209.

2. Pierce Egan, *Life in London; or, the day and night scenes of Jerry Hawthorn, Esq., and his elegant friend Corinthian Tom, accompanied by Bob Logic, the Oxonian, in their Rambles and Sprees through the Metropolis* (London: Sherwood, Neely and Jones, 1820–1), p. 329.

3. The terms King's Theatre or Italian Opera House are used interchangeably in the 1820s. I have chosen to use Italian Opera House, unless referring to a specific source.

4. See Egan, *Life* and Bernard Blackmantle, *The English Spy* (London: Sherwood, Jones & Co., 1825).

5. Amateur, *Real*, v. 1, pp. 209–10.

6. Egan, *Life*, p. 29.

7. The archives for the Italian Opera House are held at the Theatre Museum and contain a number of useful documents. Other useful primary sources include Edward Wedlake Brayley, *Accounts of the London Theatres* (London: J. Taylor Architectural Library, 1827); J. Britton, *The Original Picture of London enlarged and improved being a correct guide for the stranger as well as for the inhabitant of the Metropolis of the British Empire together with a description of the environs*, 26th edition (London: Longman, Rees, Orme, Brown & Green, 1827); J. Britton and A. Pugin, *Illustrations of the Public Buildings of London*, 2nd edition (London: John Wedle, 1838), v. 1; John Ebers, *Seven Years of the King's Theatre* (London: William Harrison Ainsworth, 1828) and Papworth, *Illustrations of the Public Buildings of London* (London: 1825). See also drawings by John Nash and G. S. Repton, 'Ground Plan, South and East Elevations of "The King's Opera House"' (1817), ref. K2/2, (1–3), Royal Institute of British Architects Drawings Collection, London. See also A. Pugin (del.), J. Roffe (Sculpt.), 'Plans, South Elevation, East Front Elevation from Haymarket' (1818). For secondary sources see H. Barton Barker, *The London Stage its History and Traditions from 1576–1888* (London: W. H. Allen, 1889); Daniel Nalbach, *The King's Theatre 1704–1867* (London: The Society for Theatre Research, 1972); F. H. W. Shepperd (ed.), 'The Parish of St. James's Westminster, Part 1, South of Piccadilly', *The Survey of London* (London: The Athlone Press, University of London, 1960), v. 29 and William Charles Smith, *The Italian Opera and Contemporary Ballet in London 1789–1820* (London: Society for Theatre Research, 1955).

8. Britton, *Original*, p. 363. See also John Feltham, *Picture of London for 1818*,

19th edition (London: Longman, Hurst, Rees, Orme & Brown, 1818), pp. 294–5.

9. See 'An Act for the Better preventing Thefts and Robberies, and for regulating Places of Publick Entertainment, and Punishing Persons Keeping Disorderly Houses', 25 George II, cap. 36, n. 4 (1752), *Statutes at Large, 23 George II – 26 George II (1750–2)* (Cambridge: Charles Bathurst, 1765), v. 20, pp. 375–80, p. 375.

10. Britton, *Original*, pp. 353 and 356.

11. Prince Puckler-Muskau, *Tour in England, Ireland, and France* (London: Effingham Wilson, 1832), (18 February 1927), v. 3, p. 364. See, for example, King's Theatre Playbill, 'Il Flauto Magico', 'Blue Devils', 'Adolphe et Mathilde' (29 May 1820), King's Theatre Archives, 1820, Theatre Museum, London.

12. Ebers, *Seven*, p. xix. English Opera was performed at the English Opera House in the Strand. See Britton, *Original*, p. 357.

13. John Feltham, *The Picture of London for 1821*, 22nd edition (London: Longman, Hurst, Rees, Orme & Brown, 1821), p. 285. For a full discussion of this point, see Iain Mackintosh, 'Departing Glories of the British Theatre', Celina Fox (ed.), *London: World City 1800–40* (New Haven & London: Yale University Press, 1992), pp. 199–208, pp. 199–201. Mackintosh argues that the two main changes in theatre design in the early nineteenth century were the increase in theatre size and the removal of proscenium arches.

14. See Britton, *Illustrations*, v. 1, pp. 305–6; George Saunders, *A Treatise on Theatres* (London: private, 1790), pp. 80–1 and Shepperd (ed.), *Survey*, v. 29, pp. 239–40.

15. Barker, *London*, p. 254; Brayley, *Accounts*, p. 31 and Britton, *Original*, pp. 365–6.

16. Mackintosh, 'Departing', p. 202.

17. Saunders, *Treatise*, p. 79.

18. Richard Cumberland, *Memoirs* (1806), pp. 57–8, quoted in James Redmond, 'Georgian Theatres and Temples', Dana Arnold (ed.), *George IV and the Metropolitan Improvements: The Creation of a Royal Image* (London: The Georgian Society, 1996), pp. 37–43, p. 39.

19. 'On Living to One's-Self', P. P. Howe (ed.), *The Complete Works of William Hazlitt*, centenary edition (London & Toronto: J. M. Dent & Sons, 1930–4), v. 8, p. 97, quoted in Redmond, 'Georgian', p. 39.

20. Nalbach, *King's*, p. 80.

21. *The Times* (16 January 1815), quoted in Smith, *Italian*, p. 131.

22. 'King's Theatre', *Morning Herald* (22 January 1824), King's Theatre Archives, 1824, Theatre Museum, London and Barker, *London*, p. 251.

23. Ebers, *Seven*, p. 78.

24. Nalbach, *King's*, p. 80.
25. 'King's Theatre', *Morning Herald* (22 January 1824), King's Theatre Archives, 1824, Theatre Museum, London.
26. Shepperd (ed.), *Survey*, v. 29, p. 240, footnote 191 and v. 30, plate 29b.
27. The *Royal Opera Arcade* consists of eighteen groin-vaulted bays each with ground-floor shop, basement and mezzanine. See Margaret MacKeith, *Shopping Arcades: a Gazetteer of British Arcades 1817–1939* (London: Mansell, 1985), p. 82; Margaret MacKeith, *The History of Shopping Arcades* (London: Mansell, 1986); Johann Friedrich Geist, *Arcades: the History of a Building Type*: (Cambridge, MA: The MIT Press, 1983), pp. 311–18 and Shepperd (ed.), *Survey*, v. 29, pp. 248–9 and v. 30, plates 38 and 39 for a detailed description of the arcade.
28. Brayley, *Accounts*, pp. 30–1; Britton, *Original*, pp. 356–6 and Papworth, *Illustrations*, v. 1, pp. 307–8.
29. See drawings by John Nash and G. S. Repton, 'South and East Elevations of "The King's Opera House"' (1817) and 'Ground Plan of "The King's Opera House"' (1817), ref. K2/2 (1–3), Royal Institute of British Architects Drawings Collection, London. See also A. Pugin (del.), J. Roffe (sculpt.), 'Plans, South Elevation, East Front Elevation from Haymarket' (1818), Britton, *Illustrations*.
30. Clive Barker, 'A Theatre for the People', Kenneth Richards and Peter Thomas (eds.), *Nineteenth Century British Theatre* (London: Methuen, 1971), pp. 3–24, p. 18.
31. See, for example, P. J. Atkins, 'The Spatial Configuration of Class Solidarity in London's West End 1792–1939', *Urban History Year Book* (1990), v. 17, pp. 36–65, pp. 37–8.
32. See, for example, Robert Cruikshank, 'The Hall of Infamy. Alias Oyster Saloon in Brydges-Street or New Covent Garden Hell', Blackmantle, *English*, v. 1, p. 399, plate 29; Amateur, 'Attractions of the Theatre Drury Lane' and 'Covent Garden and Modern Drury', *Real*, v. 1, pp. 218–20, 227 and 523–5; George and Robert Cruikshank, '*Tom* and *Jerry* taking Blue Ruin after the Spell is Broke Up', Egan, *Life*, pp. 170–9.
33. Amateur, *Real*, v. 1, p. 523.
34. Francis Grose, *A Classical Dictionary* (London: S. Hooper, 1788), n. p.
35. Amateur, *Real*, v. 1, pp. 209 and 213.
36. Britton, *Illustrations*, 2nd edition, v. 1, pp. 301–2.
37. Shepperd (ed.), *Survey*, v. 29, p. 238, footnote 191.
38. Eluned Brown (ed.), *The London Theatre 1811–66: Selections from the Diary of Henry Crabb Robinson* (London: The Society for Theatre Research, 1966), (6 February 1821), p. 95.
39. *New Monthly Magazine* (1815), referred to in Clifford John Williams, *Madame Vestris: a Theatrical Biography* (London: Sidgwick & Jackson, 1973), p. 15.

40. Britton, *Illustrations*, v. 1, p. 301, footnote to the word saloon.
41. Walley Chamberlain Oulton, *The History of the Theatres of London: Containing an Annual Register of New Pieces Revivals Pantomimes and with Occasional Notes and Anecdotes being a Continuation of Victor's and Oulton's Histories from the Year 1795 to 1817* (London: C. Chappel, 1818), v. 3, pp. 262 and 259–60, footnote.
42. *Morning Chronicle* (9 January 1797), quoted in Smith, *Italian*, pp. 40–1.
43. Tracey C. Davis and Linda Nochlin have explored the erotic geography of theatres in relation to actresses and prostitutes in a slightly later period. See Tracey C. Davis, 'Actresses and Prostitutes in Victorian London', *Theatre Research International* (1988), v. 13, n. 3, pp. 221–34; Tracey C. Davis, *Actresses as Working Women: their Social Identity in Victorian Culture* (London: Routledge, 1991), p. 147; Tracey C. Davis, 'Spectacles of Women and Conduits of Ideology', *Nineteenth Century Theatre* (Summer 1991), v. 19, n. 1, pp. 52–66; Tracey C. Davis, 'Private Women and the Public Realm', *Theatre Survey: The Journal of the American Society for Theatre Research* (May 1994), v. 35, n. 1, pp. 65–71 and Linda Nochlin, 'Manet's Masked Ball at the Opera', Linda Nochlin (ed.), *The Politics of Vision: Essays on Nineteenth-Century Art and Society* (London: Thames & Hudson, 1991), pp. 75–94. See also Norma Clarke, 'From Plaything to Professional', *Gender and History* (1993), v. 5, n. 1, pp. 120–4.
44. Amateur, *Real*, v. 1, pp. 209–15 and Egan, *Life*, pp. 173–7.
45. Marguerite Gardiner, *The Magic Lantern or Sketches of Scenes in the Metropolis* (London: Longman, Hurst, Rees, Orme & Brown, 1823), pp. 101–2.
46. See H. Alken, 'The Hon'ble Tom Dashall and his Cousin Bob, in the Lobby at Drury Lane Theatre', Amateur, *Real*, v. 1, p. 212; George and Robert Cruikshank, '*Tom* and *Jerry* in the Saloon of Covent-Garden Theatre', Egan, *Life*, p. 173 and William Heath, *Fashion and Folly: or the Buck's Pilgrimage* (London: William Sams, 1822), plate 20. This plate is untitled in the 1822 edition but given the title 'A Lounge in Saloon to Quiz the Women', William Heath, *Fashion and Folly illustrated in a series of 23 Humorous Coloured Engravings* (London: William Sams, 1833), plate 10.
47. Puckler-Muskau, *Tour* (21 November 1826), v. 3, p. 128.
48. Egan, *Life*, pp. 173–7.
49. Amateur, *Real*, v. 1, pp. 212–14.
50. Blackmantle, *English*, v. 1, p. 225–7.
51. Ebers, *Seven*, p. 360.
52. King's Theatre Playbill, 'La Chaumière Hongroise' (24 May 1813), King's Theatre Archives, 1813, Theatre Museum, London.
53. James Grant, *The Great Metropolis* (London: Saunders & Otley, 1838), v. 1, p. 30 and Ebers, *Seven*, p. 357.
54. Saunders, *Treatise*, p. 83.
55. Britton, *Illustrations*, v. 1, pp. 281–2.

56. Britton, *Illustrations*, v. 1, p. 284, see chart of dimensions.
57. Britton, *Illustrations*, v. 1, pp. 286–7.
58. Blackmantle, *English*, v. 1, p. 227.
59. Blackmantle, *English*, v. 1, p. 228.
60. Ebers, *Seven*, chapters 1 and 2, Shepperd (ed.), *Survey*, v. 29, pp. 236–43.
61. Felix MacDonogh, 'Confusion of Persons and Ranks in a Scene at the Opera', *The Hermit in London*, 5 volumes in 3 (London: Henry Colburn, 1819), v. 2, pp. 183–5.
62. *Opera House Calculation of the Annual Income or Value According to the Master's Particular of Sale viz. until 1826*, King's Theatre Archives, Theatre Museum, London, rule 1.
63. Britton, *Original*, p. 356.
64. See G. Jones (artist), H. Cook (eng.), 'Proscenium of the Opera House Entrance in the Haymarket' (London: Robert Wilkinson, 1 October 1816). This shows boxes with curtains and full-height partitions occupied by women.
65. Brayley, *Accounts*, p. 31.
66. Blackmantle, *English*, v. 1, p. 225.
67. Blackmantle, *English*, v. 1, p. 226 and Gardiner, *Magic*, pp. 84 and 90–1.
68. In 1789 there were 43 titled female subscribers to the first tier of opera boxes, 12 untitled female subscribers, 49 titled male subscribers and 20 untitled male subscribers.
69. Gardiner, *Magic*, pp. 84–90 and Blackmantle, *English*, v. 1, p. 228.
70. Britton, *Illustrations*, v. 1, p. 282.
71. Benjamin Lumley, *Reminiscences of the Opera* (London: Hurst & Blackett, 1864), pp. 62–3, quoted in Nalbach, *King's*, p. 88. See also Nalbach, *King's*, p. 129.
72. Ivor Guest, 'Dandies and Dancers', *Dance Perspectives* (Spring 1969), n. 37, pp. 3–25, p. 9.
73. Egan, *Life*, p. 329 and Puckler-Muskau, *Tour* (18 February 1927), v. 3, p. 364.
74. Fop: a fool, applied to a girl or one who is foolishly attentive to and vain of his appearance, dress, or manners; a dandy, an exquisite. Fop's Alley: 'a passage up the centre of the pit in the Old Opera House where dandies congregated'. See *Oxford English Dictionary*, CD ROM, 2nd edition, 1989.
75. Gardiner, *Magic*, pp. 80–1 and 96.
76. Nalbach, *King's*, p. 88.
77. Ebers, *Seven*, pp. 358–60.
78. Britton, *Illustrations*, v. 1, p. 298.
79. *The Illustrated London News* (25 March 1843), p. 32.
80. Ballet in mid- to late nineteenth-century Paris has been linked to feminist theories of performance and fetishism. See Lynn Garafola, 'The Travesty Dancer in Nineteenth-Century Ballet', Lesley Ferris (ed.), *Crossing the Stage:*

Controversies on Cross-Dressing (London: Routledge, 1993), pp. 96–106; Kathy Fletcher, 'Review of Lesley Ferris (ed.), *Crossing the Stage: Controversies on Cross-Dancing*', *Nineteenth Century Theatre* (Summer 1994), v. 22, n. 1, pp. 73–9, p. 74 and Abigail Solomon-Godeau, 'The Legs of the Countess', *October* (Winter, 1986), pp. 65–108.

81. See Ebers, *Seven*, p. 113 and King's Theatre Playbill, 'Camilla' (12 May 1812), King's Theatre Archives, 1812, Theatre Museum, London.
82. Blackmantle, *English*, v. 1, p. 226.
83. The last male opera singer appeared on the stage in 1832, thereafter women played the male roles.
84. Captain Gronow, *Reminiscences of Captain Gronow formerly of the Grenadier Guards and M.P. for Stafford being Anecdotes of the Camp, the Court and the Clubs at the close of the last War with France related by himself* (London: Smith, Elder, 1862), p. 180.
85. Puckler-Muskau, *Tour* (21 November 1826), v. 3, p. 114.
86. Anon., *Memoirs of the Life of Madame Vestris of the Theatre Royal Drury Lane and Covent Garden* (London: privately printed, 1830), p. 63.
87. See Garafola, 'Travesty', p. 99 and Solomon-Godeau, 'Legs', p. 98.
88. See Solomon-Godeau, 'Legs', p. 94, footnote 22 and Christy Adair, *Women and Dance: Sylphs and Sirens* (Basingstoke: Macmillan, 1992), pp. 63–9.
89. Joan Lawson, *A History of Ballet and its Makers* (London: Sir Isaac Pitman & Sons, 1964), p. 44.
90. See illustrations of female dancers who performed at the Italian Opera House in the 1820s, M. W. Sharp (painter), Rob Cooper (eng.), 'Madlle Noblet in Cendrillon' (1822) and M. W. Sharp (painter), Rob Cooper (eng.), 'Madlle Mercandotti in Cendrillon' (1822), King's Theatre, King's Theatre Archives, 1822, Theatre Museum, London. For a discussion of similar themes in the context of the later development of romantic ballet, see James Laver, *Costume in the Theatre* (London: George G. Harrap, 1964), p. 170 and Ivor Guest, *The Romantic Ballet In England: Its Development, Fulfilment, and Decline* (London: Phoenix House, 1954). See also illustrations of dancers in Sacheverell Sitwell, *The Romantic Ballet from Contemporary Prints* (London: Batsford Press, 1948).
91. Beth H. Friedman-Romell, 'Breaking the Code: Toward a Reception Theory of Theatrical Cross-Dressing in Eighteenth-Century London', *Eighteenth-Century Representations* (December 1995), v. 47, n. 4, pp. 459–80, p. 467.
92. Anon., *Memoirs of the Life Public and Private Adventures of Madame Vestris* (London: John Duncombe, 1836), pp. 73–4 and 77. See also William W. Appleton, *Madame Vestris and the London Stage* (New York: Columbia University Press, 1974); Charles Pearce, *Madame Vestris and Her Times* (London: Stanley Paul, 1923) and Clifford John Williams, *Madame Vestris: a Theatrical Biography* (London: Sidgwick & Jackson, 1973).

93. Noblet came to the King's Theatre on 21 March 1821 as 'Terpsichore' in a ballet by Monsieur Deshayes called 'Le Prix de la Danse'. See *Dancing Times* (December 1916), King's Theatre Archives, 1821, Theatre Museum, London; Blackmantle, *English*, v. 1, p. 231 and Ebers, *Seven*, pp. 69–72.
94. Ebers, *Seven*, pp. 134 and 185–8 .
95. Blackmantle, *English*, v. 1, p. 209, footnote 43.
96. Brown (ed.), *London* (7 July 1825), p. 111.
97. Anon., *Memoirs* (1836), pp. 73–4.
98. Gronow, *Reminiscences* (1862), p. 180 and Blackmantle, *English*, v. 1, p. 232.
99. Saunders, *Treatise*, p. 36.
100. Blackmantle, *English*, v. 1, p. 330.
101. Marvin Carlson, *Theatre Semiotics: Signs of Life* (Bloomington & Indianapolis: Indiana University Press, 1990), p. 44.
102. The pit was linked to the front of the house via a passage in the basement under the side boxes with a door at the end. See, for example, Richard Southern, *The Georgian Playhouse* (London: Pheiades Books, 1948), p. 35.
103. Ebers, *Seven*, p. 80.
104. Gronow, *Reminiscences* (1862), p. 180.
105. 'Advertisement for the King's Theatre', King's Theatre Archives, 1824, Theatre Museum, London.
106. See Robert Cruikshank, 'The Green Room of the King's Theatre, or Noble Amateurs viewing Foreign Curiosities' (Portraits of ten noble and distinguished patrons of the opera, with those *certain* daughters of Terpsichore), Blackmantle, *English*, v. 1, pp. 208–9 and p. 225, plate 11.
107. Blackmantle, *English*, v. 1, pp. 230–2.
108. Blackmantle, *English*, v. 1, p. 209, footnote 43.
109. See George and Robert Cruikshank, 'The Green-Room at Drury-Lane Theatre – Tom and Jerry introduced to the Characters in Don Giovanni', Egan, *Life*, pp. 323–7.

CHAPTER 6

1. Pierce Egan, *Finish to the Adventures of Tom, Jerry and Logic in their Pursuits through Life in and out of London* (London: J. S. Virtue, 1828).
2. See, for example, Anthony R. Henderson, *Female Prostitution in London 1730–1830* (London: Unversity of London, 1992) and Stanley Dana Nash, *Social Attitudes to Prostitution 1752–1829* (New York: New York University, 1980).
3. Nash, *Social*, p. 26. According to Nash the law was not clear to the Police in 1816, 1817, 1818 and 1822. See *Report from the Select Committee on the State of the Police of the Metropolis, House of Commons, Parliament, Great Britain* (Shannon,

Ireland: Irish University Press, 1816, 1817, 1818, 1822, 1827 and 1828).

4. Nash, *Social*, pp. 18 and 22 and Clive Emsley, *Crime and Society 1750–1900* (London: Longman, 1987), p. 134.

5. See 'An Act for the Better preventing Thefts and Robberies, and for regulating Places of Publick Entertainment, and Punishing Persons Keeping Disorderly Houses', 25 George II, cap. 36, n. 4 (1752), *Statutes at Large, 23 George II – 26 George II (1750–2)* (Cambridge: Charles Bathurst, 1765), v. 20, pp. 375–80 and 'An Act for Making Perpetual an Act passed in the twenty-fifth year of the Reign of His present Majesty, for the better preventing Thefts and Robberies, and for regulating Places of Publick Entertainment, and punishing Persons Keeping Disorderly Houses, for the further punishing persons selling Ale or other liquors without license', 28 George II, cap. 19 (1755), *Statutes at Large, 26 George II – 30 George II (1753–6)* (Cambridge: Charles Bathurst, 1765), v. 21, pp. 290–2.

6. See 'An Act for Consolidating into one Act and Amending the Laws relating to Idle and Disorderly Persons, Rogues and Vagabonds, Incorrigible Rogues and other Vagrants in England', 3 George IV, cap. 40 (1822), *Statutes at Large, 3 George IV (1822)* (London: His Majesty's Statute and Law Printers, 1822), v. 62, pp. 133–42 and 'An Act for the Punishment of Idle and Disorderly Persons, and Rogues and Vagabonds, in that part of Great Britain called England', 5 George IV, cap. 83 (1824), *Statutes at Large, 5 George IV (1824)* (London: His Majesty's Printers, 1839), v. 64, pp. 281–9.

7. For commentaries on the activities of these societies see, for example, Eric Bristow, *Vice and Vigilance: Purity Movements in Britian since 1700* (Totowa, NJ: Rowman & Littlefield, 1977); Maurice Quinlan, *Victorian Prelude: a History of English Manners 1700–1830* (Hamden CT: Archon Books, 1965); M. J. D. Roberts, 'Making Victorian Morals: the Society for the Suppression of Vice and its Critics 1802–86', *Historical Studies* (1981), v. 21, n. 83, pp. 157–73; M. J. D. Roberts, 'The Society for the Suppression of Vice and its Early Critics', *History Journal* (1983), v. 26, n. 1, pp. 315–29 and M. J. D. Roberts, 'Public and Private in Early Nineteenth Century London: the Vagrant Act of 1822 and its Enforcement', *Social History* (1988), v. 13, n. 3, pp. 273–94.

8. See, for example, William Hale, *Considerations on the Causes and the Prevalence of Female Prostitution: and on the Most Practicable and Efficient Means of Abating and Preventing that, and, all other crimes against the virtue and safety of the community* (London: E. Justing, 1812).

9. See, for example, Lock Asylum, *A Brief Account of the Institution of the Lock Asylum for the Reception of Penitent Female Patients, when discharged cured from the Lock Hospital* (London: C. Watts, 1796); Lock Asylum, *A Brief Account of the Institution of the Lock Asylum for the Reception of Penitent Female Patients, when discharged cured from the Lock Hospital with an abstract of the accounts from the first*

Institution to Lady-Day 1802 (London: Philanthropic Society, 1802); R. J. W. Cunningham, *To provide a Refuge for the Criminal is to give a Bounty on the Crime. This principal examined in its application to the Guardian Society and other similar institutions in a Sermon preached for the benefit of that Society* (London: J. Hatchard, L. B. Seeley, J. Low, 1817); Guardian Society, *Report of the Provisional Committee of the Guardian Society for the Preservation of Public Morals providing Temporary Asylums for Prostitutes Removed by the Operation of the Laws from the Public Streets and Affording to such as Them as are Destitute Employment and Relief Submitted to a General Meeting held at the City of London Tavern on Wednesday 13th December 1815* (London: James Low, 1816); Guardian Society, *Report of the Committee of the Guardian Society for the Preservation of Public Morals providing Temporary Asylums for Prostitutes Removed by the Operation of the Laws from the Public Streets and Affording to such of Them as are Destitute Employment and Relief Submitted to a General Meeting held at the Egyptian Hall, Mansion House on Thursday 30th October* (London: James Low, 1817) and Guardian Society, *Report of the Committee of the Guardian Society for the Preservation of Public Morals by providing a Temporary Asylum, with Suitable Employment, for Females who have deviated from the paths of virtue, and who have either been removed, by the operation of the laws, from the public streets, or have been awakened by conscience to a sense of their guilt and danger* (London: printed for the Society, 1827, 1828, 1832 and 1848).
10. Luce Irigaray, *Elemental Passions* (London: The Athlone Press, 1992), p. 63.
11. *A Letter to the Right Rev. the Lord Bishop of London containing a statement of the Immoral and Disgraceful scenes which are every evening Exhibited in the Public Streets by Crowds of half Naked and Unfortuneate Prostitutes to which is added a postscript containing an address to the magistrates of London Westminster and the Borough of Southwark by a Citizen* (London: Williams & Smith, 1808), pp. 13–14.
12. Luce Irigaray, 'Women on the Market', *This Sex which is Not One* (Ithaca: Cornell University Press, 1985), pp. 170–91.
13. Hale, *Considerations*, pp. 14–15 and *A Letter to the Right Rev.*, pp. 4 and 10.
14. *A Letter to the Right Rev.*, pp. 11 and 15; Guardian Society, *Report* (1816), p. 9 and George Smeeton, *Doings in London; or Day and Night Scenes of the frauds, frolics, manners and depravities of the Metropolis* (London, Southwark: Smeeton, 1828), p. 101.
15. Hale, *Considerations*, pp. 14–15.
16. Roberts, 'Making' (1981), p. 166. See also 'An Act' (1822), p. 134 and 'An Act' (1824), p. 282.
17. Roberts, 'Public' (1988), pp. 220 and 276.
18. John Badcock, *A Living Picture of London, for 1823, and Strangers guide thro' the Streets of the Metropolis, shewing the frauds and wiles of all descriptions of rogues* (London: W. Clarke, 1828), p. 70. See also Beresford E. Chancellor, *The Lives of the Rakes* (London: Philip Allan & Co., 1924), pp. 35–6; Beresford E.

NOTES TO PAGES 132-5

Chancellor, *The Pleasure Haunts of London* (London: Constable, 1925), pp. 187–8 and Hilary Evans, *The Oldest Profession: an Illustrated History of Prostitution* (London: David & Charles, 1979), p. 90.

19. See Richard King, *The Complete London Spy for the present year 1781* (London: King's Authority, 1781), p. 76.

20. M. D. Archenholz, *Picture of England containing a description of the laws , customs and manners of England interspersed with curious and interesting anecdotes* (Dublin: P. Byrne, 1791), p. 189.

21. For full descriptions of these nunneries see *Nocturnal Revels: Sketches and Portraits of the Most Celebrated Demi-Reps and Courtesans of this Period* (London: M. Goadby, 1779) and Egan, *Life*, pp. 167–8.

22. See, for example, E. J. Burford and J. Wotton, *Private Vices and Public Virtues: Bawdry in London from Elizabethan Times to the Regency* (London: Robert Hale, 1995), pp. 154–5 and 157.

23. Amateur, *Real*, v. 1, p. 571.

24. Bernard Blackmantle, *The English Spy* (London: Sherwood, Jones & Co., 1825), v. 2, p. 23. See also Phebe Philips, *The Woman of the Town* (London: J. Roe & Ann Lemoine, 1809), pp. 14 and 18 and Harriette Wilson, *Memoirs of Harriette Wilson written by herself* (London: J. J. Stockdale, 1825), v. 1, p. 68.

25. Amateur, *Real*, v. 1, p. 570.

26. Egan, *Finish*, pp. 294–331, p. 250 and Philips, *Woman*, pp. 25–7.

27. Amateur, *Real*, pp. 204–5 and Charles Hindley, *The True History of Tom and Jerry, or, The Day and Night Scenes, of Life in London, from the Start to the finish! With a key to the persons and places, together with a vocabulary and glossary of the flash and slang terms, occurring in the course of the work* (London: Reeves & Turner, 1890), p. 179.

28. Smeeton, *Doings*, pp. 92–3.

29. Amateur, *Real*, v. 1, p. 571.

30. Egan, *Finish*, pp. 214–21.

31. Egan, *Finish*, pp. 337–43. Fires in brothels appear as motifs for hell, damnation and destruction through sexual licentiousness, for example, the fire in the Chandos Brothel, the fire in Charlotte Haye's brothel in King's Place and 'the Bagnio in Flames' in an earlier spy tale. See King, *Complete*, p. 82.

32. Egan, *Finish*, pp. 311–15.

33. Smeeton, *Doings*, p. 93.

34. Blackmantle, *English*, v. 1, p. 233.

35. Smeeton, *Doings*, p. 103.

36. Amateur, *Real*, v. 2, p. 341; Blackmantle, *English*, v. 2, p. 249 and Egan, *Finish*, p. 129.

37. Egan, *Finish*, pp. 276–80.

38. See, for example, 23 May 1820, 20 November 1821, 15 January 1821, 17

May 1822, 13 December 1822, *Report Books of the Captain of the Watch Patrol D2099* (02.11.1819 – 17.01.1824) and 12 July 1824, *Report Books of the Captain of the Watch Patrol D2100* (19.01.1824 – 21.02.1827), for the Parish of St James's, Pall Mall Division, Westminster City Archives, London.

39. Pierce Egan, *Life in London; or, the day and night scenes of Jerry Hawthorn, Esq., and his elegant friend Corinthian Tom, accompanied by Bob Logic, the Oxonian, in their Rambles and Sprees through the Metropolis* (London: Sherwood, Neely & Jones, 1820–1), p. 185.

40. Egan, *Finish*, pp. 294–6 and 313. See also Philips, *Woman*, pp. 25–7.

41. Irigaray, *Elemental Passions*, p. 63.

42. *Rambler's Magazine or Annals of Gallantry or Glee, Pleasure and Bon Ton; a delicious bouquet of amorous, bacchanalian, whimsical, humorous, theatrical and literary entertainment* (London: J. Mitford, 1828), v. 1, n. 1, p. 32 and v. 2, n. 1, p. 212.

43. Archenholz, *Picture*, pp. 193–4.

44. Appendix. Rev. Henry George Watkins, Guardian Society, *Report* (1816), p. 33.

45. *A Letter to the Right Rev.*, pp. 12–13.

46. Hale, *Considerations*, pp. 4–5 and *A Letter to the Right Rev.*, pp. 12–3.

47. Hale, *Considerations*, p. 35.

48. Smeeton, *Doings*, p. 92.

49. Peter Fryer, *The Man of Pleasure's Companion: a Nineteenth Century Anthology of Amorous Entertainment* (London: Arthur Barker, 1968), p. 49.

50. Julia Johnstone, *Confessions of Julia Johnstone written by herself in contradiction to the fables of Harriett Wilson* (London: Benbow, 1825), p. 194.

51. Chancellor, *Lives*, p. 36.

52. Amateur, *Real*, v. 1, p. 524.

53. *Nocturnal Revels*, v. 1, p. 179.

54. King, *Complete*, pp. 58–9.

55. *Nocturnal Revels*, v. 2, p. 145.

56. Egan, *Life*, p. 167.

57. *The Rambler or Fashionable Companion for April being a complete register of Gallantry* (London: T. Holt, 1824), (November 1824), v. 1, n. 8, p. 280.

58. *Letter to the Right Rev.*, p. 11.

59. Egan, *Finish*, p. 214.

60. Luce Irigaray, *The Speculum of the Other Woman* (Ithaca: Cornell University Press, 1985), p. 116.

61. Philips, *Woman*, p. 14.

62. See, for example, *La Belle Assemblée, or, Bell's Court and Fashionable Magazine* (London: J. Bell, 1806), (July 1806), p. 231 and (February 1806), p. 20. See also *La Belle Assemblée, or, Bell's Court and Fashionable Magazine* (London: J. Bell,

1809), (July 1809), pp. 42–3; (August 1809), p. 82 and (September 1809), p. 132.

63. Blackmantle, *English*, pp. 233–4.
64. See, for example, *La Belle Assemblée* (July 1806), p. 231 and *La Belle Assemblée, or, Court and Fashionable Magazine containing interesting and original literature and records of the Beaumonde* (London: Whittaker, Treacher & Co., 1829), (December 1829), v. 10, p. 271.
65. *La Belle Assemblée* (March 1806), p. 93.
66. Mary Wilson, *The Whore's Catechism* (London: Sarah Brown, 1830), translated from Baron Dominique Vivant Denon, *Le Point de Lendemain* (Paris, 1800), p. 76.
67. Archenholz, *Picture*, p. 193 and King, *Complete*, p. 76.
68. Smeeton, *Doings*, p. 93.
69. William Hutton, *A Journey to London* (London: William Hutton, 1818), p. 46.
70. In the saloons and lobbies of theatres, rambling tales describe women employed by brothels to ensure that the clothes borrowed were not stolen. See Amateur, *Real*, pp. 566–7 and 571.
71. Anon., *A Fortnight's Ramble through London, or a complete display of all the Cheats and Frauds practised in that Great Metropolis with the best Methods for eluding them being a true and pleasing narrative of the Adventures of a farmer's son* (London: Dean & Munday, 1817), p. 13.
72. George A. Stevens, *The Adventures of a Speculist or, a Journey through London compiled from papers written by George Alexander Stevens (Author of a Lecture upon Heads)* (London: S. Bladon, 1788), p. 181.
73. *Rambler's Magazine or Fashionable Emporium of Polite Literature* (London: Benbow, 1822), (April 1822), v. 1, n. 4, p. 161. See also Anne Clarke, *Authentic Memoirs of Mrs Clarke in which is portrayed the Secret History and Intrigues of many Characters in the first circles of fashion and high life and containing the whole of the correspondence during the time she lived under the protection of his Royal Highness the Duke of York* (London: Thomas Tegg, 1809), pp. 45–6 and Blackmantle, *English*, pp. 238–9.
74. Stevens, *Adventures*, p. 174.
75. Egan, *Life*, p. 169.
76. Blackmantle, *English*, v. 1, pp. 233–4.
77. Egan, *Life*, pp. 168–9.
78. Egan, *Life*, pp. 168–9.
79. Johnstone, *Confessions*, p. 196.
80. *Rambler's Magazine* (March 1822), v. 1, n. 3, p. 106.
81. Amateur, *Real*, v. 2, p. 441.
82. C. A. G. Goede, *The Stranger in England or Travels in Great Britain containing Remarks on the Politics, Laws, Manners, Customs, and Distinguished Characters of the*

Country and chiefly its Metropolis with Criticism on the Stage (London: Mathews & Leigh, 1807), pp. 79–80.

83. *Nocturnal Revels*, v. 1, p. 141.

84. Egan, *Finish*, pp. 355–7 and 364–7.

85. Gayle Rubin, 'The Traffic in Women: Notes on the "Political Economy" of Sex' (1975), Joan W. Scott (ed.), *Feminism and History* (Oxford: Oxford University Press, 1996), p. 118.

Bibliography

DRAWINGS AND VISUAL MATERIAL

The British Museum Drawings Collection, London

William Herbert, 'Nash Plan for a New Arcade and a New Street at the West End of the Strand and Improvements at Charing Cross' (December 1830), Crace Collection, XVII, view 33.

William Herbert, 'Interior Perspective of the Lowther Arcade' (1830), Crace Collection, XVII, view 33.

Royal Institute of British Architects Drawings Collection, London

John Nash and G. S. Repton, 'Ground Plan, South and East Elevations of the King's Opera House' (1817), ref. K2/2 (1–3).

J. B. Papworth, 'Designs for Alterations to the Morning Room and to the Façade, Boodle's Club, 28 St. James's St., London' (1821), ref. PAP 93 (33), 2–16.

J. B. Papworth, 'Addition of a Kitchen and Dining Room, Boodle's Club, 28 St. James's St., London' (1834), ref. PAP 93 (33), 17–21.

J. B. Papworth, 'Designs for Alterations and Decorations to the Interior, White's Club, 37–8 St. James's St., London' (1842–3), ref. PAP 122 (2).

Sir John Soane Museum, London

Henry Holland, 'Two Alternative Plans and a Perspective for Brooks's Club, St. James's St., London' (1776).

ARCHIVES

Boodle's Archives, Boodle's Club, St James's Street, London

Boodles's Archives are held unindexed at Boodle's Club and include the items listed below, as well as other records for the twentieth century including 'Candidate Books', 'Honorary Members' Books', 'Building Repairs and Alterations', 'Minutes of Committees and Sub-Committees', 'Members'

Requirements', 'Day Books (with Lists of Wine and Food bought by Members)'.

'Boodle's Rules' (no date).

'Rules and List of Members for Boodle's Club' (1762–4).

'Rules and List of Members for Boodle's Club' (1762–93).

'Rules and List of Members for Boodle's Club' (1787–9).

'Boodle's Club Rules' (1857–80).

'Names of the Managers' (1766–1896).

'Members' Signatures' (1782–).

'Boodle's Membership Book' (1814–20).

'Betting Book' (1783–1855).

'Particulars of a Valuable Leasehold Estate called the Sçavoir Vivre, St. James's Street' (November 1802).

'Boodle's Inventory and Valuation of the Tenants Fixtures, Furniture, Books, Linen, China, Glass and other Effects at no. 28 St. James's Street, S. W.'

'The Property of the Proprietors of "Boodle's Club" and agreed to be purchased by a "Syndicate" of the Members' (December 1896).

'Plans for a Ladies' Side' (June 1960).

'Southby's Inventory and Valuation of Furniture, Clocks, Pictures and Prints at 28 St. James's Street, S. W. 1, the property of Boodle's. Taken for the Purpose of Insurance' (September 1985).

'History of the Purchase of the New Crown Lease on the Main Club House of Boodle's at 28 St James's Street from 1st January 1985 to 31st December 2084.'

Brooks's Archives, The Greater London Record Office, Northampton Street, London

Brooks's Archives are unindexed and include documents of Brooks's, Fox's, St James's and the Dilettante Club. The Subscription Books (1764–1880) include the names of club members and the payment of annual subscriptions. The Subscription Books (1765–1821) contain club rules to which members subscribed.

'Subscription Book' (1764–74).

'Subscription Book' (1779–82).

'Subscription Book' (1794–8).

'Subscription Book' (1799–1805).

'Subscription Book' (1806–13).

'Subscription Book' (1814–21).

'Subscription Book' (1822–8).

King's Theatre Archives, Theatre Museum, London

The King's Theatre Archives are held at the Theatre Museum and consist of Box 2482 (historical items concerning the building fabric) and various miscellaneous items filed according to year. Those which have been most relevant to this research are listed below.

'List of Subscribers for 1783' (Box 2482).

'List of Subscribers for 1789' (Box 2482).

'Particular and Conditions of Sale of King's Theatre or Opera House with Machinery, Scenes, Wardrobe, Music and all other Properties belonging to which will be sold Pursuant to an Order of the High Court of Chancery date 5th Day of August 1816' (Box 2482).

'Opera House Calculation of the Annual Income or Value According to the Master's Particular of Sale viz. until 1826' (Box 2482).

'King's Theatre or Opera House to be sold by Private Contract together with its extensive Scenery, Machinery, Wardrobe, Music and other Properties belonging thereof, n. 32' (London: private, n. d.), (Box 2482).

King's Theatre Playbills (1811–25).

J. Hartley (3 October 1826), 'The King v. Duncombe', Court of King's Bench (25 November 1826), (File 1826).

Anon. (Student of the Inner Temple), 'A Commentary on the Licentious Liberty of the Press, in which the recent Publication, entitled, *Memoirs of Harriette Wilson*, is severely censured' (London: Printed for the Author, 1825), (File 1825).

Westminster City Archives, London

'Beadles Reports on Activities during the Night Patrols with the Constables and at the Watch Houses', Pall Mall Division, Parish of St James's, London.

'Charge Books', Pall Mall Division, Parish of St James's, London.

'Report Book of the Captain of the Watch Patrol', Pall Mall Division, Parish of St James's, London'.

'Report Books of the Captains of the Watch Patrol', Pall Mall Division, Parish of St James's, London.

'Church Rates', Pall Mall Division, Parish of St James's, London (1790).

'Water Rates', Pall Mall Division, Parish of St James's, London (1790).

'Paving Rates', Pall Mall Division, Parish of St James's, London (1790 and 1820).

'Poor Rates', Pall Mall Division, Parish of St James's, London (1790, 1800, 1810, 1820 and 1830)

'Watch Rates', Pall Mall Division, Parish of St James's, London (1800, 1810 and 1820).

Ephemera Collection, Museum of London, London

'Whig Club Book May 1784' (Clubs A1).

GOVERNMENT PUBLICATIONS

'An Act for the Better preventing Thefts and Robberies, and for regulating Places of Publick Entertainment, and Punishing Persons Keeping Disorderly Houses', 25 George II, cap. 36, n. 4 (1752), *Statutes at Large, 23 George II – 26 George II (1750–2)* (Cambridge: Charles Bathurst, 1765), v. 20, pp. 375–80.

'An Act for Making Perpetual an Act passed in the twenty-fifth year of the Reign of His present Majesty, for the better preventing Thefts and Robberies, and for regulating Places of Publick Entertainment, and punishing Persons Keeping Disorderly Houses, for the further punishing persons selling Ale or other liquors without license', 28 George II, cap. 19 (1755), *Statutes at Large, 26 George II – 30 George II (1753–6)* (Cambridge: Charles Bathurst, 1765), v. 21, pp. 290–2.

'An Act to extend the Provisions of an Act, (entitled, An act to Amend and make more effectual the Laws relating to Rogues, Vagabonds, and other Idle and Disorderly Persons, and to Houses of Correction) *to certain cases not therein mentioned*', 23 George III, cap. 88 (1783), *Statutes at Large, 22 George III – 24 George III (1782–4)* (Cambridge: Charles Bathurst, 1782), v. 34, pp. 392–3.

'An Act for Consolidating into one Act and Amending the Laws relating to Idle and Disorderly Persons, Rogues and Vagabonds, Incorrigible Rogues and other Vagrants in England', 3 George IV, cap. 40 (1822), *Statutes at Large, 3 George IV (1822)* (London: His Majesty's Statute and Law Printers, 1822), v. 62, pp. 133–42

'An Act for the Punishment of Idle and Disorderly Persons, and Rogues and Vagabonds, in that part of Great Britain called England', 5 George IV, cap. 83 (1824), *Statutes at Large, 5 George IV (1824)* (London: His Majesty's Printers, 1839), v. 64, pp. 281–9.

INTERVIEWS

Interview with Mr Edmunds (Secretary of Boodle's Club), St James's Street, London (July 1995).

Interview with Mr Parkinson (Oxford and Cambridge Club), Pall Mall, London (August 1995).

Interview with Michael Lock (Beadle of the Burlington Arcade), Piccadilly, London (August 1995).

Interview with John Simpson (Beadle of the Burlington Arcade), Piccadilly, London (September 1995).

CATALOGUES

Cruikshank 200 (London: John Lordroper, 1992).
Masquerade: Catalogue to an Exhibition (2 July – 2 October 1983), Museum of London, London.

PERIODICALS

Architectural Journal.
Architectural Review.
La Belle Assemblée, or, Bell's Court and Fashionable Magazine.
La Belle Assemblée, or, Bell's Court and Fashionable Magazine, New Series.
La Belle Assemblée, or, Court and Fashionable Magazine containing interesting and original literature and records of the Beaumonde, Third Series.
Builder.
Country Life.
Covent Garden Magazine or Amorous Repository calculated solely for the Entertainment of the Polite World and the finishing of a Young Gentleman's Education.
Gentleman's Magazine.
Harris's List of Covent Garden Ladies or the Man of Pleasures Kalender, for the Year 1788, containing the histories and some curious anecdotes of the most celebrated Ladies now on the Town, or in keeping and also many of their keepers.
Illustrated London News.
Man of Pleasure's Pocket-Book or the Bon Vivant's Vade Mecum for the Year 1780.
Oxberry's Dramatic Biography (New Series Oxberry's Dramatic Biography and Green Room Spy).
Oxberry's Theatrical Biographies.
Racing Calendar.
Rambler's Magazine or the Annals of Gallantry, Glee, Pleasure, and the Bon Ton; calculated for the entertainment of the Polite World and to furnish a Man of Pleasure with a most delicious bouquet of amorous, bacchanalian, whimsical, humorous, theatrical and literary entertainment.
Rambler's Magazine or the Annals of Gallantry, Glee, Pleasure and Bon Ton.
Rambler's Magazine or the Annals of Gallantry or Glee, Pleasure and Bon Ton; a delicious bouquet of amorous, bacchanalian, whimsical, humorous, theatrical and literary entertainment.

Rambler's Magazine or Fashionable Companion.

Rambler's Magazine or Fashionable Emporium of Polite Literature.

Ranger's Magazine or the Man of Fashion's Companion, being the XXXXX of the Month and general assemblage of Love, Gallantry, Wit, Pleasure, Harmony, Mirth, Glee, and Fancy, containing monthly List of Covent Garden Cyprians; or, the Man of Pleasures Vade Mecum.

Roach's New and Complete History of the Stage from its Original to its Present State including all the entertaining anecdotes of London, Dublin and Edinburgh.

Sportsman's Dictionary.

Sportsman's Repository.

Sporting Magazine or Monthly Calendar of the Transactions of the Turf, the Chase, and every other Pleasure interesting to the Man of Pleasure and Enterprise.

Sporting Almanack and Olympic Ephermeris.

The Times.

World of Fashion and Continental Feuilletons: A Monthly Publication dedicated to High Life, Fashionables, Fashions, Polite Literature, Fine Arts, the Operas, Theatres, embellished with London and Parisian Fashions, and Costumes of all Nations.

BOOKS AND ARTICLES

Anon., 'The Public and Private Life, Amorous Adventures and wonderful exploits at home and abroad of M. Vestris'; 'The Public and Private Life of Miss Paton'; 'The Life, Armours, and Intrigues of Miss Chester'; 'The Extraordinary Life and Private Memoirs of the Marchioness of Cunningham'; 'The Amorous Adventures by Sea and Land of our present monarch William the Fourth [. . .] interspersed with Sketches of the Life of the unfortunate Mrs Jordan'; 'The Public and Private Life of Miss Waylett, the Actress'; *Amatory Biography or Lives of the most seductive Characters of the present day in Monthly Numbers, at Sixpence each, embellished with highly finished full-length portraits* (London: Stockdale, Duncombe, Mitford & Kelly, n. d.).

Anon., *The History of Mary Wood: the Housemaid or the Danger of False Excuses* (Dublin: William Watson & Sons, 1810).

Anon., *Observations on a late Publication: entitled 'A Treatise on the Police of the Metropolis', by P. Colquhoun Esq., by a Citizen of London but no Magistrate* (London: H. D. Symonds, 1800).

Anon., *Tricks of the Town laid open; or a Companion for a Country Gentleman* (London: H. Slater & R. Adams, 1747).

Anon., *The Country Spy or a Ramble through London* (London: n. p., 1750).

Anon., *The Devil upon Crutches in England or Night Scenes in London* (London: Phillip Hodges, 1755).

Anon., *The Midnight Spy or London from 10 in the Evening to 5 in the Morning, exhibiting a Great Variety of Scenes in High Life and Low Life* (London: J. Cooke, 1766).

Anon., *A Sunday Ramble: or a modern Sabbath-day Journey in and about the Cities of London and Westminster* (London: n. p., 1776).

Anon., *The Grecian Courtezan or the Adventures of Lycoris containing a particular description of the Manner of celebrating the ancient Rites of Venus, Bacchus, Cupid & c. with an Account of the Amours of Danae, Lamia, Lais, Thais, and other Devotees of the Temples of Public Pleasure in medio tutissimus ibis King's Place. Printed for M. Hayes, Mitchell, Windsor and other Priestesses of the Cytherean Deity and sold by appointment by all booksellers in Town and Country* (King's Place, London: n. p., 1779).

Anon., *Courtesans of this Period* (London: M. Goadby, 1779).

Anon., *Tricks of the Town laid open; a true caution to both Sexes in Town and Country* (London: Sabine, 1780).

Anon., *Characters of the present most celebrated Courtezans interspersed with a variety of Secret Anedotes never before published* (London: M. James, 1780).

Anon., *Poetical Epistle to the Rev'd Mr Madan on his Thelypthora or a Treatise on Female Ruin in its Causes, Effects, Consequences, Prevention and Remedy by a Nymph of King's-Place* (London: Fielding & Walker, 1781).

Anon., *London unmasked or the New Town Spy* (London: n. p., 1784).

Anon., *The Secret History of the Green Room containing Authentic and Entertaining Memoirs of the Actors and Actresses in the Three Theatres Royal* (London: J. Owen, 1795).

Anon., *Thoughts on Means of Alleviating the Miseries Attendant Upon Common Prostitution* (London: T. Caddell and W. Davies, 1799).

Anon., *An Address to the Benevolent Public in Behalf of the London Female Penitentiary* (London: Shacklewell, 1807).

Anon., *A Letter to the Right Rev. the Lord Bishop of London containing a statement of the Immoral and Disgraceful scenes which are every evening Exhibited in the Public Streets by Crowds of half Naked and unfortunate Prostitutes to which is added a postscript containing an address to the magistrates of London, Westminster and the Borough of Southwark by a Citizen* (London: Williams & Smith, 1808).

Anon., *The Authentic and Impartial Life of Mrs Mary Anne Clarke including numerous original letters* (London: T. Kelly, 1809).

Anon., *Authentic Memoirs of the Green Room for 1801–1804 involving sketches (Biographical, Critical and Characteristic) of the performers of the Theatre Royal, Drury Lane Covent-Garden, and the Haymarket, containing Original Lives and Anecdotes, never before published* (London: J. Roach, 1806, 1815 and 1816).

Anon., *Report from the Select Committee on the State of the Police of the Metropolis, House of Commons, Parliament, Great Britain* (Shannon, Ireland: Irish University Press, 1816, 1817, 1818, 1822, 1827 and 1828).

Anon., *A Fortnight's Ramble through London, or a complete display of all the Cheats and*

Frauds practised in that Great Metropolis with the best Methods for eluding them, being a true and pleasing narrative of the adventures of a farmer's son (London: Dean & Munday, 1817).

Anon., *An Address to the Guardian Society* (London: W. Marchant, 1817).

Anon., *The Actress of the Present Day* (London: James Harper, 1817).

Anon., *Brief Statement of Facts Relative to the King's Theatre* (London: n. p., 1818).

Anon., *Bye Laws and Regulations of the Magdalen Hospital* (London: W. Pew, 1821).

Anon. ('by an amateur'), *Real Life in London, or the furthur Rambles and Adventures of Bob Tallyho, Esq. and his cousin the Hon. Tom Dashall, through the metropolis; exhibiting a living picture of fashionable characters, manners and amusements in high and low life* (London: Jones & Co., 1821–2). This book has been attributed to both Pierce Egan and Richard Dighton by the Guildhall Library Catalogue, and to Jon Bee or John Badcock by Edmund Reid.

Anon., *The Biography of the British Stage being Correct Narratives of the Lives of all the Principal Actors and Actresses at Drury Lane, Covent Garden, the Haymarket* (London: Sherwood, Jones & Co., 1824).

Anon., *A Tale of the Last Century, the Secret Memoirs of Harriott Pumpkin, a Celebrated Actress: from her Infancy to her Seduction of, and subsequent marriage with, a Banker* (London: Duncombe, 1825).

Anon., *The History and Adventures of Miss Betsy Warwick the Female Rambler* (London: T. Sabine, 1825).

Anon., 'Madame Vestris v. the Pamphlet Sellers', *News* (26 November 1826).

Anon., 'Review of Marianne Hudson, *Almack's 1827–8*' (Brighton: Taylor & Son, 1827).

Anon, *Memoirs of the Life of Madame Vestris of the Theatre Royal Drury Lane and Covent Garden* (London: privately printed, 1830).

Anon. (K. Griffenhoofe), *Memoirs of the Life Public and Private Adventures of Madame Vestris* (London: John Duncombe, 1836).

Anon., 'Obituary – Pierce Egan', *Gentleman's Magazine* (November 1849), v. 32, p. 548.

Anon. (Editorial), 'Article on White's Club', *Builder* (17 April 1852), v. 10, n. 480, p. 241.

Anon., *The London Clubs* (London: Henry James, 1853).

Anon., 'Proposed Regent-Street and Bond-Street Arcade', *Builder* (20 February 1864), v. 22, pp. 132–3.

Anon., *Memorials of Brooks's: from the Foundation of the Club 1764 to the Close of the Nineteenth Century compiled from the Records of the Club* (London: Ballantyne, 1907).

Anon., *Athenaeum (founded 1824) Rules and List of Members* (London: Printed for the use of Members only, 1910).

Anon., 'Bond Street', *Country Life* (1 May 1937), pp. i–iv.

Anon., 'Arthur's: the End of a Famous London Club', *Country Life* (1 June 1940), pp. 546–9.

Anon., *The Athenaeum: Club and Social Life in London* (London: Heinemann, 1975).

William Acton, *Prostitution considered in its Moral, Social and Sanitary aspects in London and other large Cities* (London: John Churchhill, 1857).

Christy Adair, *Women and Dance: Sylphs and Sirens* (Basingstoke: Macmillan, 1992).

Parveen Adams and Elizabeth Cowie (eds.), *The Woman in Question* (London: Verso, 1990).

Alison Adburgham, *Shopping in Style* (London: Thames & Hudson, 1979).

Alison Adburgham, *Silver Fork Society: Fashionable Life and Literature* (London: Constable, 1983).

Alison Adburgham, *Shops and Shopping 1800–1914* (London: George Allen & Unwin, 1964).

Kathleen Adler, 'The Suburban, the Modern and une Dame de Paissy', *Oxford Art Journal* (1989), v. 12, n. 1, pp. 3–13.

Diane Agrest, *Architecture from Without: Theoretical Framings for a Critical Practice* (Cambridge, MA: The MIT Press, 1993).

Diane Agrest, Patricia Conway and Leslie Kanes Weisman (eds.), *The Sex of Architecture* (New York: Abrams, 1997).

Sally Alexander, *Women's Work in the Nineteenth Century: a Study of the Years 1820–50* (London: The Journeyman Press, 1983).

Robert J. Allen, *Clubs of London* (Cambridge, MA: Harvard University Press, 1933).

Robert Altick, *The Shows of London* (Cambridge, MA: Harvard University Press, 1978).

Amanda Anderson, 'Review of Judith Walkowiz, *City of Dreadful Delight: Narratives of Sexual Danger in Late Victorian London*', *Victorian Studies* (Summer 1993), v. 36, n. 4, pp. 474–5.

Kay Anderson and Fay Gale (eds.), *Inventing Places* (Australia: Longman Cheshire, 1992).

Patricia Anderson, *The Printed Image and the Transformation of Popular Culture 1790–1860* (Oxford: Clarendon Press, 1994).

Donna Andrew, 'Aldermen and the Big Bourgeoisie of London reconsidered', *Social History* (1981), v. 6, n. 3, pp. 359–64.

George Andrewes, *The Stranger's Guide or the Frauds of London detected etc.* (London: J. Bailey, 1808).

George Andrewes, *A Dictionary of the Slang and other Cant Languages* (London: G. Smeeton, 1809).

William W. Appleton, *Madame Vestris and the London Stage* (New York: Columbia University Press, 1974).

Louis Aragon, *Paris Peasant* (Boston: Exact Change, 1994).

Body:

M. D. Archenholz, *Picture of England containing a description of the laws, customs and manners of England interspersed with curious and interesting anecdotes* (Dublin: P. Byrne, 1791).

Shirley Ardener (ed.), *Women and Space: Ground Rules and Social Maps* (Oxford: Berg, 1993).

Dana Arnold, 'George IV and the Metropolitan Improvements: The Creation of a Royal Image', Dana Arnold (ed.), *Squanderous and Lavish Profession: George IV, his Image and Patronage of the Arts* (London: The Georgian Group, 1995), pp. 51–6.

P. J. Atkins, 'The Spatial Configuration of Class Solidarity in London's West End 1792–1939', *Urban History Year Book* (1990), v. 17, pp. 36–65.

J. D. Aylward, *The House of Angelo* (London: The Batchworth Press, 1953).

John Badcock, *Slang: a Dictionary of the Turf, the ring, the chase, the pit, the bon-ton and the varieties of life, forming the completest and most authentic lexicon balatronicum [. . .] of the sporting world* (London: T. Hughes, 1823).

John Badcock, *A Living Picture of London, for 1823, and Strangers guide thro' the streets of the metropolis shewing the frauds and wiles of all descriptions of rogues* (London: W. Clark, 1828).

John Badcock, *A Living Picture of London, for 1828, and a stranger's guide through the streets* (London: W. Clark, 1828).

Marc Baer, *Theatre and Disorder in Late Georgian London* (Oxford: Clarendon Press, 1992).

Alexander F. Baillie, *The Oriental Club and Hanover Square* (London: Longman, Green, 1901).

Michele Barret and Anne Phillips (eds.), *Destabilising Theory: Contemporary Feminist Debates* (Cambridge: Polity Press, 1992).

Françoise Barret-Ducrocq, *Love in the Time of Victoria: Sexuality, Class and Gender in Nineteenth Century London* (London: Verso, 1991).

Clive Barker, 'A Theatre for the People', Kenneth Richards and Peter Thomas (eds.), *Nineteenth Century British Theatre* (London: Methuen, 1971), pp. 3–24.

H. Barton Barker, *The London Stage: its History and Traditions from 1576–1888* (London: W. H. Allen, 1889).

George Barrington, *Barrington's New London Spy for 1805, or the frauds of London detected, also a Treatise on the Art of Boxing by Mr. Belcher*, 4th edition (London: T. Tegg, 1805).

Roland Barthes, 'Semiology and Urbanism', Joan Ockman (ed.), *Architecture Culture 1943–1968: a Documentary Anthology* (New York: Rizzoli, 1993), pp. 413–18.

Christine Battersby, 'Gender and the Picturesque: Recording Ruins in the Landscape of Patriarchy', Jane Brettle and Sally Rice (eds.), *Public Bodies – Private States: New Views on Photography, Representation and Gender* (Manchester: Manchester University Press, 1994), pp. 78–95.

Charles Baudelaire, *The Parisian Prowler* (London: The University of Georgia Press, 1997).

David Bell and Gill Valentine (eds.), *Mapping Desires* (London: Routledge, 1995).

Shannon Bell, *Reading, Writing and Rewriting the Prostitute Body* (Bloomington & Indianapolis: Indiana University Press, 1994).

Seyla Benhabib, *Situating the Self: Gender: Community and Postmodernism in Contemporary Ethics* (Cambridge: Polity Press, 1992).

Thelma H. Benjamin, *London Shops and Shopping* (London: Herbert Joseph Ltd, 1934).

Walter Benjamin, *Charles Baudelaire: a Lyric Poet in the Era of High Capitalism* (London: Verso, 1997).

Walter Benjamin, *One Way Street and Other Writings* (London: Verso, 1985).

Klaus van den Berg, 'The Geometry of Culture: Urban Space and Theatre Buildings in Twentieth-Century Berlin', *Theatre Research International* (1991), v. 16, n. 1, pp. 1–16.

Maurice Berger, Brian Wallis and Simon Watson (eds.), *Constructing Masculinity* (London: Routledge, 1996).

Ann Bergren, 'Dear Jennifer', *ANY* (January–February 1994), n. 4, pp. 12–15.

Ellen Perry Berkeley (ed.), *Architecture: a Place for Women* (London & Washington: Smithsonian Institution Press, 1989).

Charles Bernheimer, *Figures of Ill-Repute: Representing Prostitution in Nineteenth-Century France* (Cambridge, MA: Harvard University Press, 1989).

Aaron Betsky, *Building Sex: Men, Women, Architecture and the Construction of Sexuality* (New York: William Morrow, 1995).

Derek Birley, 'Bonaparte and the Squire: Chauvinism, Virility and Sport in the Period of the French Wars', J. A. Mangan (ed.), *Pleasure, Profit, Proselytism* (London: Frank Cass, 1988), pp. 21–41.

Derek Birley, *Sport and the Making of Britain* (Manchester: Manchester University Press, 1993).

Bernard Blackmantle (pseud.), *The English Spy: an original work* (London: Sherwood, Jones & Co., 1825). This has been attributed to Charles Westmacott by the British Library Catalogue.

Juliet Blair, 'Private Parts in Public Places: the Case of Actresses', Shirley Ardener (ed.), *Women and Space: Ground Rules and Social Maps* (Oxford: Berg, 1993), pp. 200–22.

Lesley Blanche, *The Game of Hearts: Harriette Wilson and her Memoirs* (London: Gryphon Books, 1957).

Horace Bleakley, *Ladies Fair and Frail: Sketches of the Demi-Monde During the Eighteenth Century* (New York: Dodd, Mead, 1926).

Jennifer Bloomer, 'Big Jugs', Arthur Kroker and Marilouise Kroker (eds.),

The Hysterical Male: New Feminist Theory (London: Macmillan, 1991), pp. 13–27.

Jennifer Bloomer, *Architecture and the Text: the (S)crypts of Joyce and Piranesi* (New Haven & London: Yale University Press, 1993).

Henry Blyth, *Hell and Hazard or William Crockford versus the Gentlemen of England* (London: Weidenfeld & Nicolson, 1969).

James Boaden (ed.), *Memoirs of Mrs. Inchbald including her familiar correspondence with the most distinguished persons of her time to which are added the massacre and a case of conscience now first published from her autographed copies* (London: Richard Bentley, 1833).

Robert Bocock, *Consumption* (London: Routledge, 1993).

Arthur T. Bolton, 'Eighteenth Century Club-Houses – White's', *Country Life* (3 June 1916), pp. 10–14.

Arthur T. Bolton, 'London Clubs: Boodle's', *Country Life* (9 December 1916), pp. 12–20.

Arthur T. Bolton (ed.), *Portrait of Sir John Soane* (London: Soane Museum Publications, 1927).

Liz Bondi, 'Feminism, Postmodernism and Geography: a Space for Women?', *Antipode* (August 1990), v. 22, n. 2, pp. 156–67.

Liz Bondi, 'Gender Symbols and Urban landscapes', *Progress in Human Geography* (1992), v. 16, n. 2, pp. 157–70.

Liz Bondi, 'Locating Identity Politics', Michael Keith and Steve Pile (eds), *Place and the Politics of Identity* (London: Routledge, 1993), pp. 84–101.

Liz Bondi, 'Gender and Geography: Crossing Boundaries', *Progress in Human Geography* (1993), v. 17, n. 2, pp. 241–6.

Liz Bondi and Mona Domosh, 'Other Figures in the Other Places: on Feminism, Postmodernism and Geography', *Environment and Planning D: Space and Society* (1992), v. 10, pp. 199–213.

Iain Borden, Joe Kerr, Alicia Pivaro and Jane Rendell (eds), *Strangely Familiar: Narratives of Architecture in the City* (London: Routledge, 1996).

Iain Borden, Helen Thomas and Jane Rendell, 'Knowing Different Cities: Reflections on Recent European City and Planning History', Leonie Sandercock (ed.), *Making the Invisible Visible: New Historiographies for Planning* (University of California Press, 1997).

Iain Borden, Joe Kerr, Jane Rendell (eds.) with Alicia Pivaro, *Unknown City: Contesting Architecture and Social Space* (Cambridge MA: The MIT Press, 2000).

Iain Borden and Jane Rendell (eds.), *Intersections: Architectural Histories and Critical Theories* (London: Routledge, 2000).

Susan Bordo, 'Postmodern Subjects, Postmodern Bodies', *Feminist Studies* (1992), v. 18, n. 1, pp. 176–90.

Mary Cathcart Borer, *An Illustrated Guide to London 1800* (London: Robert Hale, 1988).

Peter Borsay (ed.), *The Eighteenth Century Town 1688–1820* (Harlow: Longman, 1990).

Brian Boru, esq., *Real Life in Ireland, or the Day and Night Scenes, Rovings, Rambles and Sprees, Bulls, Blunders, Bidderarions, and Blarney of Brian Boru, Esq. and his elegant friend Sir Shawn O'Dogherty, By a Real Paddy* (London: B. Bensley, 1821).

Paul Gabriel Boucé (ed.), *Sexuality in Eighteenth Century Culture* (Manchester: Manchester University Press, 1982).

Pierre Bourdieu, *Distinction: a Social Critique of the Judgement of Taste* (London: Routledge & Kegan Paul, 1984).

Algernon Bourke, *History of White's Club* (London: Algernon Bourke, n. d.).

Sara Boutelle, 'Julia Morgan', Susana Torre (ed.), *Women in American Architecture: a Historic and Contemporary Perspective* (New York: Whitney Library of Design, 1977), pp. 79–87.

Rachel Bowlby, 'The Judgement of Paris (and the Choice of Kristeva)', *New Formations* (Winter 1989), n. 9, pp. 51–60.

Lindsay Boynton, 'Scandal and Society', Dana Arnold (ed.), *George IV and the Metropolitan Improvements: The Creation of a Royal Image* (London: The Georgian Society, 1995), pp. 44–50.

Frances Bradshaw, 'Working with Women', Matrix, *Making Space: Women and the Man-Made Environment* (London: Pluto Press, 1984), pp. 89–105.

Rosa Braidotti, 'Body-Images and the Pornography of Representation', Kathleen Lennon and Margaret Whitford (eds.), *Knowing the Difference: Feminist Perspectives in Epistemology* (London: Routledge, 1994), pp. 17–30.

Rosi Braidotti, *Nomadic Subjects* (New York: Columbia University Press, 1994).

Dennis Brailsford, *Sport, Time and Society* (London: Routledge, 1991).

Dennis Brailsford, *British Sport: a Social History* (Cambridge: Lutterworth Press, 1992).

Dennis Brailsford, *Bareknuckles: a Social History of Prize-Fighting* (Cambridge, Lutterworth Press, 1988).

J. S. Bratton, 'Pomp Circuses: Secular Ritual and Theatrical Hegemony 1788–1832', *Nineteenth Century Theatre* (Winter 1994), v. 22, n. 2, pp. 93–118.

Edward Wedlake Brayley, *Accounts of the London Theatres* (London: J. Taylor Architectural Library, 1827).

Theresa Brennam, 'An Impasse in Psychoanalysis and Feminism', Sneja Gunew (ed.), *A Reader in Feminist Knowledge* (London: Routledge, 1991), pp. 114–38.

André Breton, *Mad Love* (London: University of Nebraska Press, 1987).

Jane Brettle and Sally Rice (eds.), *Public Bodies – Private States: New Views on Photography, Representation and Gender* (Manchester: Manchester University Press, 1994).

John Brewer and Roy Porter (eds.), *Consumption and the World of Goods* (London: Routledge, 1993).

Asa Briggs, *The Age of Improvement 1783–1867* (London: Longman, 1979).

Edward Bristow, *Vice and Vigilance: Purity Movements in Britain since 1700* (Totowa, NJ: Rowman & Littlefield, 1977).

J. Britton, *The Original Picture of London enlarged and improved being a correct guide for the stranger as well as for the inhabitant of the Metropolis of the British Empire together with a description of the environs*, 26th edition (London: Longman, Rees, Orme, Brown & Green, 1827).

J. Britton and A. Pugin, *Illustrations of the Public Buildings of London*, 2nd edition (London: John Wedle, 1838).

Harry Brod (ed.), *The Making of Masculinities: the New Men's Studies* (London: Routledge, 1987).

Percy Rudolph Broemel, *Paris and London in 1815* (London: Murray & Co., 1929).

Denise Scott Brown, 'Room at the Top? Sexism and the Star System in Architecture', Ellen Perry Berkeley (ed.), *Architecture: a Place for Women* (London & Washington: Smithsonian Institution Press, 1989), pp. 237–46.

Eluned Brown (ed.), *The London Theatre 1811–66: Selections from the Diary of Henry Crabb Robinson* (London: The Society for Theatre Research, 1966).

Arthur Bryant, *The Age of Elegance 1812–22* (London: Collins, 1950).

James Buchanan, *Observations on the Penitentiary System in the U. S.: Cause and Prevention of Crime in the U. K. with a Proposition as respects the Unfortunate Female abandoned to Prostitution in the Cities of London, Dublin and Edinburgh* (London: Black, Young & Young, 1829).

Susan Buck-Morss, *The Dialectics of Seeing: Walter Benjamin and the Arcades Project* (Cambridge, MA: The MIT Press, 1991).

Rosemarie Buikema and Anneke Smelik (eds.), *Women's Studies and Culture: a Feminist Introduction* (London: Zed Books, 1993).

Vern L. Bullough, Bonnie Bullough, Elcano Barrett and Margaret Deacon, *A Bibliography of Prostitution* (London: Garland Reference Library of Social Science, 1977).

Vern L. Bullough and Bonnie Bullough, *Women and Prostitution: a Social History* (New York: Prometheus Books, 1987).

Vern L. Bullough and Lilli Sentz, *Prostitution: a Guide to the Sources 1960–90* (London: Garland Publishing, 1992).

Vern L. Bullough, 'Prostitution and Reform in Eighteenth Century Britain', *Eighteenth Century Life* (May 1985), v. 9, n. 3, pp. 61–74.

E. J. Burford, *Royal St. James's being a Story of Kings, Clubmen and Courtesans* (London: Robert Hale, 1988).

E. J. Burford, *London: The Synfulle Citie* (London: Robert Hale, 1990).

E. J. Burford, *Wits, Wenches, and Wantons* (London: Robert Hale, 1990).

E. J. Burford and Joy Wotton, *Private Vices and Public Virtues: Bawdry in London from Elizabethan Times to the Regency* (London: Robert Hale, 1995).

Thomas Burke, *The Streets of London* (London: B. T. Batsford, 1940).

Frances Burney, *Female Life in London, being the History of a Young Lady's Introduction to Fashionable Life and the Gay Scenes of the Metropolis Displaying a Highly Humorous, Satirical, and Entertaining Description of Fashionable Characters, Manners and Amusements in the Higher Circles of Metropolitan Society* (London: Jones & Co., 1822).

Fanny Burney, *The Wanderer* (1816) (Oxford: Oxford University Press, 1991).

Judith Butler, *Gender Trouble: Feminism and the Subversion of Identity* (London: Routledge, 1990).

James Butterworth, *Clubland* (London: Epworth Press, 1932).

Colin Campbell, 'The Sociology of Consumption', Daniel Miller (ed.), *Acknowledging Consumption* (London: Routledge, 1995), pp. 96–126.

David Cannadine, *Lords and Landlords: the Aristocracy and the Towns 1774–1967* (Leicester: Leicester University Press, 1980).

David Cannadine, *Aspects of Aristocracy: Grandeur and Decline in Modern Britain* (New Haven & London: Yale University Press, 1994).

Kathleen Canning, 'Feminist History After the Linguistic Turn: Historicizing Discourse and Experience', *Signs* (Winter, 1994), pp. 368–404.

Jane Caplan, 'The Politics of Prostitution', *History Workshop Journal* (1982), v. 13, pp. 77–8.

David Carey, *Life in Paris: comprising the Rambles, Sprees and Amours of Dick Wildfire, of Corinthian Celebrity, and his Bang-up Companions, Squire Jenkins and Captain O'Shuffleton* (London: John Fairburn, 1822).

William Carey, *The Strangers Guide through London: or a view of the British Metropolis in 1808* (London: James Cundee, 1808).

Marvin Carlson, *Theories of the Theatre* (Ithaca: Cornell University Press, 1984).

Marvin Carlson, *Places of Performance: the Semiotics of Theatre Architecture* (Ithaca & London: Cornell University Press, 1989).

Marvin Carlson, 'Theatre History, Methodology and Distinctive Features', *Theatre Research International* (Winter 1989), v. 20, n. 2, pp. 90–6.

Marvin Carlson, *Theatre Semiotics: Signs of Life* (Bloomington & Indianapolis: Indiana University Press, 1990).

Terry Castle, *The Female Thermometer: Eighteenth Century Culture and The Invention of the Uncanny* (Stanford: Stanford University Press, 1994).

Jeremy Catnach, *Life in London, or the Sprees of Tom and Jerry, attempted in cuts and verse*, 5th edition (London: Jas. Catnach, 1822).

Zeynep Çelik, 'Le Corbusier, Orientalism, Colonialism', *Assemblage* (April 1992), n. 17, pp. 66–77.

Michael de Certeau, *The Practice of Everyday Life* (Berkeley, Los Angeles & Oxford: University of California Press, 1988).

Beresford E. Chancellor, *The Eighteenth Century in London: an Account of its Social Life and Arts* (London: B. T. Batsford, 1920).

Beresford E. Chancellor, *Memorials of St. James's Street, together with the Annals of Almacks* (London: Grant Richards, 1922).

Beresford E. Chancellor, *The Pleasure Haunts of London* (London: Constable, 1925).

Beresford E. Chancellor, *Life in Regency and Early Victorian Times* (London: B. T. Batsford, 1926).

Kellow Chesney, *The Victorian Underworld* (London: Temple Chesney, 1970).

Farid Chevianne, *A History of Men's Fashion* (Paris: Flammarion, 1993).

Hélène Cixious, 'The Laugh of the Medusa', Elaine Marks and Isabelle de Courtivron (eds.), *New French Feminisms: an Anthology* (London: Harvester, 1981), pp. 243–64.

Mark Clapson, *A Bit of a Flutter: Gambling and English Society 1823–1961* (Manchester: Manchester University Press, 1992).

Anna Clark, *Women's Silence, Men's Violence, Sexual Assault in England 1770–1845* (London: Pandora Press, 1987).

Anna Clark, 'The Sexual Crisis and Popular Religion in London 1770–1820', *International Labour and Working Class History* (1988), v. 34, pp. 56–69.

A. Clark, 'Whores and Gossips, Sexual Regulation in London 1770–1825', J. Angernem (ed.), *Current Issues in Women's History* (London: Routledge, 1989), pp. 231–48.

Anna Clark, 'Queen Caroline and the Sexual Politics of Popular Culture in London 1820', *Representations* (1990), v. 31, pp. 47–68.

Anna Clark, *The Struggle for Breeches* (Berkeley, Los Angeles & Oxford: University of California Press, 1995).

Anne Clarke, *Authentic Memoirs of Mrs Clarke in which is portrayed the Secret History and Intrigues of many Characters in the first circles of fashion and high life and containing the whole of the correspondence during the time she lived under the protection of his Royal Highness the Duke of York* (London: Thomas Tegg, 1809).

Linda Clarke, *Building Capitalism* (London: Routledge, 1992).

Norma Clarke, 'From Plaything to Professional', *Gender and History* (1993), v. 5, n. 1, pp. 120–4.

Mary Anne Clawson, *Constructing Brotherhood: Gender/Class and Fraternity* (Princeton: Princeton University Press, 1989).

Hollis Clayson, *Painted Love* (New Haven & London: Yale University Press, 1991).

John Cleland, *Fanny Hill: Memoirs of a Woman of Pleasure* (Hertfordshire: Wordsworth Editions, 1993).

Catherine Clément, *Opera, or the Undoing of Women* (London: Virago Press, 1989).

Cynthia Cockburn and Jonathan Rutherford (eds.), *Unwrapping Masculinity* (London: Lawrence & Wishart, 1988).

Reginald Colby, 'Shopping off the City Streets', *Country Life* (19 November 1964), v. 136, pp. 1343–9.

Debra Coleman, Elizabeth Danze and Carol Henderson (eds.), *Architecture and Feminism* (New York: Princeton Architectural Press, 1996).

John Coleman, *Players and Playwrights I have known* (London: Chatto & Windus, 1888).

Beatriz Colomina (ed.), *Architectureproduction* (New York: Princeton Architectural Press, 1988).

Beatriz Colomina, 'The Split Wall: Domestic Voyeurism', Beatriz Colomina (ed.), *Sexuality and Space* (New York: Princeton Architectural Press, 1992), pp. 73–98.

Beatriz Colomina (ed.), *Sexuality and Space* (New York: Princeton Architectural Press, 1992).

Beatriz Colomina, *Privacy and Publicity: Modern Architecture as Mass Media* (Cambridge, MA: MIT Press, 1994).

Patrick Colquhoun, *Observations and Facts relative to Licensed Ale-Houses in the City of London and its Environs humbly submitted to the consideration of Magistrates in every part of Great-Britian by a Magistrate Acting for the Counties of Middlesex Surry Kent and Essex* (London: n. p., 1794).

Patrick Colquhoun, *A Treatise on the Police of the Metropolis* (London: H. Fry, 1797).

Percy Colson, *White's 1693–1950* (London: Heinemann, 1951).

Howard M. Colvin, *A Biographical Dictionary of British Architects, 1660–1840* (New Haven & London: Yale University Press, 1995).

Susan P. Conner, 'Prostitution and the Jacobin Agenda for Social Control', *Eighteenth Century Life* (1988), v. 12, n. 1, pp. 42–51.

Susan P. Conner, 'Politics, Prostitution and the Pox in Revolutionary Paris 1789–99', *Journal of Social History* (1989), v. 22, n. 4, pp. 713–34.

Dutton Cook, *A Book of the Play* (London: Sampson, Law, Marston, Searle & Rivington, 1876).

Alain Corbin, 'Commercial Sexuality in Nineteenth Century France: a System of Images and Regulations', *Representations* (1986), v. 14, pp. 209–19.

Penelope J. Corfield, 'The Capital City', *The Impact of English Towns 1700–1800* (Oxford: Oxford University Press, 1982), pp. 66–81.

P. J. Corfield (ed.), *The Impact of English Towns 1700–1800* (Oxford: Oxford University Press, 1982).

Penelope Corfield, 'Walking the City Streets, an Eighteenth Century Odyssey', *Historical Perspectives* (1990), v. 16, pp. 132–74.

John Corry, *The English Metropolis or London in the Year 1820* (London: Sherwood, Neely & Jones, 1820).

John Corry, *The English Metropolis or London in the Year 1825* (London: Barnard & Farley, 1825).

Rosalind Coward and John Ellis, *Language and Materialism: Developments in Semiology and the Theory of the Subject* (London: Routledge & Kegan Paul, 1977).

Rosalind Coward, *Patriarchal Precedents: Sexuality and Social Relations* (London: Routledge & Kegan Paul, 1983).

Frank Richard Cowell, *The Athenaeum: Club and Social Life in London 1824–1974* (London: Heinemann, 1975).

Elizabeth Cowie, 'Woman as Sign', Parveen Adams and Elizabeth Cowie (eds.), *The Woman in Question* (London: Verso, 1990), pp. 117–33.

Dan Cruikshank and Neil Burton, *Life in the Georgian City* (London: Viking, 1990).

George Cruikshank, *The Betting Book* (London: W. & F. G. Cash, 1852).

Richard Cumberland, *Memoirs* (London: Lackington, 1806).

Rev. J. W. Cunningham, *To provide a Refuge for the Criminal is to give a Bounty on the Crime. This principal examined in its application to the Guardian Society and other similar institutions in a Sermon preached for the benefit of that Society* (London: J. Hatchard, L. B. Seeley, J. Low, 1817).

Julia Curtis, 'Review of Tracy C. Davis, *Actresses as Working Women: their Social Identity in Victorian Culture*', *Theatre Survey* (November 1992), v. 33, n. 2, pp. 219–22.

Ruth Daley, 'An Imperfect, Inadequately and Wretched System: Policing London Before Peel', *Criminal Justice History* (1989), v. 10, pp. 95–130.

George Daniel, *Garrick in the Green Room* (London: James Webb, 1829).

Leonore Davidoff, 'Gender and Class in Victorian England', Judith L. Newton, Mary P. Ryan and Judith R. Walkowitz (eds.), *Sex and Class in Women's History* (London: Routledge & Kegan Paul, 1983), pp. 17–71.

Leonore Davidoff and Catherine Hall, 'The Architecture of Public and Private Life', Derek Fraser and Anthony Sutcliffe (eds.), *The Pursuit of Urban History* (London: Edward Arnold, 1983), pp. 327–45.

Leonore Davidoff, *The Best Circles* (London: Croom Helm, 1986).

Leonore Davidoff and Catherine Hall, *Family Fortunes: Men and Women of the English Middle Class 1750–1850* (Chicago: Chicago University Press, 1987).

Leonore Davidoff, *Worlds Between: Historical Perspectives on Gender and Class* (Cambridge: Polity Press, 1995).

Dorothy Davis, *A History of Shopping* (London: Routledge & Kegan Paul, 1966).

Terence Davis, *The Architecture of John Nash* (London: Studio, 1960).

Terence Davis, *John Nash: The Prince Regent's Architect* (London: Country Life, 1966).

Tracey C. Davis, 'Actresses and Prostitutes in Victorian London', *Theatre Research International* (1988), v. 13, n. 3, pp. 221–34.

Tracey C. Davis, *Actresses as Working Women: their Social Identity in Victorian Culture* (London: Routledge, 1991).

Tracey C. Davis, 'Spectacles of Women and Conduits of Ideology', *Nineteenth Century Theatre* (Summer 1991), v. 19, n. 1, pp. 52–66.

Tracey C. Davis, 'Private Women and the Public Realm', *Theatre Survey: the Journal of the American Society for Theatre Research* (May 1994), v. 35, n. 1, pp. 65–71.

Jan De Vries, 'Purchasing Power and the World of Goods', Neil McKendrick, John Brewer and Roy Porter (eds.), *The Birth of a Consumer Society: the Commercialisation of Eighteenth Century England* (London, Europa Publications, 1982), pp. 85–132.

Leonard De Vries and Peter Fryer, *Venus Unmasked* (London: Arthur Barker, 1967).

Deale, *Crockfords or Life in the West* (London: Saunders & Otley, 1828).

Guy Debord, 'Theory of the Dérive', *Internationale Situationniste* (December 1958), n. 2., republished in Ken Knabb (ed.), *Situationist International Anthology* (1989), pp. 50–4.

Thomas Dekker, *The Belman of London* (London: Nathaniell Butter, 1608).

Patrick Delaforce, *Wellington the Beau: the Life and Loves of the Duke of Wellington* (Gloucestershire: The Windrush Press, 1990).

Phyllis Dianne Deutsch, 'Fortune and Chance: Aristocratic Gambling and English Society' (Dissertation Ref. DK 69133/DK 69134 Y, 1991).

Rosalyn Deutsche, 'Men in Space', *Strategies* (1990), n. 3, pp. 130–7.

Rosalyn Deutsche, 'Boys Town', *Environment and Planning D: Space and Society* (1991), v. 9, pp. 5–30.

Charles Dibdin, *History and Illustrations of the London Theatre comprising an account of the origin and progress of the drama in England with historical and descriptive of the Theatres Royal, Covent Garden, Drury Lane, Haymarket, English Opera House and Royal Amphitheatre* (London: Printed for the Proprietors of the Illustrations of London Buildings, 1826).

M. Wilson Disher, *Pleasures of London* (London: Robert Hale, 1950).

R. H. Ditchfield, *London's West End* (London: Jonathan Cape, 1925).

Mary Ann Doane, 'Film and the Masquerade: Theorising the Female Spectator', *Screen* (September–October 1982), v. 23, ns. 2–4, pp. 74–87.

Ellen Donkin, 'Review of Tracy C. Davis, *Actresses as Working Women: their Social Identity in Victorian Culture*', *Nineteenth Century Theatre* (Summer 1992), v. 20, n. 1, pp. 64–6.

Mary Douglas, *Purity and Danger: an Analysis of Concepts of Pollution and Danger* (Harmondsworth: Penguin, 1966).

Robyn Dowling, 'Femininity, Place and Commodities: a Retail Case Study', *Antipode* (October 1993), v. 25, n. 4, pp. 295–319.

T. S. Duncombe, *Life and Correspondence* (London: Blackett, 1868).

Charles Dunne, *The Academicians of 1823* (London: Lawler & Quick, 1823).

Gary Dyer, 'The "Vanity Fair" of Nineteenth Century England: Commerce, Women and the East in the Ladies Bazaar', *Nineteenth Century Literature* (1991), v. 46, n. 2, pp. 196–222.

E. J. Dyos and Michael Wolff (eds.), *The Victorian City: Images and Realities* (London: Routledge & Kegan Paul, 1973).

H. J. Dyos, *Exploring the Urban Past* (Cambridge: Cambridge University Press, 1982).

John Ebers, *Seven Years of the King's Theatre* (London: William Harrison Ainsworth, 1828).

Henry S. Eeles and Earl Spencer, *Brooks's: 1764–1964* (London: Country Life, 1964).

Pierce Egan, *Boxiana or Sketches of Pugilism by One of the Fancy (Boximania, or Sketches of Ancient and Modern Pugilism)* (London: G. Smeeton, 1812).

Pierce Egan, *Boxiana* (London: Sherwood, Neely & Jones, 1818).

Pierce Egan, *Boxiana: New Series* (London: G. Virtue, 1828–9).

Pierce Egan, *Life in London: or, the day and night scenes of Jerry Hawthorn, Esq., and his elegant friend Corinthian Tom, accompanied by Bob Logic, the Oxonian, in their Rambles and Sprees through the Metropolis* (London: Sherwood, Neely & Jones, 1820–1).

Pierce Egan, *The Finish to the Adventures of Tom, Jerry and Logic in their Pursuits through Life in and out of London* (London: J. S .Virtue & Co., 1828).

Pierce Egan, *Life in London; or, the day and night scenes of Jerry Hawthorn, Esq., and his elegant friend Corinthian Tom, accompanied by Bob Logic, the Oxonian, in their Rambles and Sprees through the Metropolis* (London: Chatto & Windus, 1870).

Pierce Egan, *The Mistress of Royalty or the Loves of Florizel and Perdita. Portrayed in the Amatory Epistles between an Illustrious Personage and a Distinguished Female* (London: P. Egan, 1814).

Pierce Egan, *Walks through Bath* (London: Sherwood, Neely & Jones, 1819).

Norbert Elias, *Power and Civility: The Civilising Process* (Oxford: Blackwell, 1982).

Robert Elkin, *The Old Concert Rooms of London* (London: Edward Arnold, 1955).

Aytoun Ellis, *The Penny Universities* (London: Secker & Warburg, 1956).

Clive Emsley, *Crime and Society 1750–1900* (London: Longman, 1987).

Carolly Erickson, *Our Tempestuous Day: a History of Regency England* (London: Robson Books, 1996).

Don Manuel Alvarez Espriella, *Letters from England* (London: Longman, Hurst, Rees & Orme, 1807).

Hilary Evans, *The Oldest Profession: an Illustrated History of Prostitution* (London: David & Charles, 1979).

Louis Alexander Fagan, *The Reform Club: Its Founder and Architect 1838–86* (London: Quaritch, 1887).

Pasi Falk, *The Consuming Body* (London: Sage, 1994).

Mike Featherstone, 'The Body in Consumer Culture', Mike Hepworth, Mike Featherstone and Bryan S. Turner (eds.), *The Body: Social Process and Cultural Theory* (London: Sage 1991), pp. 170–96.

David Feldman and Gareth Stedman Jones (eds.), *Metropolis London: Representations and Histories since 1800* (London: Routledge, 1989).

Jessica R. Feldman, *Gender on the Divide: the Dandy in Modernist Literature* (New York: Cornell University Press, 1993).

John Feltham, *Picture for London for 1818*, 19th edition (London: Longman, Hurst, Rees, Orme & Brown, 1818).

John Feltham, *The Picture of London for 1821*, 22nd edition (London: Longman, Hurst, Rees, Orme & Brown, 1821).

John Feltham, *Picture for London for 1824*, 23rd edition (London: Longman, Hurst, Rees, Orme & Brown, 1824).

Lesley Ferris (ed.), *Crossing the Stage: Controversies on Cross-Dressing* (London: Routledge, 1993).

C. W. Firebrace, *The Army and Navy Club 1837–1933* (London: John Murray, 1934).

Edward Fitzball, *35 Years of a Dramatic Author's Life* (London: n. p., 1859).

Almeric Fitzroy, *History of the Travellers' Club* (London: George Allen & Unwin, 1927).

Jane Flax, 'Postmodernism and Gender Relations in Feminist Theory', Linda Nicholson (ed.), *Feminism/Postmodernism* (London: Routledge, 1990), pp. 39–62.

Jane Flax, *Thinking Fragments: Psychoanalysis, Feminism and Postmodernism in the Contemporary West* (Berkeley, Los Angeles & Oxford: University of California Press, 1991).

Peter Fleetwood-Hesketh, 'The Travellers' Club, London', *Country Life* (17 November, 1966), pp. 1270–4.

Lon Fleming, 'Lévi-Strauss, Feminism and the Politics of Representation', *Block* (1983), v. 9, pp. 15–26.

Kathy Fletcher, 'Review of Lesley Ferris (ed.), *Crossing the Stage: Controversies on Cross-Dressing*', *Nineteenth Century Theatre* (Summer 1994), v. 22, n. 1, pp. 73–9.

Denys Forrest, *The Oriental: Life Story of a West End Club* (London: B. T. Batsford, 1968).

Denys Forrest, *Foursome in St. James's – The Story of the East India, Devonshire, Sports and Public Schools Club* (Brighton: Dolphin Ltd, 1982).

F. S. Forrester, *Ballet In England: A Bibliography and Survey c. 1700 – June 1966* (London: The Library Association, 1968).

Celina Fox, *London: World City 1800–40* (Newhaven & London: Yale University Press, 1992).

Celina Fox and Aileen Ribeiro, *Masquerade* (London: Museum of London, 1983).

Karen A. Frank, 'A Feminist Approach to Architecture: Acknowledging Women's Ways of Knowing', Ellen Perry Berkeley (ed.), *Architecture: a Place for Women* (London & Washington: Smithsonian Institution Press, 1989), pp. 201–16.

Arthur W. Frank, 'For a Sociology of the Body: An Analytic Overview', Mike Hepworth, Mike Featherstone and Bryan S. Turner (eds.), *The Body: Social Process and Cultural Theory* (London: Sage 1991), pp. 36–102.

Derek Fraser and Anthony Sutcliffe (eds.), *The Pursuit of Urban History* (London: Edward Arnold, 1983).

Anne Friedberg, *Window Shopping* (Berkeley, Los Angeles & Oxford: University of California Press, 1993).

Alice Friedman, 'A Feminist Practice in Architectural History?', 'Gender and Design', *Design Book Review* (Summer 1992), n. 25, pp. 16–18.

Alice Friedman, 'Architecture, Authority and the Gaze: Planning and Representation in the Early Modern Country House', *Assemblage* (August 1992), v. 18, pp. 40–61.

Beth H. Friedman-Romell, 'Breaking the Code: Toward a Reception Theory of Theatrical Cross-Dressing in Eighteenth-Century London', *Eighteenth-Century Representations* (December 1995), v. 47, n. 4, pp. 459–80.

David Frisby, *The Fragments of Modernity* (Cambridge, MA: The MIT Press, 1988).

Peter Fryer, *The Man of Pleasure's Companion: a Nineteenth Century Anthology of Amorous Entertainment* (London: Arthur Baker, 1968).

Diane Fuss, *Essentially Speaking: Feminism, Nature and Difference* (London: Routledge, 1989).

Jane Gallop, *Feminism and Psychoanalysis: The Daughter's Seduction* (London: Macmillan, 1982).

Eva Gamamikow *et al.* (eds.), *The Public and the Private* (London: Heinemann, 1983).

Lorraine Gamman and Margaret Marshment (eds), *The Female Gaze: Women as Viewers of Popular Culture* (London: Women's Press, 1988).

Lorraine Gamman and Merja Makinen, *Female Fetishism: a New Look* (London: Lawrence & Wishart, 1994).

Lynn Garafola, 'The Travesty Dancer in Nineteenth-Century Ballet', Lesley Ferris (ed.), *Crossing the Stage: Controversies on Cross-Dressing* (London: Routledge, 1993), pp. 96–106.

Tamar Garb, 'Unpicking the Seams of her Disguise – Self-Representation in the Case of Marie Bashkirtseff', *Block* (August 1987–8), n. 13, pp. 79–85.

Marguerite Gardiner, *The Magic Lantern or Sketches of Scenes in the Metropolis* (London: Longman, Hurst, Rees, Orme & Brown, 1823).

David Garrioch, 'House, Shop Signs and Social Organisation in Western European Cites, 1500–1900', *Urban History* (April 1994), v. 21, part 1, pp. 21–48.

Moira Gatens, 'A Critique of the Sex/Gender Distinction', Sneja Gunew (ed.), *A Reader in Feminist Knowledge* (London: Routledge, 1991), pp. 139–60.

John Gay, *Trivia: or the Art of Walking the Streets of London* (London: B. Lintott, 1715).

Erik Gustaf Geijer, *Impressions of England 1809–10* (London: n. p., 1809–10).

Johann Friedrich Geist, *Arcades: the History of a Building Type* (Cambridge, MA: The MIT Press, 1983).

M. D. George, *Hogarth to Cruikshank: Social Change in Graphic Satire* (Harmondsworth: Penguin, 1967).

M. D. George, *London Life in the Eighteenth Century* (Harmondsworth: Penguin, 1992).

Ian Gibson, *The English Vice, Beating, Sex, Prostitution in Victorian England and After* (London: Duckworth, 1978).

Timothy J. Gilfoyle, *City of Eros: New York City, Prostitution and the Commercialization of Sex 1790–1920* (London: W. W. Norton, 1992).

Mark Girouard, 'Moonlit Matchmaking: Assembly Rooms of the Eighteenth Century', *Country Life* (1978), v. 180, ns. 4644, 4647 and 4650, pp. 540–4, 766–8 and 1057–9.

Tom Girtin, *The Abominable Clubmen* (London: Hutchinson, 1964).

Joan Glasheen, *St. James's London* (London: Phillimore, 1987).

C. A. G. Goede, *The Stranger in England or Travels in Great Britain containing Remarks on the Politics, Laws, Manners, Customs, and Distinguished Characters of the Country and chiefly its Metropolis with Criticism on the Stage* (London: Mathews & Leigh, 1807).

Erving Goffman, *The Presentation of Self in Everyday Life* (New York: Anchor Books, 1959).

James Grant, *The Great Metropolis* (London: Saunders & Otley, 1838).

Charles Graves, *Leather Armchairs* (London: Collins, 1963).

Clara H. Greed, *Women and Planning: Creating Gendered Realities* (London: Routledge, 1994).

W. R. Greg, 'Prostitution', *Westminster Review* (July 1850), v. 53, pp. 448–508.

Derek Gregory, *Geographical Imaginations* (Oxford: Blackwell, 1994).

Arthur Griffiths, *Clubs and Clubmen* (London: Hutchinson, 1907).

Paul Griffiths, 'The Structure of Prostitution in Elizabethan London', *Continuity and Change* (1993), v. 8, pp. 39–63.

Captain Gronow, *Reminiscences of Captain Gronow formerly of the Grenadier Guards and M. P. for Stafford being Anecdotes of the Camp, the Court and the Clubs at the close of the last War with France related by himself* (London: Smith, Elder, 1862).

Captain Gronow, *Recollections and Anecdotes being a Second Series of Reminiscences of the Camp, the Court and the Clubs by Captain R. H. Gronow (formerly of the Grenadier Guards and M. P. for Stafford)* (London: Smith, Elder, 1863).

Captain Gronow, *Celebrities of London and Paris being a Third Series of Reminiscences and*

Anecdotes of the Camp, the Court and the Clubs containing a correct account of the Coup D'etat by Captain R. H. Gronow formerly of the Grenadier Guards and M. P. for Stafford (London: Smith, Elder, 1865).

Captain Gronow, *Captain Gronow's last Recollections being the Fourth and Final Series of the Reminiscences and anecdotes with a portrait* (London: Smith, Elder, 1866).

Francis Grose, *A Classical Dictionary of the Vulgar Tongue* (London: S. Hooper, 1788).

Francis Grose, *A Provincial Glossary, with a collection of local proverbs and popular superstitions* (London: S. Hooper, 1790).

Francis Grose, *A Classical Dictionary of the Vulgar Tongue*, 3rd edition (London: Hooper & Wigstead, 1796).

Francis Grose, *Lexicon Balatronicum: a Dictionary of Buckish Slang, University Wit and Pickpocket Elegance* (London: C. Chappel, 1811).

Francis Grose, *Grose's Classical Dictionary of the Vulgar Tongue, revised and corrected, with the addition of numerous slang phrases, collected from tried authorities by Pierce Egan* (London: Sherwood, Neely & Jones, 1823).

Francis Grose, *A Classical Dictionary* (London: Routledge & Kegan Paul, 1963).

Elizabeth Grosz, *Sexual Subversions* (London: Allen & Unwin, 1989).

Elizabeth Grosz, 'Women, Chora, Dwelling', *ANY* (1994), n. 4, pp. 22–7.

Elizabeth Grosz, *Space, Time and Perversion* (London: Routledge, 1996).

Guardian Society, *Report of the Provisional Committee of the Guardian Society for the Preservation of Public Morals providing Temporary Asylums for Prostitutes Removed by the Operation of the Laws from the Public Streets and Affording to such of Them as are Destitute Employment and Relief Submitted to a General Meeting held at the City of London Tavern on Wednesday 13th December 1815* (London: James Low, 1816).

Guardian Society, *Report of the Committee of the Guardian Society for the Preservation of Public Morals providing Temporary Asylums for Prostitutes Removed by the Operation of the Laws from the Public Streets and Affording to such of Them as are Destitute Employment and Relief Submitted to a General Meeting held at the Egyptian Hall, Mansion House on Thursday 30th October* (London: James Low, 1817).

Guardian Society, *Report of the Committee of the Guardian Society for the Preservation of Public Morals by providing a Temporary Asylum, with Suitable Employment, for Females who have deviated from the paths of virtue, and who have either been removed, by the operation of the laws, from the public streets, or have been awakened by conscience to a sense of their guilt and danger* (London: Printed for the Society, 1827, 1828, 1832 and 1848).

Ivor Guest, *The Romantic Ballet In England: its Development, Fulfilment, and Decline* (London: Phoenix House, 1954).

Ivor Guest, 'Dandies and Dancers', *Dance Perspectives* (Spring 1969), n. 37, pp. 3–25.

Ivor Guest, *The Romantic Ballet in Paris* (London: Dance Books, 1980).

Sneja Gunew (ed.), *A Reader in Feminist Knowledge* (London: Routledge, 1991).

John Habakkuk, *Marriage, Debt and the Estates System: English Landownership 1650–1950* (Oxford: Clarendon Press, 1994).

William Hale, *An Address to the Public Upon the Dangerous Tendency of the London Female Penitentiary; with Hints Relative to the Best Means of Lessening the Sum of Prostitution* (London: W. Nicholson, 1809).

William Hale, *A Reply to the Pamphlets Lately Published in Defence of the London Female Penitentiary: With Further Remarks Upon the Dangerous Tendency of the Institution* (London: G. Auld, 1809).

William Hale, *Considerations on the Causes and the Prevalence of Female Prostitution: and on the Most Practicable and Efficient Means of Abating and Preventing that, and, all other crimes against the virtue and safety of the community* (London: E. Justing, 1812).

Catherine Hall, *White, Male and Middle Class: Explorations in Feminism and History* (Cambridge: Polity Press, 1992).

Molly Hankwitz, 'The Right to Rewrite: Feminism and Architectural Theory', *Inland Architect* (January–February 1991), pp. 52–5.

Donna Haraway, 'Situated Knowledges: the Science Question in Feminism and the Privilege of Partial Knowledge', *Feminist Studies* (Fall 1988), v. 14, n. 3, pp. 575–603.

Thomas Harman, *A Caueat, Warening for Common Cursetors Vulgarely called Vagabones* (London: William Gryffith, 1567).

C. C. Harris, *Kinship* (Milton Keynes: Open University, 1990).

Olivia Harris, 'Households and their Boundaries', *History Workshop Journal* (1982), v. 13, pp. 140–52.

Brian Harrison, 'Underneath the Victorians', *Victorian Studies* (1967), v. 10, pp. 239–62.

Brian Harrison, *Drink and the Victorians: the Temperance Question in England 1815–72* (London: Faber and Faber, 1971).

Susan Jill Harsin, *Policing Prostitution in Nineteenth Century Paris* (Princeton: Princeton University Press, 1985).

A. D. Harvey, *Sex in Georgian England* (London: Duckworth, 1994).

David Harvey, *The Condition of Postmodernity* (Oxford: Blackwell, 1989).

Joseph Haslewood, *The Secret History of the Green Room containing Authentic and Entertaining Memoirs of the Actors and Actresses in the Three Theatres Royal* (London: H. D. Symmonds, 1793).

Joseph Haslewood, *Green Room Gossip or Gravity Gallinipt* (London: J. Barker, 1809).

Gail L. Hawkes, 'Dressing Up – Cross-dressing and Sexual Dissonance', *Journal of Gender Studies* (1995), v. 4, n. 3, pp. 261–70.

Dolores Hayden, *The Grand Domestic Revolution* (Cambridge, MA: The MIT Press, 1981).

Dolores Hayden, *Redesigning the American Dream* (New York & London: W. W. Norton & Company, 1986).

Richard Head, *The Canting Academy or Villanies Discovered* (London: F. Leach, 1674).

Jeff Hearn, *Men in the Public Eye* (London: Routledge, 1991).

William Heath, *Fashion and Folly: or the Buck's Pilgrimage* (London: William Sams, 1822).

William Heath, *Fashion and Folly illustrated in a series of 23 Humorous Coloured Engravings* (London: William Sams, 1833).

J. J. Hecht, *The Domestic Servant Class in the Eighteenth Century* (London: Routledge & Kegan Paul, 1955).

Henriette A. Gram Heiny, 'Boxing in British Sporting Art: 1730–1824' (Dissertation Ref. CV 61446/CV 61447 Y, 1987).

Bracebridge Hemyng, 'The Prostitution Class Generally', Henry Mayhew and Bracebridge Hemyng (eds.), *London Labour and the London Poor, London Morning Chronicle 1861–2*, v. 4 (London: Frank Cass, 1967).

A. R. Henderson, 'Female Prostitution in London 1730–1830' (PhD thesis, University of London, 1992).

Fernando Henriques, *Prostitution and Society, Prostitution in Europe and the Americas* (New York: Citadel Press, 1965).

Fernando Henriques, *Modern Sexuality* (London: MacGibbon & Kee, 1968).

Mike Hepworth, Mike Featherstone and Bryan S. Turner (eds.), *The Body: Social Process and Cultural Theory* (London: Sage, 1991).

Liz Heron, *Streets of Desire: Women's Fiction of the Twentieth Century* (London: Routledge, 1993).

Christopher Hibbert, *London: the Biography of a Town* (Harmondsworth: Penguin, 1977).

Christopher Hibbert, *The English: a Social History 1066–1945* (London: Harper Collins, 1994).

Douglas Hill, *One Hundred Years of Georgian London* (London: Macmillan, 1970).

Jonathan Hill (ed.), *Occupying Architecture: Between the Architect and the User* (London: Routlege, 1998).

Charles Hindley, *The True History of Tom and Jerry, or, The Day and Night Scenes of Life in London, from the Start to the Finish! With a key to the persons and places, together with a vocabulary and glossary of the flash and slang terms, occurring in the course of the work* (London: C. Hindley, 1890).

René Hirschon, *Women and Property – Women as Property* (London: Croom Helm, 1984).

Hermione Hobhouse, *History of Regent Street* (London: Queen Anne Press, 1975).

Jane Aiken Hodge, *Passion and Principle: the Lives and Loves of Regency Women* (London: John Murray, 1996).

Joan Hoff, 'Gender as a Postmodern Category of Paralysis', *Women's History Review* (1994), v. 3, n. 2, pp. 149–68.

Ann Catherine Holbrook, *Memoirs of an Actress comprising a faithful narrative of her theatrical career from 1798 to the present period giving a lively picture of the stage in general and interspersed with a variety of anecdotes humorous and pathetic* (Manchester: J. Harrop, 1807).

Christel Hollevoet, 'Wandering in the City', *The Power of the City/The City of Power* (Whitney Museum of American Art, 1991–2).

Christine Holmlund, 'I love Luce: the Lesbian, Mimesis and Masquerade in Irigaray, Freud, and Mainstream Film', *New Formations* (Winter 1989), n. 9, pp. 105–23.

bell hooks, *Yearnings: Race, Gender and Cultural Politics* (London: Turnaround Press, 1989).

Marianne Hudson, *Almack's 1827–8* (Brighton: Taylor & Son, 1827).

Francesca Hughes, *The Architect: Reconstructing Her Practice* (Cambridge, MA: The MIT Press, 1996).

Maggie Humm (ed.), *Feminisms: a Reader* (London: Harvester Wheatsheaf, 1992).

A. L. Humphreys, *Crockfords, or the Goddess of Chance in St. James's 1828–44* (London: Hutchinson, 1953).

Anne Humphries, 'Needle Women Forced into Prostitution', Anne Humphries (ed.), *Voices of the Poor: Selections from Letters to the Morning Chronicle, Labour and the Poor 1849–59* (London: Frank Cass, 1971).

Christopher Hussey, 'Famous Clubs and Their Story – Boodle's Club London', *Country Life* (24 December 1932), pp. 716–20.

William Hutton, *A Journey to London* (London: William Hutton, 1818).

Ronald Hyam, *Empire and Sexuality: the British Experience* (Manchester: Manchester University Press, 1990).

Stephen Inwood, 'Policing London's Morals: the Metropolitian Police Force and Popular Culture', *London Journal* (1990), v. 15, n. 2, pp. 129–46.

Luce Irigaray, 'When the Goods Get Together', Elaine Marks and Isabelle de Courtivron (eds.), *New French Feminisms: An Anthology* (Amherst: University of Massachusetts Press, 1980), pp. 107–10.

Luce Irigaray, *The Speculum of the Other Woman* (1974), trans. Gillian C. Gill (Ithaca: Cornell University Press, 1985).

Luce Irigaray, *This Sex Which Is Not One* (1977), trans. Catherine Porter with Carolyn Burke (Ithaca: Cornell, 1985).

Luce Irigaray, *Elemental Passions* (1982), trans. Joanne Collie and Judith Still (London, The Athlone Press, 1992).

Luce Irigaray, *An Ethics of Sexual Difference* (1984), trans. Carolyn Burke and Gillian C. Burke (London, The Athlone Press, 1993).

Luce Irigaray, 'Women, the Sacred and Money', *Paragraph* (1986), v. 8, pp. 6–18.

Luce Irigaray, *Thinking the Difference: For a Peaceful Revolution* (1989), trans. Karin Montin (London: The Athlone Press, 1994).

Luce Irigaray, *Je, Tu, Nous: Towards a Culture of Difference* (1990), trans. Alison Martin (London, Routledge, 1993).

Luce Irigaray, *I Love to You: Sketches of a Possible Felicity in History*, trans. Alison Martin (London, Routledge, 1996).

David C. Itzkowitz, 'Victorian Bookmakers and their Customers', *Victorian Studies* (1988), v. 32, n. 1, pp. 7–30.

Louis C. Jackson, *History of the United Services Club* (London: Committee of the United Service Club, 1937).

Mary Jacobus, Evelyn Fox Keller and Sally Shuttleworth (eds.), *Body/Politics: Women and the Discourses of Science* (London: Routledge, 1990).

Louis James, *Fiction for the Working Man* (Oxford: Oxford University Press, 1963).

Louis James, *Print and the People 1819–51* (London: Allen Lane, 1976).

Louise C. Johnson, 'What Future for Feminist Geography?', *Gender, Place and Culture* (1994), v. 1, n. 1, pp. 103–13.

Nicola Johnson, *Eighteenth Century London* (London: HMSO, 1991).

Julia (Storer) Johnstone, *Confessions of Julia Johnstone written by herself in contradiction to the fables of Harriette Wilson* (London: Benbow, 1825).

Edward Jones and Christopher Woodward, *A Guide to the Architecture of London* (London: Weidenfeld & Nicolson, 1992).

Gareth Stedman Jones, *Outcast London: a Study in the Relationship Between Classes in Victorian Society* (Harmondsworth: Penguin, 1984).

Gareth Stedman Jones, 'The Cockney and the Nation 1780–1988', David Feldman and Gareth Stedman Jones (eds.), *Metropolis London: Representations and Histories since 1800* (London: Routledge, 1989), pp. 272–325.

Louis C. Jones, *The Clubs of the Georgian Rakes* (New York: Columbia University Press, 1842).

Steve Jones, *London Through the Keyhole* (Nottingham: Wicked Publishers, 1991).

Barbara Kanner, *Women in English Social History 1800–1914: A Guide to Research* (New York: Garland, 1987–90).

Ann E. Kaplan, *Women and Film: Both Sides of the Camera* (New York: Methuen, 1983).

Kojin Karatani, *Architecture as Metaphor: Language, Number, Money* (Cambridge, MA: The MIT Press, 1995).

Patrick Keiller, *London* (1995).

Patrick Keiller, *Robinson in Space* (1997).

Michael Keith and Steve Pile (eds.), *Place and the Politics of Identity* (London: Routledge, 1993).

Joan Kelly, 'The Doubled Vision of Feminist Theory', Judith L. Newton, Mary P.

Ryan and Judith R. Walkowitz (eds.), *Sex and Class in Women's History* (London: Routledge & Kegan Paul, 1983), pp. 259–70.

Michael Kelly, *Reminiscences of Michael Kelly of the King's Theatre and Theatre Drury Lane including a period of nearly half a century with original anecdotes of many distinguished persons political literary and musical* (London: New Burlington Street, 1826).

Magrit Kennedy, 'Seven Hypotheses on Male and Female Principles', 'Making Room: Women and Architecture', *Heresies: A Feminist Publication on Art and Politics* (1981), v. 3, n. 3, issue 11, pp. 12–13.

M. Kimmel (ed.), *Changing Men: New Directions in Research on Men and Masculinity* (Newbury Park: Sage, 1987).

Anthony D. King (ed.), *Buildings and Society: Essays on the Social Development of the Built Environment* (London: Routledge & Kegan Paul, 1980).

Anthony King, *The Bungalow* (Oxford: Oxford University Press, 1995).

Richard King, *The Complete London Spy for the present year 1781* (London: Alex Hogg, 1781).

Francis Kirkham, *A Trip through London containing Observations on Men and Things* (London: J. Roberts, 1728).

Julia Kristeva, *Desire in Language: A Semiotic Approach to Literature and Art* (Oxford: Blackwell, 1980).

Arthur Kroker and Marilouise Kroker (eds.), *The Hysterical Male: New Feminist Theory* (London: Macmillan, 1991).

Annette Kuhn, *Women's Pictures; Feminism and Cinema* (London: Verso, 1994).

Donna Landry and Gerald Maclean, *Materialist Feminisms* (Oxford: Blackwell, 1993).

Thomas Laqueur, 'Making Sex', *Journal of Modern History* (1982), v. 54, pp. 417–66.

Jacob Larwood, *The Story of the London Parks* (London: Francis Harvey, 1872).

C. Lasch, *The Culture of Narcissism* (New York: Norton, 1979).

James Laver, *Costume in the Theatre* (London: George G. Harrap and Co., 1964).

James Laver, *Dandies* (London: Weidenfeld & Nicolson, 1968).

James Laver, *Modesty in Dress: an Inquiry into the Fundamentals of Fashion* (London: Heinemann, 1969).

James Laver, *Costume and Fashion: a Concise History of Fashion* (London, Thames & Hudson, 1995).

Joan Lawson, *A History of Ballet and its Makers* (London: Sir Isaac Pitman & Sons, 1964).

Helen Leacroft and Richard Leacroft, *Theatre and Playhouse: an Illustrated Survey of Theatre Building from Ancient Greece to the Present Day* (London: Methuen, 1984).

James Lees-Milne, 'Brooks's Club, St. James's Street', *Country Life* (14 September 1978), pp. 710–13.

Henri Lefebvre, *The Production of Space* (Oxford: Blackwell, 1991).

Samuel Leigh, *Leigh's New Picture of London*, 3rd edition (London: Leigh, 1819).

Anthony Lejeune, *The Gentlemen's Clubs of London* (London: MacDonald & Jane's, 1979).

Anthony Lejeune, *White's: the First Three Hundred Years* (London: A. & C. Black, 1993).

Kathleen Lennon and Margaret Whitford (eds.), *Knowing the Difference: Feminist Perspectives in Epistemology* (London: Routledge, 1994).

Claude Lévi-Strauss, *The Elementary Structures of Kinship* (Boston: Beacon Press, 1969).

Donald Levine (ed.), *Georg Simmel: On Individuality and Social Forms* (Chicago: Chicago University Press, 1971).

Phillipa Levine, 'Consistent Contradiction: Prostitution and Protective Labour Legislation in Nineteenth Century England', *Social History* (1994), v. 19, n. 1, pp. 17–35.

Philippa Levine, 'Women and Prostitution: Metaphor, Reality, History', *Canadian Journal of History* (December 1993), v. 28, n. 3, pp. 479–94.

Brenda Ralph Lewis, 'Hummus and Whore Houses', *British Heritage* (1982), v. 3, n. 3, pp. 20–5.

Clare Lewis and Steve Pile, 'Woman, Body, Space: Rio Carnival and the Politics of Performance', *Gender, Place and Culture* (1996), v. 3, n. 1, pp. 23–41.

Bryant Lillywhite, *London Coffee Houses* (London: George Allen & Unwin, 1963).

Gilles Lipovestsky, *The Empire of Fashion: Dressing Modern Democracy* (Princeton: Princeton University Press, 1994).

Genevieve Lloyd, *The Man of Reason: 'Male' and 'Female' in Western Philosophy* (London: Methuen, 1984).

Mimi Lobell, 'The Buried Treasure', Ellen Perry Berkeley (ed.), *Architecture: a Place for Women* (London & Washington: Smithsonian Institution Press, 1989), pp. 139–57.

Lock Asylum, *A Brief Account of the Institution of the Lock Asylum for the Reception of Penitent Female Patients, when discharged cured from the Lock Hospital* (London: C. Watts, 1796).

Lock Asylum, *A Brief Account of the Institution of the Lock Asylum for the Reception of Penitent Female Patients, when discharged cured from the Lock Hospital with an abstract of the accounts from the first Institution to Lady-Day 1802* (London: Plilanthropic Society, 1802).

Donald A. Low, *Thieves Kitchen: The Regency Underworld* (Totowa, NJ: Biblio Distribution Center, 1982).

Benjamin Lumley, *Reminiscences of the Opera* (London: Hurst & Blackett, 1864).

Henry Luttrell, *Crockford-House: a Rhapsody in 2 Cantos* (London: Murray, 1827).

James J. Lynch, *Box, Pit and Gallery: Stage and Society in Johnson's London* (Berkeley, Los Angeles & Oxford: University of California Press, 1953).

Kevin Lynch, *The Image of the City* (London: The MIT Press, 1988).

Iain McCalman, 'Unrespectable Radicalism: Infidels and Pornography in Early Nineteenth Century London', *Past and Present* (1984), v. 104, pp. 74–110.

Iain McCalman, *Radical Underworld: Prophets, Revolutionaries and Pornographers in London 1795–1840* (Cambridge: Cambridge University Press, 1988).

Felix MacDonogh, *The Hermit in London*, 5 volumes in 3 (London: Henry Colburn, 1819).

Felix MacDonogh, *The Hermit in London or Sketches of English Manners*, 3 volumes in 2 (London: H. Colburn & Co., 1822).

Margaret MacKeith, *Shopping Arcades: a Gazetteer of British Arcades 1817–1939* (London: Mansell, 1985).

Margaret MacKeith, *The History of Shopping Arcades* (London: Mansell, 1986).

Neil McKendrick, John Brewer and J. H. Plumb, *The Birth of a Consumer Society: the Commercialisation of Eighteenth Century England* (London: Europa Publications 1982).

Catherine MacKinnon, *Toward a Feminist Theory of the State* (Cambridge, MA: Harvard University Press, 1989).

Iain Mackintosh, 'Departing Glories of the British Theatre', Celina Fox (ed.), *London: World City 1800–40* (New Haven & London: Yale University Press, 1992), pp. 199–208.

Mary McLeod, 'Everyday and "Other" Spaces', Debra L. Coleman, Elizabeth Ann Danze and Carol Jane Henderson (eds.), *Feminism and Architecture* (New York: Princeton Architectural Press, 1996), pp. 3–37.

W. Macqueen-Pope, *Haymarket: Theatre of Perfection* (London: W. H. Allen, 1948).

Simon McVeigh, *Concert Life in London from Mozart to Haydn* (Cambridge: Cambridge University Press, 1993).

Martin Madan, *Thelypthora: or, a Treatise on Female Ruin, in its Causes, Effects, Consequences, Prevention, and Remedy; Considered on the Basis of Divine Law: Under the Following Heads, viz. Marriage, Whoredom, Fornication, Adultery, Polygamy, Divorce With Many Other Incidental Matters Particularly Including an Examination of the Principles and Tendency of Statute 26 George II c. 33 Commonly called the Marriage Act* (London: J. Dodsley, 1780).

Maginn, *The Clubs of London with Anecdotes of their Members Sketches of Character and Conversations*, 2 volumes (London: Henry Colburn, 1828).

Maria Maitland, *The Woman of the Town or the Authentic memoirs of Maria Maitland well known in the Vicinity of Covent-Garden* (London: J. Roe & Ann Lemoine, 1809).

Robert W. Malcolmson, *Popular Recreations In British Society 1700–1850* (Cambridge: Cambridge University Press, 1973).

T. Malton, *A Picturesque Tour through the Cities of London and Westminster* (London: n. p., 1792).

Raymond Mander and Joe Mitchenson, *Lost Theatres of London* (London: New English Library, 1976).

J. A. Mangan (ed.), *Pleasure, Profit, Proselytism* (London: Frank Cass, 1988).

Michael Mansbridge, *John Nash* (Oxford: Phaidon, 1991).

Steven Marcus, *The Other Victorians: a Study of Sexuality and Pornography in Mid-Nineteenth Century England* (New York: Basic Books, 1966).

Stella Margetson, *Leisure and Pleasure in the Nineteenth Century* (London: Cassell, 1969).

Elaine Marks and Isabelle de Courtivron (eds.), *New French Feminisms: an Anthology* (London: Harvester, 1981).

Thomas A. Markus, *Buildings and Power* (London: Routledge, 1993).

James E. Marlow, 'Popular Culture, Pugilism and Pickwick', *Journal of Popular Culture* (1982), v. 15, n. 4, pp. 16–30.

Max Marquis, *Mistress of Many: Selections from the Memoirs of Harriette Wilson* (London: Bestseller Library, 1960).

Charles Marsh, *Clubs of London* (London: W. Colburn, 1832).

Dorothy Marshall, *English People in the Eighteenth Century* (London: Longman, 1956).

Thomas Marshall, *Lives of the Most Celebrated Actors and Actresses* (London: A. Appleyard, n. d.).

Karl Marx, *Capital: the Process of Production of Capital* (Harmondsworth: Penguin, 1976).

Karl Marx and Friedrich Engels, *The Communist Manifesto* (Harmondsworth: Penguin, 1967).

Doreen Massey, 'Flexible Sexism', *Environment and Planning D: Society and Space* (1991), v. 9, pp. 31–57.

Doreen Massey, *Space, Place and Gender* (Cambridge: Polity Press, 1994).

Matrix, *Making Space: Women and the Man Made Environment* (London: Pluto Press, 1984).

Cyril Maude, *The Haymarket Theatre* (London: Grant Richards, 1903).

Marcel Mauss, *The Gift: Forms and Functions of Exchange in Archaic Societies* (New York: Harvester, 1967).

Duncan McCorquodale, Katerina Rüedi and Sarah Wigglesworth (eds.), *Desiring Practices: Architecture, Gender and the Interdisciplinary* (London: Black Dog Publishing Ltd, 1996).

Grant McCracken, *Culture and Consumption* (Bloomington: Indiana University Press, 1990).

Linda McDowell, 'Space, Place and Gender Relations, Parts 1 and 2', *Progress in Human Geography* (1993), v. 17, n. 2, pp. 157–79 and v. 17, n. 3, pp. 305–18.

Count Edward de Melfort, *Impressions of England* (London: Richard Betley, 1836).

J. G. Merquior, *From Prague to Paris: a Critique of Structuralist and Post-Structuralist Thought* (London: Verso, 1986).

Judith Milhous, 'Lighting at the King's Theatre, Haymarket 1780–82', *Theatre Research International* (1991), v. 16, n. 3, pp. 215–36.

Daniel Miller (ed.), *Acknowledging Consumption* (London: Routledge, 1995).

James K. Miller, *Prostitution Considered in Relation to its Cause and Cure* (Edinburgh: Sutherland & Knox, 1859).

Rosalind Minsky, *Psychoanalysis and Gender* (London: Routledge, 1996).

Eileen Moers, *The Dandy: Brummel to Beerbohm* (Lincoln: University of Nebraska Press, 1978).

Toril Moi, *Sexual/Textual Politics: Feminist Literary Theory* (London: Methuen, 1985).

Jan Montefiore, 'Philosophical Passions', *Women: a Cultural Review* (Autumn 1992), v. 3, n. 2, pp. 196–9.

Henrietta L. Moore, *Feminism and Anthropology* (Cambridge: Polity Press, 1988).

J. Mordaunt Crook, 'The Clubhouse', Philip Ziegler and Seward Desmond (eds.), *Brooks's: a Social History* (London: Constable, 1991), pp. 153–60.

Frank Mort, *Dangerous Sexualities: Medico Moral Politics in England since 1830* (London: Routledge, 1987).

Frank Mort, *Cultures of Consumption* (London: Routledge, 1996).

Laura Mulvey (ed.), *Visual Pleasure and Narrative Cinema in Visual and Other Pleasures* (London: Macmillan, 1989).

Laura Mulvey, 'Cinematic Space: Desiring and Deciphering', Duncan McCorquodale, Katerina Rüedi and Sarah Wigglesworth (eds.), *Desiring Practices: Architecture, Gender and the Interdisciplinary* (London: Black Dog Publishing Ltd, 1996), pp. 206–15.

Roger Munting, 'Betting and Business', *Business History* (1989), v. 31, n. 4, pp. 67–85.

Daniel Nalbach, *The King's Theatre 1704–1867* (London: The Society for Theatre Research, 1972).

Gordon Nares, 'Two Centuries at Brooks's', *Country Life* (1 February 1952), pp. 290–4.

Stanley Dana Nash, 'Social Attitudes to Prostitution 1752–1829' (PhD thesis, New York University, 1980).

Stanley Nash, 'Prostitution and Charity: The Magdalen Hospital: A Case Study', *Journal of Social History* (1984), v. 17, n. 47, pp. 617–28.

Stanley D. Nash, *Prostitution in Great Britian: an Annotated Bibliography, 1485–1901* (London: The Scarecrow Press, 1994).

Lynda Nead, *Myths of Sexuality: Representations of Women in Victorian Britain* (Oxford: Blackwell, 1988).

R. S. Neale, *Bath: A Social History 1680–1800* (London: Routledge & Kegan Paul, 1981).

T. G. A. Nelson, 'Women of Pleasure', *Eighteenth Century Life* (1987), v. 11, n. 1, pp. 181–98.

Molly Nesbit, 'In the Absence of the Parisienne', Beatriz Colomina (ed.), *Sexuality and Space* (New York: Princeton Architectural Press, 1992), pp. 307–25.

Ralph Nevill, *London Clubs: their History and Treasures* (London: Chatto and Windus, 1969).

Robert Nevill, *Light Come, Light Go: Gambling – Gamesters – Wagers – The Turf* (London: Macmillan, 1909).

Judith L. Newton, Mary P. Ryan and Judith R. Walkowitz (eds.), *Sex and Class in Women's History* (London: Routledge & Kegan Paul, 1983).

Linda Nicholson (ed.), *Feminism/Postmodernism* (London: Routledge, 1990).

Linda Nochlin, 'Manet's Masked Ball at the Opera', Linda Nochlin (ed.), *The Politics of Vision: Essays on Nineteenth-Century Art and Society* (London: Thames & Hudson, 1991), pp. 75–94.

Deborah Epstein Nord, 'The City as Theatre: From Georgians to Early Victorian London', *Victorian Studies* (1988), v. 31, n. 2, pp. 159–88.

Christopher North, 'On George Cruikshank', *Blackwood's Edinburgh Magazine* (July 1823), pp. 18–26.

Felicity A. Nussbaum, *Torrid Zones: Maternity, Sexuality and Empire in Eighteenth Century English Narratives* (London: Johns Hopkins University Press, 1995).

Andrea Nye, *Feminist Theory and the Philosophy of Man* (New York: Croom Helm, 1989).

Miles Ogborn, 'Love-State-Ego: "centres" and "margins" in Nineteenth-Century Britain', *Environment and Planning D: Society and Space* (1992), v. 10, pp. 287–305.

Barbara Oldershaw, 'Developing a Feminist Critique of Architecture', 'Gender and Design', *Design Book Review* (Summer 1992), n. 25, pp. 7–15.

Donald J. Olsen, *Town Planning in London: the Eighteenth and Nineteenth Centuries* (New Haven & London: Yale University Press, 1982).

Walley Chamberlain Oulton, *The History of the Theatres of London: Containing an Annual Register of New Pieces Revivals Pantomimes and with Occasional Notes and Anecdotes being a Continuation of Victor's and Oulton's Histories from the Year 1795 to 1817* (London: C. Chappel, 1818).

Oxford English Dictionary, CD ROM, 2nd edition (1989).

Steven Parissien, *Regency Style* (London: Phaidon, 1992).

Eric Partridge, *A Dictionary of Slang and Unconventional English* (London: Routledge & Kegan Paul, 1964).

Carole Pateman, *The Sexual Contract* (Cambridge: Polity Press, 1988).

Carole Pateman, *The Disorder of Women* (Cambridge: Polity Press, 1989).

Charles Pearce, *Madame Vestris and Her Times* (London: Stanley Paul, 1923).

Ronald Pearsall, *The Worm in the Bud: the World of Victorian Sexuality* (London: Pelican, 1971).

Samuel Pegge, *Anecdotes of the English Language chiefly regarding the area around London and its Environs — whence it will appear that the Natives of the Metropolis have not corrupted the language of their ancestors* (London: J. Nichols & Son, 1803).

Thomas Pennant, *Some Account of London*, 5th edition (London: n. p., 1814).

Joan Perkin, *Women and Marriage in Nineteenth-Century England* (London: Routledge, 1989).

Michelle Perrot (ed.), *A History of Private Life: From the Fires of the Revolution to the Great War* (Cambridge, MA: The Belknap Press of Harvard University Press, 1990).

Charles Petrie, *The Carlton Club* (London: Eyre & Spottiswoode, 1955).

Frederick C. Petty, *Italian Opera in London 1760–1800* (Ann Arbor, MI: UMI Research Press, 1980).

Nikolaus Pevsner, *A History of Building Types* (London: Thames & Hudson, 1976).

Barry Phelps, *The Power and the Party* (London: Macmillan, 1984).

Phebe Phillips, *Authentic memoirs of Phepe Phillips otherwise Maria Maitland well known in the Vicinity of Covent-Garden* (London: Ann Lemoine, 1799).

Phebe Phillips, *The Woman of the Town or Authentic Memoirs of Phebe Phillips otherwise known as Maria Maitland, well known in the vicinity of Covent Garden* (London: Ann Lemoine, 1801).

Phebe Phillips, *The Woman of the Town* (London: J. Roe & Ann Lemoine, 1809).

Phebe Phillips, *The Woman of the Town or the Authentic memoirs of Phebe Phillips who at an early age left her friends and became a kept mistress delineating the various adventures she met with in that station and the delusive schemes she afterwards practised as an abandoned prostitute* (London: Dean & Munday, 1825).

Steve Pile and Nigel Thrift (eds.), *Mapping the Subject* (London: Routledge, 1995).

Steve Pile, *The Body and the City* (London: Routledge, 1996).

Steve Pile, 'The Un(known)City . . . or, an urban geography of what lies buried below the surface', Iain Borden, Joe Kerr, Jane Rendell (eds.) with Alicia Pivaro, *Unknown City: Contesting Architecture and Social Space* (Cambridge, MA: The MIT Press, 2000), pp. 263–79.

Sadie Plant, ' "Bloody Woman": Review of Margaret Whitford, *Luce Irigaray: Philosophy in the Feminine*', *Radical Philosophy* (Spring 1992), n. 60, pp. 47–8.

J. H. Plumb, *The Commercialisation of Leisure* (Reading: University of Reading, 1973).

Val Plumwood, 'Do we need a Sex/Gender Distinction?', *Radical Philosphy* (Spring 1989), n. 51, pp. 2–11.

Griselda Pollock, *Vision and Difference: Femininity, Feminism and the Histories of Art* (London: Routledge, 1988).

Griselda Pollock, 'Vicarious Excitements: London, a Pilgrimage by Gustave Doré and Blanchard Jerrold', *New Formations* (Spring 1988), n. 4, pp. 25–50.

Mary Poovey, 'Feminism and Deconstruction', *Feminist Studies* (1988), v. 14, n. 1, pp. 51–65.

Mary Poovey, *Uneven Developments: The Ideological Work of Gender in Mid-Victorian Britain* (Chicago: University of Chicago Press, 1988).

Mary Poovey, 'Speaking of the Body: Mid-Victorian Constructions of Female Desire', Mary Jacobus, Evelyn Fox Keller and Sally Shuttleworth (eds.), *Body/ Politics: Women and the Discourses of Science* (London: Routledge, 1990), pp. 29–68.

Roy Porter, *English Society in the Eighteenth Century* (Harmondswoth: Penguin, 1990).

Roy Porter, *London* (London: Hamish Hamilton, 1994).

Andrew Posner and Helaine Perchuk (eds.), *The Masculine Masquerade* (Cambridge, MA: The MIT Press, 1995).

Alex Potts, 'Picturing the Modern Metropolis: Images of London in the Nineteenth Century', *History Workshop Journal* (1988), v. 26, pp. 28–56.

Rosamond Bayne Powell, *Eighteenth Century London Life* (London: John Murray, 1937).

J. B. Priestley, *The Prince of Pleasure and his Regency 1811–20* (London: Heinemann, 1969).

Elsbeth Probyn, 'Travels in the Postmodern: Making Sense of the Local', Linda Nicholson (ed.), *Feminism/Postmodernism* (London: Routledge, 1990), pp. 176–89.

Labelle Prussin, *African Nomadic Architecture: Space, Place and Gender* (Washington: Smithsonian Institution Press, 1995).

Prince Puckler-Muskau, *Tour in England, Ireland, and France* (London: Effingham Wilson, 1832).

Maurice Quinlan, *Victorian Prelude: a History of English Manners 1700–1830* (Hamden, CT: Archon Books, 1965).

John B. Radner, 'The Youthful Harlot's Curse: the Prostitute as Symbol of the City in 18th Century English Literature', *Eighteenth Century Life* (1976), v. 2, n. 3, pp. 59–64.

Stanley C. Ramsey, 'London Clubs I – The Reform Club', *Architectural Review* (1913), v. 33, pp. 87–90.

Stanley C. Ramsey, 'London Clubs II – Brooks's', *Architectural Review* (1913), v. 34, pp. 7–11.

Stanley C. Ramsey, 'London Clubs V – Boodles', *Architectural Review* (1913), v. 34, pp. 71–76.

Stanley C. Ramsey, 'London Clubs IX – The Union Club', *Architectural Review* (1913), v. 35, pp. 115–18.

Amos Rapoport, *House Form and Culture* (Englewood Cliffs: Prentice Hall, 1969).

Amos Rapoport, *Human Aspects of Urban Form* (Oxford: Pergamon Press, 1977).

Steen Eiler Rasmussen, *London: The Unique City* (Cambridge, MA: The MIT Press, 1988).

James Redmond, 'Georgian Theatres and Temples', Dana Arnold (ed.), *George IV and the Metropolitan Improvements: the Creation of a Royal Image* (London: The Georgian Society, 1996), pp. 37–43.

J. C. Reid, *Bucks and Bruisers* (London: Routledge & Kegan Paul, 1971).

Rayna R. Reiter (ed.), *Toward an Anthropology of Women* (New York: Monthly Review Press, 1975).

Jane Rendell, *Women in an Industrializing Society: England 1750–1800* (Oxford: Blackwell, 1990).

Jane Rendell, 'Subjective Space: an Architectural History of the Burlington Arcade', Duncan McCorquodale, Katerina Rüedi and Sarah Wigglesworth (eds.), *Desiring Practices* (London: Black Dog Publishing Ltd, 1996), pp. 216–33.

Jane Rendell, 'Thresholds, Passages and Surfaces: Touching, Passing and Seeing in the Burlington Arcade', Alex Cole (ed.), *The Optics of Walter Benjamin* (London: Blackdog Publishing Ltd, 1999).

Jane Rendell, Barbara Penner and Iain Borden (eds), *Gender, Space, Architecture: An Interdisciplinary Introduction* (London: Routledge, 1999).

Jane Rendell, ' "Bazaar Beauties" or "Pleasure is our Pursuit": A Spatial Story of Exchange', Iain Borden, Joe Kerr and Jane Rendell (eds.) with Alicia Pivaro, *Unknown City* (Cambridge, MA: The MIT Press, 2000), pp. 105–22.

David Reynolds (ed.), *Weber in London 1826* (London: Oswald Wolff, 1976).

Elaine A. Reynolds, 'St. Marylebone: Local Police Reform in London 1755–1829', *Historian* (1989), v. 51, n. 3, pp. 446–66.

Aileen Ribeiro, *Dress and Morality* (London: B. T. Batsford, 1986).

Anthony Richardson, *Robert Mylne, Architect* (London: B. T. Batsford, 1955).

A. E. Richardson, *Georgian England* (London: B. T. Batsford, 1931).

Joan Riviere, 'Womanliness as Masquerade', *International Journal of Psychoanalysis* (1929), v. 10, pp. 303–13.

M. J. D. Roberts, 'Making Victorian Morals: the Society for the Suppression of Vice and its Critics 1802–86', *Historical Studies* (1981), v. 21, n. 83, pp. 157–73.

M. J. D. Roberts, 'The Society for the Suppression of Vice and its Early Critics', *History Journal* (1983), v. 26, n. 1, pp. 315–29.

M. J. D. Roberts, 'Public and Private in Early Nineteenth Century London: the Vagrant Act of 1822 and its Enforcement', *Social History* (1988), v. 13, n. 3, pp. 273–94.

Marion Roberts, *Living in Man-Made World: Gender Assumptions in Modern Housing Design* (London: Routledge, 1991).

Nickie Roberts, *Whores in History* (London: HarperCollins, 1993).

Edward Forbes Robinson, *The Early History of Coffee Houses in England* (London: Kegan Paul, 1893).

Nicholas Rogers, 'Money, Land and Lineage: the Big Bourgeoisie of Hanoverian London', Peter Borsay (ed.), *The Eighteenth Century Town 1688–1820* (Harlow: Longman, 1990), pp. 268–314.

Pat Rogers 'The Breeches Part', Paul Gabriel Boucé (ed.), *Sexuality in Eighteenth Century Culture* (Manchester: Manchester University Press, 1982), pp. 244–58.

C. H. Rolph (ed.), *Women of the Streets: a Sociological Study of the Common Prostitute* (London: Secker & Warburg, 1955).

R. C. Rome, *Union Club: an Illustrated Descriptive Record of the Oldest Members Club* (London: B. T. Batsford, 1948).

James Roose-Evans, *London Theatre: From the Globe to the National* (Oxford: Phaidon, 1977).

Michael Roper and John Tosh (eds.), *Manful Assertions: Masculinities in Britain since 1800* (London: Routledge, 1991).

Michelle Rosaldo and Louise Lamphere, *Women, Culture and Society* (Stanford: Stanford University Press, 1974).

Gillian Rose, 'Review of Edward Soja, *Postmodern Geographies* and David Harvey, *The Condition of Postmodernity*', *Journal of Historical Geography* (January, 1991), v. 17, n. 1, pp. 118–21.

Gillian Rose, *Feminism and Geography: the Limits of Geographical Knowledge* (Cambridge: Polity Press, 1993).

Gillian Rose, 'Progress in Geography and Gender: or Something Else?', *Progress in Human Geography* (1993), v. 17, n. 4, pp. 531–7.

Gillian Rose, 'Making Space for the Female Subject of Feminism', Steve Pile and Nigel Thrift (eds.), *Mapping the Subject* (London: Routledge, 1996), pp. 332–54.

Jacqueline Rose, *Sexuality in the Field of Vision* (London: Verso, 1986).

G. S. Rousseau and Roy Porter (eds.), *Sexual Underworlds of the Enlightenment* (Manchester: Manchester University Press, 1988).

A. Maude Royden, *Downward Paths: an Inquiry into the Causes which Contribute to the Making of a Prostitute* (London: G. Bill & Sons, 1916).

Gayle Rubin, 'The Traffic in Women: Notes on the "Political Economy" of Sex', Rayna Reiter (ed.), *Toward an Anthropology of Women* (New York: Monthly Review Press, 1975), pp. 157–210.

Gayle Rubin, 'Sexual Traffic: Interview with Judith Butler', *Differences: a Journal of Feminist Cultural Studies* (1994), v. 6, ns. 2 and 3, pp. 62–99.

Gayle Rubin, 'The Traffic in Women: Notes on the "Political Economy" of Sex',

Joan W. Scott (ed.), *Feminism and History* (Oxford: Oxford University Press, 1996), pp. 105–51.

George Rudé, *Hanoverian London 1714–1808* (London: Secker & Warburg, 1971).

George Rudé, *Criminal and Victim: Crime and Society in Early Nineteenth Century England* (Oxford: Clarendon Press, 1985).

John Rule, *Albion's People: English Society 1714–1815* (London: Longman, 1992).

Richard Rush, *A Residence at the Court of London* (London: Century, 1987).

Jenny Ryan, 'Women, Modernity and the City', *Theory, Culture and Society* (November 1994), v. 11, n. 4, pp. 35–64.

Mary P. Ryan, *Women in Public: Between Banners and Ballots, 1825–80* (London: Johns Hopkins University Press, 1990).

Michael Ryan, *Prostitution in London* (London: H. Bailliere, 1839).

Joseph Rykwert, *The Dancing Column: On Order in Architecture* (Cambridge, MA: The MIT Press, 1996).

Peter Sabor, 'The Censor Censured: Expurgating Memoirs of a Woman of Pleasure', *Eighteenth Century Life* (May 1985), v. 9, n. 3, pp. 192–201.

George Sala, *Twice Around the Clock, of the Hours of Day and Night in London* (London: Houlston & Wright, 1859).

E. P. Sanger, *London Theatres* (London: n. p., 1829).

Joel Sanders (ed.), *Stud: Architectures of Masculinity* (New York: Princeton Architectural Press, 1996).

George Saunders, *A Treatise on Theatres* (London: private, 1790).

Jean-Baptist-Balthazar Sauvan, *Diorama Anglais ou Promenades Pittoresque à Londres* (Paris: Didot, 1823).

Leonard D. Schwarz, 'Social Class and Social Geography: the Middle Classes in London at the End of the Eighteenth Century', *Social History* (1982), v. 7, n. 2, pp. 167–85.

L. D. Schwarz, 'Social Class and Social Geography: the Middle Classes in London at the End of the Nineteenth Century', Peter Borsay (ed.), *The Eighteenth Century Town 1688–1820* (Harlow: Longman, 1990), pp. 315–37.

Jona Schellekens, 'Courtship, The Clandestine Marriage Act and Illegitimate Fertility in England', *Journal Of Interdisciplinary History* (Winter 1993), v. 25, n. 3, pp. 433–44.

Paul Schlicke, 'The Pilgrimage of Pierce Egan', *Journal of Popular Culture* (1987), v. 21, n. 1, pp. 1–9.

George Ryley Scott, *The History of Prostitution* (London: Senate, 1996).

J. M. Scott, *The Book of Pall Mall* (London: Heinemann, 1965).

Joan W. Scott, 'Deconstructing Equality Versus Difference: or, the Uses of Post-structuralist Theory for Feminists', *Feminist Studies* (Spring 1981), v. 14, n. 1, pp. 33–50.

Joan W. Scott, *Gender and the Politics of History* (New York: Columbia University Press, 1988).

Joan W. Scott, 'The Evidence of Experience', *Critical Enquiry* (Summer 1991), v. 17, pp. 773–99.

Joan Wallach Scott (ed.), *Feminism and History* (Oxford: Oxford University Press, 1996).

Eve Kosofsky Sedgwick, *Between Men: English Literature and Male Homosexual Desire* (New York: Columbia University Press, 1985).

Richard Sennett, *The Fall of Public Man* (New York: First Vintage Books Edition, 1978).

Richard Sennett, *The Conscience of the Eye* (London: Faber, 1990).

Richard Sennett, *Flesh and Stone* (London: Faber, 1994).

Tristram Shandy, *Miss C—y's Cabinet of Curiosities, or the Green Room broke open* (London: Maiden's Head, 1765).

Ann Sheldon, *Authentic and Interesting Memoirs of Miss Ann Sheldon (now Mrs Archer)* (London: Printed for the Authoress, 1787).

Thomas Shepherd, 'Metropolitan Improvements or London in the Nineteenth Century [. . .] from the Original Drawings of Thomas H. Shepherd with notes by James Elmes', *London in the Nineteenth Century* (London: Jones & Co., 1 November 1829), v. 1.

Thomas Shepherd, 'London and its Environs in the Nineteenth Century from the Original Drawings by Thomas E. Shepherd', *London in the Nineteenth Century* (London: Jones & Co., 1 November 1829), v. 2.

F. H. W. Shepperd (ed.), 'The Parish of St. James's Westminster, Part 1, South of Piccadilly', *The Survey of London* (London: The Athlone Press, University of London, 1960), v. 29.

F. H. W. Shepperd (ed.), 'The Parish of St. James's Westminster, Part 2, South of Piccadilly', *The Survey of London* (London: The Athlone Press, University of London, 1960), v. 30.

F. H. W. Shepperd (ed.), 'The Parish of St. James's Westminster, Part 1, North of Piccadilly', *The Survey of London* (London: The Athlone Press, University of London, 1963), v. 31.

F. H. W. Shepperd (ed.), 'The Parish of St. James's Westminster, Part 2, North of Piccadilly', *The Survey of London* (London: The Athlone Press, University of London, 1963), v. 32.

Michael Sheringham (ed.), *Parisian Fields* (London: Reaktion Press, 1996).

Erroll Sherson, *London's Lost Theatres of the Nineteenth Century* (London: John Lane, The Bodley Head Ltd, 1925).

Rob Shields (ed.), *Lifestyle Shopping* (London: Routledge, 1992).

Rob Shields, 'Fancy Footwork', Keith Tester (ed.), *The Flâneur* (London: Routledge, 1994), pp. 61–80.

Laurie Shrage, *Moral Dilemmas of Feminism* (London: Routledge, 1994).

Georg Simmel, 'Fashion', Donald Levine (ed.), *Georg Simmel: On Individuality and Social Forms* (Chicago: Chicago University Press, 1971), pp. 294–323.

Louis Simond, *Journal of a Tour and a Residence in Great Britain during the Years 1810 and 1811* (London: Longman, Hurst, Rees, Orme & Brown, 1817).

Abraham A. Sion, *Prostitution and the Law* (London: Faber, 1977).

Sacheverell Sitwell, *The Romantic Ballet from Contemporary Prints* (London: B. T. Batsford, 1948).

George Smeeton, *The Flash Dictionary and The Art of Boxing* (London: G. Smeeton, 1821).

George Smeeton, *Doings in London; or Day and Night Scenes of the frauds, frolics, manners and depravities of the Metropolis* (London: Smeeton, 1828).

Olivia Smith, *The Politics of Language* (Oxford: Clarendon Press, 1984).

William Charles Smith, *The Italian Opera and Contemporary Ballet in London 1789–1820* (London: Society for Theatre Research, 1955).

Edward Soja, *Postmodern Geographies: the Reassertion of Space in Social Theory* (London: Verso, 1989).

David Solkin, *Painting for Money: Eighteenth Century Conversation Piece* (New Haven & London: Yale University Press, 1994).

Abigail Solomon-Godeau, 'The Legs of the Countess', *October* (Winter, 1986), pp. 65–108.

Richard Southern, *The Georgian Playhouse* (London: Pheiades Books, 1948).

Patricia Meyer Spacks, 'Review of Terry Castle, *Masquerade and Civilization*', *Eighteenth-Century Studies* (Fall, 1987), v. 21, n. 1, pp. 98–102.

Daphne Spain, *Gendered Spaces* (Chapel Hill: University of North Carolina Press, 1992).

Marianne Spencer Stanhope, *Almack's: a Novel in Three Volumes* (London: Saunders & Otley, 1826).

Judith Squires, 'Private Lives, Secluded Places: Privacy as Political Possibility', *Environment and Planning D: Society and Space* (1994), v. 12 , pp. 387–410.

Peter Stallybrass and Allon White, *The Politics and Poetics of Transgression* (London: Methuen, 1986).

Christine Stansell, *City of Women, Sex and Class in New York 1789–1860* (New York: Illini Books ed., 1986).

Susan Staves, *Married Women's Separate Property in England 1660–1833* (Cambridge, MA: Harvard University Press, 1990).

Andrew Steinmetz, *The Gaming Table: its Votaries and Victims in all Time and Countries especially in England and in France* (London: Tinsley Brothers, 1870).

George Alexander Stevens, *The Adventures of a Speculist or, a Journey through London compiled from papers written by George Alexander Stevens (Author of a Lecture upon Heads)* (London: S. Bladon, 1788).

Damie Stillman, *English Neo-Classical Architecture* (London: A. Zwemmer, 1988).

Catharine R. Stimpson *et al.* (eds.), *Women and the American City* (Chicago: University of Chicago Press, 1979).

M. Veronica Stokes, 'The Lowther Arcade in the Strand', *The London Topographical Record*, v. 32 (London: London Topographical Record, 1974)

Lawrence Stone, *The Family, Sex and Marriage in England 1500–1800* (Harmondsworth: Penguin, 1990).

Dorothy Stroud, *Henry Holland: His Life and Architecture* (London: Country Life, 1966).

John Summerson, *John Nash: Architect to King George IV* (London: George Allen & Unwin, 1935).

John Summerson, *Georgian London* (London: Pelican, 1962).

John Summerson, *The Life and Work John Nash Architect* (London: George Allen & Unwin, 1980).

T. S. Surr, *A Winter in London or Sketches of Fashion* (London: Richard Phillips, 1806).

Gillian Swanson, 'Drunk with the Glitter: Consuming Spaces and Sexual Geographies', Sophie Watson and Katherine Gibson (eds.), *Postmodern Cities and Spaces* (Oxford: Blackwell, 1995), pp. 80–99.

William Tait, *Magdalenism: an Inquiry into the Extent Causes and Consequences of Prostitution in Edinburgh* (Edinburgh: P. Rickard, 1842).

James Beard Talbot, *The Miseries of Prostitution* (London: James Madden, 1844).

John Tallis, *Tallis's London Street Views: Exhibition Upwards of One Hundred Buildings* (London: John Tallis, 1838–40).

John Tallis, *Tallis's Street Views and Pictorial Directory of England, Scotland and Ireland* (London: J. & F. Tallis, 1847).

John Tallis, *Tallis's Illustrated London: in Commemoration of the Great Exhibition* (London: J. Tallis & Co., 1851).

John Tallis, *John Tallis's London Street Views 1838–40* (London: Published in Association with the London Topographical Society, Nattali and Maurice, 1969).

Reay Tannihill, *Sex in History* (London: Abacus, 1992).

Miss Taylor, *Authentic Memoirs of Mrs. Clarke* (London: n.p., 1809).

Keith Tester (ed.), *The Flâneur* (London: Routledge, 1994).

W. M. Thackeray, *Sketches and Travels in London* (Gloucester: Alan Sutton Publishing, 1989).

Mary Thale, 'The London Debating Societies in the 1790s', *Historical Journal* (1989), v. 32, n. 1, pp. 57–86.

Angela Thirkell, *The Fortunes of Harriette: the Surprising Career of Harriette Wilson* (London: Hamish Hamilton, 1936).

E. P. Thompson, *Customs in Common* (Harmondsworth: Penguin, 1993).

John Timbs, *Club Life in London* (London: Richard Bentley, 1866).

John Timbs, *Curiosities of London* (London: John Camden Hotten, 1867).

Rosemary Tong, *Feminist Thought: a Comprehensive Introduction* (London: Routledge, 1992).

Susana Torre, 'The Pyramid and Labyrinth', Susana Torre (ed.), *Women in American Architecture: A Historic and Contemporary Perspective* (New York: Whitney Library of Design, 1977), pp. 186–202.

Susana Torre (ed.), *Women in American Architecture: A Historic and Contemporary Perspective* (New York: Whitney Library of Design, 1977).

Susana Torre, 'Space as Matrix', *Heresies: A Feminist Publication on Art and Politics* (1981), v. 3, n. 3, issue 11, pp. 51–2.

John Tosh, 'Domesticity and Manliness in the Victorian Middle-class', Michael Roper and John Tosh (eds.), *Manful Assertions: Masculinities in Britain since 1800* (London: Routledge, 1991), pp. 43–73.

Flora Tristan, *Flora Tristran's London Journal 1842* (Boston: Charles River Books, 1981).

Eric Trudgill, 'Prostitution and Paterfamilias', E. J. Dyos and Michael Wolff (eds.), *The Victorian City: Images and Realities* (London: Routledge & Kegan Paul, 1973), pp. 693–705.

Rudolph Trumbach, 'Modern Prostitution and Gender in Fanny Hill: Libertine and Domesticated Fantasy', G. S. Rousseau and Roy Porter (eds.), *Sexual Underworlds of the Enlightenment* (Manchester: Manchester University Press, 1988), pp. 69–85.

Rudolph Trumbach, 'Sex, Gender, and Sexual Identity in Modern Culture: Male Sodomy and Female Prostitution in Enlightenment London', *Journal of the History of Sexuality* (1991), v. 2, pp. 186–203.

Stephen Turner, 'Almack's and Society', *History Today* (April 1976), v. 26, n. 4, pp. 241–9.

Geoffrey Tyack, 'James Pennithorne and the London Street Improvements 1838–55', *London Journal* (1990), v. 15, n. 1, pp. 38–56.

Henry Urbach, 'Closets, Clothes, Disclosure', Duncan McCorquodale, Katerina Rüedi and Sarah Wigglesworth (eds.), *Desiring Practices: Architecture, Gender and the Interdisciplinary* (London: Black Dog Publishing Ltd, 1996), pp. 246–63.

John Urry, *Consuming Places* (London: Routledge, 1995).

Wray Vamplew, 'Sport and Industrialisation: An Economic Interpretation of the changes in Popular Sport in Nineteenth-Century England', J. A. Mangan (ed.), *Pleasure, Profit, Proselytism* (London: Frank Cass, 1988), pp. 7–20.

Thorstein Veblen, *The Theory of the Leisure Class* (Harmondsworth: Penguin, 1979).

Mariana Verde, 'The Love of Finery: Fashion and the Fallen Woman in Nineteenth Century Social Discourse', *Victorian Studies* (Winter 1989), v. 32, pp. 169–88.

H. T. Waddy, *The Devonshire Club and Crockfords* (London: Eveleigh Nash, 1919).

Peter Wagner, 'The Pornographer in the Courtroom', Paul-Gabriel Boucé (ed.), *Sexuality in Eighteenth Century Britain*, (Manchester: Manchester University Press, 1982), pp. 120–39.

Sylvia Walby, *Theorising Patriarchy* (Oxford: Blackwell, 1990).

Edward Walford, *Old and New London* (London: Cassell, Petter & Galpin, 1873).

Lynne Walker, *British Women in Architecture 1671–1951* (London: Sorello Press, 1984).

Lynne Walker, 'Women and Architecture', Judy Attfield and Pat Kirkham (eds.), *A View from the Interior: Feminism, Women and Design* (London: The Women's Press, 1989), pp. 90–105.

Judith Walkowitz, 'Notes on the History of Victorian Prostitution', *Feminist Studies* (1972), v. 1, pp. 105–14.

Judith Walkowitz, 'The Politics of Prostitution', *Signs* (1980), v. 6, n. 1, pp. 123–35.

Judith Walkowitz, *Prostitution and Victorian Society: Women, Class and the State* (Cambridge: Cambridge University Press, 1980).

Judith Walkowitz, 'Jack the Ripper and the Myth of Male Violence', *Feminist Studies* (1982), v. 8, n. 3, pp. 543–74.

Judith Walkowitz, 'Male Vice and Female Virtue: Feminism and the Politics of Prostitution in Nineteenth-Century Britain', *History Workshop Journal* (1982), v. 13, pp. 79–93.

Judith Walkowitz, *City of Dreadful Delight: Narratives of Sexual Danger in Late Victorian London* (London: Virago Press, 1992).

Claire Walsh, 'Shop Design and the Display of Goods in Eighteenth Century London', *Journal of Design History* (1995), v. 8, n. 3, pp. 157–75.

Edward Ward, *The London Spy* (London: J. Nutt & J. How, 1698–9).

Edward Ward, *The Secret History of London Clubs* (London: J. Phillips, 1710).

H. Ward, *The Athenaeum 1824–1925* (London: Printed for the Club, 1926).

Marina Warner, *Monuments and Maidens: the Allegory of the Female Form* (London: Picador, 1988).

Norah Waugh, *The Cut of Men's Clothes* (London: Faber, 1964).

Sophie Watson and Katherine Gibson (eds.), *Postmodern Cities and Spaces* (Oxford: Blackwell, 1995).

W. M. Weare, *The Fatal Effects of Gambling* (London: T. Kelly, 1824).

Ben Weinreb and Christopher Hibbert, *The London Encyclopaedia* (London: Papermac, 1983).

Leslie Kanes Weisman, *Discrimination by Design* (Chicago: University of Illinois Press, 1992).

Gebhardt Fredrich August Wendeborn, *A View of England towards the close of the Eighteenth Century* (Dublin: William Sleater for P. Wogan, 1791).

Paul W. Werth, 'Through the Prism of Prostitution: State, Society and Power', *Social History* (1994), v. 19, n. 1, pp. 1–15.

Nathaniel S. Wheaton, *A Journal of a Residence During Several Months in London: Including Excursions through various parts of England and a short Tour in France and Scotland in the Years 1823 and 1824* (Hartford: H. & F. J. Huntingdon, 1830).

Charles White, *Almack's Revisited* (London: Saunders & Otley, 1828).

R. J. White, *Life in Regency England* (London: B. T. Batsford, 1963).

Margaret Whitford, *The Irigaray Reader* (Oxford: Blackwell, 1991).

Margaret Whitford, *Luce Irigaray: Philosophy in the Feminine* (London: Routledge, 1991).

William Wilding, *The Man of Pleasure or Memoirs of Will'm Wilding Esq.* (London: Ann Lemoine, 1800).

Clifford John Williams, *Madame Vestris: a Theatrical Biography* (London: Sidgwick & Jackson, 1973).

Raymond Williams, *Marxism and Literature* (Oxford: Oxford University Press, 1977).

Judith Williamson, *Consuming Passions: the Dynamics of Popular Culture* (London: Marian Boyers, 1986).

C. Baron Wilson, *Our Actresses: or Glances at Stage Favourites Past and Present* (London: Smith, Elder, 1844).

Elizabeth Wilson, *Adorned in Dreams* (London: Virago Press, 1985).

Elizabeth Wilson, *Sphinx in the City: Urban Life, the Control of Women and Disorder* (London: Virago Press, 1991).

Elizabeth Wilson, 'The Invisible Flâneur', *The New Left Review* (1992), v. 191, pp. 90–110.

Elizabeth Wilson, 'The Rhetoric of Urban Space', *New Left Review* (1995), v. 209, pp. 146–60.

Harriette Wilson, *Harriette Wilson's Memoirs of herself and others* (London: T. Douglas, 1825).

Harriette Wilson, *The Interesting Memoirs and Amourous Adventures of Harriette Wilson one of the most Celebrated Women of the Present Day interpersed with numerous Anecdotes of Illustrious Persons* (London: W. Chubb, T. Blackfeter, T. Reed, 1825).

Harriette Wilson, *Memoirs of Harriette Wilson written by herself* (London: J. J. Stockdale, 1825).

Harriette Wilson, *Paris Lions and London Tigers* (London: J. J. Stockdale, 1825).

Harriet Wilson, *Memoirs of Herself and Others* (London: Peter Davies, 1929).

Mabel O. Wilson, 'Black Bodies/White Cities: Le Corbusier in Harlem', *ANY* (1996), n. 16, pp. 35–9.

Mary Wilson, *The Voluptuous Night* (London: Sarah Brown, 1830), translated from Baron Dominique Vivant Denon, *La Nuit Merveilleuse ou le Ne·plus Ultra du Plaisir* (Paris, n. p., 1800).

Mary Wilson, *The Whore's Catechism* (London: Sarah Brown, 1830), translated from Baron Dominique Vivant Denon, *Le Point de Lendemain* (Paris, n. p., 1800).

Hilary Winchester, 'The Construction and Deconstruction of Women's Roles in the Urban Landscape', Kay Anderson and Fay Gale (eds.), *Inventing Places* (Australia: Longman Cheshire, 1992), pp. 139–55.

Jeanette Winterson, *The Passion* (Harmondsworth: Penguin, 1988).

Janet Wolff, 'The Invisible Flâneuse', *Theory, Culture and Society* (1985), v. 2, n. 3, pp. 37–46.

Janet Wolff, *Feminine Sentences: Essays on Women and Culture* (Cambridge: Polity Press, 1990).

Janet Wolff, 'Memoirs and Micrologies: Walter Benjamin, Feminism and Cultural Analysis', *New Formations: The Actuality of Walter Benjamin* (Summer 1993), n. 20, pp. 113–22.

Sybil Wolfram, *In-Laws and Out-Laws: Kinship and Marriage in England* (London: Croom Helm, 1987).

George Woodbridge, *The Reform Club 1836–1978: a History from the Club's Records* (London: Reform Club, 1978).

Gwendolyn Wright, 'On the Fringe of the Profession: Women in American Architecture', Spiro Kostof (ed.), *The Architect: Chapters in the History of the Profession* (Oxford: Oxford University Press, 1977), pp. 280–309.

G. Yates, *The Ball or a Glance at Almack's in 1829* (London: Henry Colburn, 1829).

Philip Ziegler and Desmond Seward (eds.), *Brooks's: a Social History* (London: Constable, 1991).

Susan Zimmerman (ed.), *Erotic Politics: Desire on the Renaissance Stage* (London: Routledge, 1992).

Index

Note: Page references in *italics* are to illustrations

quadrille, the 98–9

rambling 6–7, 18, 23–9, 32–40, 49–51,
    55–62, 126, 131–3
  definition of 31
  texts on 32–5, 45, 51, 55, 57, 60,
    70–1, 75, 79, 82, 85, 102–3, 110,
    114–15, 118, 123–5, 135–40 *passim*
Reform Club 65, 72
Regency period 19
Regent Street 45, 50–1, 54, 109
Repton, G. S. 106, 108
Rose, Gillian 9
Roxborough, the (club) 65
Royal Opera Arcade 108, 111
Royal Saloon 41, 135, 137–9
Rubin, Gayle 13

St Giles in the Fields 54
St James's 4–6, 5, 64–7, 70, 78, 94, 104
'sanctum sanctorium' 79–81
scopophilia 18, 49
season, the 6, 91–2
segregation, social 34
Sennett, Richard 26
'separate spheres' ideology 19–20,
    22–3, 55, 63
Simmel, Georg 25–7
situated knowledge 16
Slade, Stephen 89
slang 39, 47–8
Soane, John 72
social production of space 9
Soja, Edward 9
Solomon-Godeau, Abigail 15
spectacle 50
sporting skills 48
'spy' tales 32

standpoint theory 16
subscription houses 67, 73

taverns 66–7, 70
Thatched House Tavern 66
Travellers' Club 65, 68, 74
travesty dancers 121
'trickle down' theory 25

Union Club 65
United Services Club 65, 74

Vagrancy Acts 21, 57, 60, 80, 130–2
value in exchange and in use 13–14, 19,
    95–6
Vauxhall 100
Veblen, Thorstein 25–7
Vestris, Madame 60, 121, 123
Vice Society 132
Vitruvius 39–40
voyeurism 18

Walby, Sylvia 21
waltz, the 96, 98–9
Watier's (club) 65, 74
Whip club 76
White House brothel 136
White's (club) 28, 63–5, 71–5, 78
Whitford, Margaret 15
Wilson, Elizabeth 22
Wilson, Harriette 95
Wolff, Janet 22
women
  as commodities 3–4, 13–15, 19, 57,
    89–90, 97, 103, 140
  property rights of 90–1
Wyatt, Benjamin and Phillip 66
Wyatt, James 73